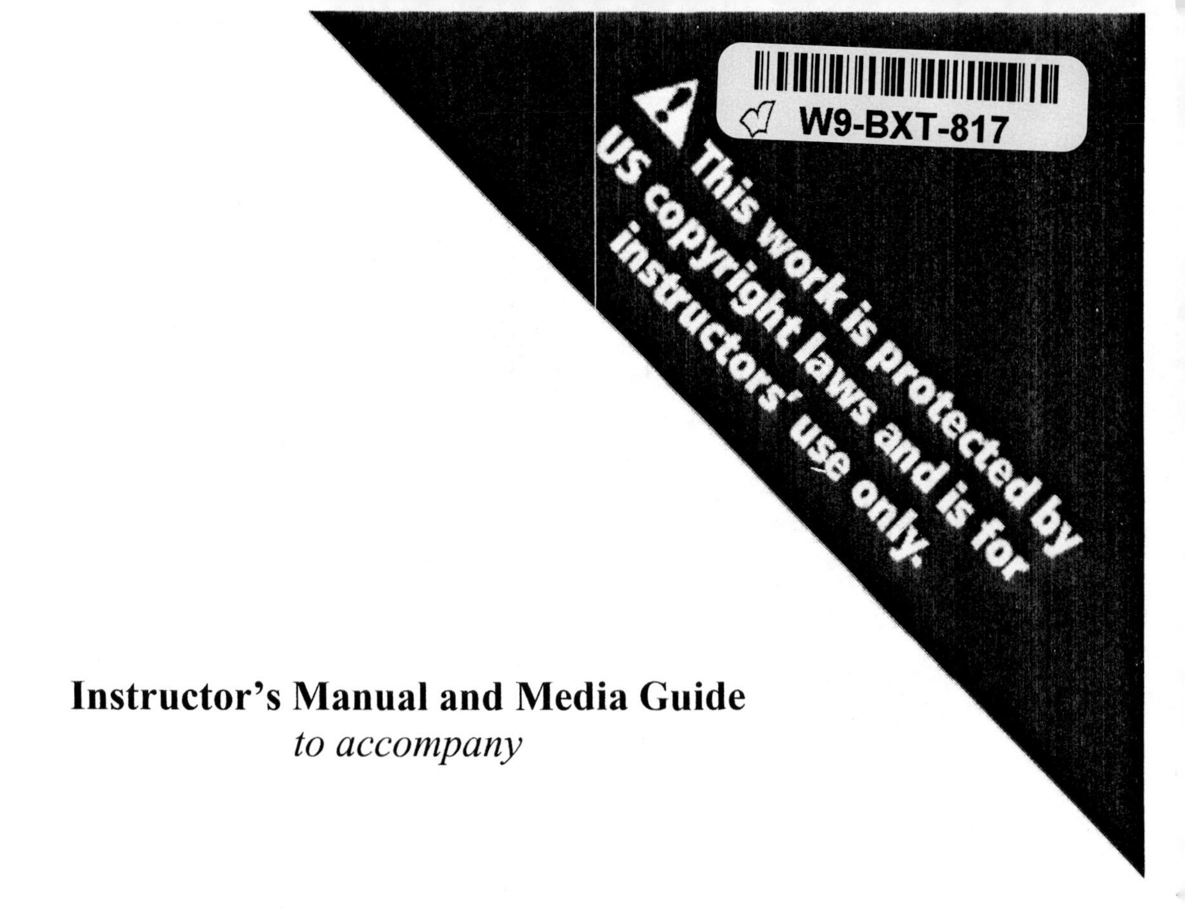

Instructor's Manual and Media Guide
to accompany

Educational Psychology
Windows on Classrooms

Seventh Edition

Paul Eggen
University of North Florida

Don Kauchak
University of Utah

Upper Saddle River, New Jersey
Columbus, Ohio

---

10 9 8 7 6 5 4 3 2

ISBN: 0-13-172449-5

TABLE OF CONTENTS

DVD Episodes

Two DVDs are found at the back of each textbook. These DVDs contain 25 classroom vignettes that range in length from 4 to 15 minutes. These classroom episodes illustrate specific chapter concepts, and references to them appear in the text.

An overview of the DVD Episodes that accompany the Seventh Edition of *Educational Psychology: Windows on Classrooms* is found in Table 1 that follows. Specific references to each episode are inserted into different chapters, provide a brief overview, and direct students to a specific DVD episode. These can be shown in class as a classroom instructional activity or given as homework.

Table 1: Overview of DVDs That Accompany the Text (New to This Edition)

Episode	Chapter	Title	Description	Approx Len (minu
1 DVD 1	1	Demonstrating knowledge in classrooms	This episode illustrates a kindergarten teacher, middle school teacher, and two high school teachers demonstrating different forms of teacher knowledge.	14
2 DVD 1	2	Examining learner thinking: Piaget's conservation tasks	In this episode, students of different ages respond to Piaget's famous conservation tasks.	5
3 DVD 1	2	Developmental differences: Studying properties of air in first grade	This episode illustrates the thinking of first graders as they try to explain why water doesn't enter a glass inverted in a bowl of water and why a card doesn't fall off an inverted cup full of water.	4
4 DVD 1	3	Moral reasoning: Examining a moral dilemma	This episode illustrates the moral reasoning of students at different ages when they are presented with a moral dilemmas	4
5 DVD 1	4	Culturally responsive teaching	In this episode a teacher discusses with an interviewer the accommodations she has made in her classroom for a student of Islamic faith, and the support her other students provide.	5
6 DVD 1	5	Reviewing an IEP	In this episode a teacher team discusses an IEP with a concerned parent	5
7 DVD 1	5	Using peer tutoring with students having exceptionalities	This episode illustrates children conducting a flashcard drill as a form of peer tutoring	5
8 DVD 1	6	Using reinforcement in classrooms	In this episode a second-grade teacher uses a considerable amount of positive reinforcement combined with some presentation punishment as a part of her classroom management system.	7

9 DVD 1	6	Demonstrating problem solving in high school chemistry	This episode illustrates a high-school teacher using direct modeling to demonstrate the steps involved in solving chemistry problems.	8
10 DVD 1	7	Applying information processing: Attracting students attention	This episode illustrates two teachers attempting to begin their lesson with a demonstration that will attract students' attention.	8
11 DVD 1	7	Applying information processing: Organizing information	This episode includes four teachers using different ways of organizing information for students.	6
12 DVD 1	7	Applying information processing: The *Scarlet Letter* in high school English	This episode illustrates a teacher's attempts to help her students understand the characters in the novel *The Scarlet Letter*. (It is also chapter's closing case study.)	9
13 DVD 1	8	Constructing knowledge of beam balances	This episode illustrates the thinking of fourth graders as they attempt to construct understanding of the principle that makes beams balance. (It is also the chapter's opening case study, and it is integrated throughout the chapter.)	9
14 DVD 1	8	Constructing concepts: Using concrete examples	In this episode one middle school teacher uses a concrete example to illustrate the concept *bilateral symmetry* and a second middle school teacher uses the same strategy to teach the concept *concrete poem.*	10
15 DVD 1	9	Using a problem solving model: Finding area in elementary math	This episode involves fifth-graders' attempts to find the area of the carpeted portion of their classroom, which is an irregular shape. (It is also the chapter's opening case study.)	11
16 DVD 2	9	Guiding students' problem solving: Graphing in second grade	In this episode a second-grade teacher uses a problem solving approach to help her students understand bar graphs. (It is also the chapter's closing case study.)	14
17 DVD 2	10	Applying cognitive motivation theory: Writing paragraphs in 5th grade	In this episode a fifth-grade teacher has her students involved in writing, displaying and evaluating each others' paragraphs.	13
18 DVD 2	11	Applying the motivation model: Studying arthropods in 5th grade	The same teacher as in Episode 17 is attempting to use an intrinsically interesting activity to help her students understand the concept *arthropod.* (It is also the chapter's opening case study.)	13

19 DVD 2	12	Establishing and practicing classroom rules	In this episode, a second-grade teacher is attempting to help her students understand a set of classroom rules, and later in the episode she conducts a review of the rules.	6
20 DVD 2	13	Analyzing instructional alignment	In this episode a fifth-grade teacher covers a variety of topics related to the Civil War.	10
21 DVD 2	13	Essential teaching skills in an urban classroom	The teacher in this episode is attempting to demonstrate the Essential Teaching Skills with his middle school students.	13
22 DVD 2	13	Guided discovery in an elementary classroom	In this episode, a fifth-grade teacher uses *Guided Discovery* to help her students understand Haiku poetry.	10
23 DVD 2	14	Laptops for data in fifth grade	Students in this episode gather and enter information on laptop computers in their classroom	5
24 DVD 2	14	Using PowerPoint in the classroom	In this episode a world history teacher uses a PowerPoint presentation to provide her students with information on ancient Greece	5
25 DVD 2	15	Using assessment in decision making	The teacher in this episode uses a variety of assessment data to make instructional decisions about teacher her students to add fractions.	15

POWERPOINT SLIDES

INTRODUCTION:
TO THE INSTRUCTOR

New to This Edition

As we prepared the seventh edition of *Educational Psychology: Windows on Classrooms* we attempted to make our book, already the most applied in the field, even more usable and reader friendly. To reach this goal we have adopted a *Guided Learning System.* The *Guided Learning System* is a feature designed to maximize students' understanding of the text content. Grounded in principles of learning and teaching, it provides learners with structure, opportunities to actively process the chapter content, feedback, and reviews, each an essential factor for learning from both text and classroom activities.

The ***Guided Learning System*** has the following features:
- A *specific learning objective* is written for each major section of each chapter.
- A set of *"Checking Your Understanding" questions* directly aligned with the learning objective is then included at the end of the section.
- *Feedback* for the "Checking Your Understanding" questions is provided in Appendix B at the end of the text.
- *"Knowledge Extension" questions* that help learners relate the content to topics they've already studied are provided on the book's Companion Website (CW). Feedback for the questions is included on the CW.
- *"Meeting Your Learning Objectives" review sections* that restate the learning objectives are provided with bulleted summaries of the topics covered in that section.

In addition to the ***Guided Learning System,*** the following features are new to this edition.

- **Learning and Teaching in Urban Environments:** A rapidly increasing number of our nation's students attend urban schools, and it is likely that new teachers' first job offers will be in urban environments. Integrated sections in Chapters 1, 3, 8, 11, 12, 13, and 15 in addition to the thematic emphasis in Chapter 4, directly address the unique challenges and rewards related to social development, learning, motivation, classroom management, instruction, and assessment that exist in urban environments.
- **New Chapter: *Learning and Instruction and Technology*:** Technology is now an integral part of our lives, and it is having an increasing impact on teaching and learning. Chapter 14, relates technology to theories of learning and provides readers with description of instructional applications of technology.
- **"Analyzing Classrooms" DVDs**: Two DVD's that are packaged with the book include 25 episodes that provide real-world examples of various aspects of the teaching-learning process. Margin notes in each of the chapters refer readers to the episodes.
- **Expanded coverage of social constructivism:** Increasing attention is being placed on the social construction of knowledge in the learning-teaching process. Expanded coverage of social constructivism in Chapter 8 includes detailed discussions of cognitive apprenticeships, situated learning, sociocultural learning theory, and classrooms as learning communities.
- **Thematic Coverage of Teacher Professionalism:** Teacher professionalism is increasingly emphasized in education today. Professionalism and the role of professional knowledge in learning to teach is now a theme for the text.
- **Connections to Prentice Hall's *Teacher Prep* Website:** Prentice Hall's *Teacher Prep* website provides a variety of resources for text users, and each chapter of the text identifies links to the *Teacher Prep* website in its *Exploring Further* feature.
- **Increased Integration of Case Studies:** Instead of merely presenting a beginning-of-chapter case study, the content of each chapter begins with a series of questions that provide a bridge from the case to the topics in the chapter. The questions are specifically addressed as the content is presented, and the case study is elaborated and integrated with the content, making the theory and research presented in the chapter concrete, meaningful, and applicable.

- **Increased Coverage of Instructional Principles and Models of Instruction:** Each chapter includes sections that provide principles of instruction for applying the content of the section in classrooms. *Principles of Instruction* sections are included for each major topic of the book. In addition detailed coverage of models of instruction, including *Direct Instruction, Lecture Discussion, Guided Discovery,* and *Cooperative Learning* sections are presented in Chapter 13.

Integrated Companion Website. The book's companion website at www.prenhall.com/eggen is now more closely integrated with each of the chapters in the text. It includes:

- *Integrated Online Cases:* An online case integrated with the content of each chapter gives students additional experience with applying the topics covered in the chapter. Multiple-choice and short-answer questions similar to those found on the PRAXIS™ exam are included with the case study.
- *"Exploring Further" Topics:* The "Exploring Further" feature allows students to study sleected topics in greater depth. At least one of the "Exploring Further" topics in each chapter is linked to Prentice Hall's *Teacher Prep* website.
- *Feedback for Short-Answer Questions Following the End-of-Chapter Cases:* The feedback provides students with ideal answers consistent with the requirements of the PRAXIS™ exam.
- *Knowledge Extensions*: The "Knowledge Extension" questions and feedback that are part of the *Guided Learning System* are on the companion website.
- *Practice Quiz and Essay Questions:* Practice quiz items in multiple-choice format and essay questions in the *Self-Assessment* module of each chapter help students study for quizzes and exams. The practice quiz and essay questions are similar to those found on the PRAXIS™ exam.
- *Portfolio Activities:* Suggested portfolio activities help students begin the process of preparing a professional portfolio.

USING THE INSTRUCTOR'S MANUAL AND MEDIA GUIDE

The *Instructor's Manual and Media Guide* is organized into five sections each of which was designed to provide you with strategies to model effective instruction.

- **Teaching Suggestions.** Teaching suggestions are general suggestions for teaching your course, together with the rationale for each suggestion. They are designed to help you "practice what you preach." We emphasize that they are merely "suggestions." You are the best judge of what will produce the most learning in your students.

- **Suggested Projects.** The Suggested Projects offer ideas for student activities, one or more of which you may choose to assign your students.

- **Observing in Classrooms.** If you have a field component attached to your course, or you have access to schools, you may want your students to complete some of the field activities outlined in this section. Guidelines are presented in this section to inform your students of appropriate protocol when making school visits.

- **Chapter-by-Chapter Guides.** The chapter-by-chapter guides are set up as follows:
  - *Chapter Overview:* The overview provides you with a short summary of the major concepts in each chapter.
  - *Chapter Objectives:* The objectives describe the important learning outcomes for each chapter.
  - *PowerPoint Slides:* A list of PowerPoint slides designed to be used with the chapter is included. They are listed by chapter and number, e.g., PP 2.1 is the first PowerPoint slide on the list for Chapter 2.
  - *DVD Episodes:* The DVD episodes suggested for use with the chapter are listed and described.
  - *Chapter Outline*: The chapter outline includes all the headings for all sections of the chapter.
  - *Presentation Outline:* The presentation outline provides suggestions, including suggested PowerPoint slides and DVD episodes, for teaching the content of the chapter.
  - *Enrichment Materials.* Suggested readings from the Teacher Prep website, additional "Exploring Further" suggestions, Discussion Starters, and Background Readings, are offered as enrichment materials.
  - *Feedback:* Feedback for the Developing as a Professional: Praxis Practice short-answer questions and the Online Casebook questions are provided. *Students do not have access to the Online Casebook questions, so you may choose to assign the questions for homework.*
  - *Classroom Exercises:* The classroom exercises are questions that you may also choose to assign as homework. *Students do not have access to either the questions or the feedback.* The feedback immediately follows the questions in this manual.
- **The Media Guide**. The Media Guide begins on page 271.

We hope you find these materials useful. If you have any questions or comments about the information in the text, this *Instructor's Manual and Media Guide*, or any other support materials, please feel free to contact us. Our e-mail addresses are peggen@unf.edu and kauchak@ed.utah.edu. We would enjoy hearing from you.

The best of luck in your teaching.

Paul Eggen
Don Kauchak

TEACHING SUGGESTIONS

Suggestion	Rationale	Text Reference
If your classes aren't too large, try to learn your students' names.	Knowing their names is a form of personalization, and students appreciate your efforts.	Chapter 10 Chapter 11
Begin your classes on time, and have your materials prepared and ready	Research on effective teaching indicates that effective teachers maximize their time available for instruction, and this allows you to model effective instruction	Chapter 6 Chapter 12 Chapter 13
Establish routines for turning in and collecting materials and other procedural activities.	Expert teachers have as many of their procedures routinized as possible.	Chapter 7 Chapter 9 Chapter 13
Present problems and questions as application exercises.	Working on problems and questions, either individually or in groups, helps students apply their understanding to the real world of teaching.	Chapter 8 Chapter 13
Begin your lessons with a question, problem, or some other attention getter. (Suggestions are offered in the presentation outlines.)	Attention is the beginning point for information processing, and attention getters can induce curiosity, which is a characteristic of intrinsically motivating activities.	Chapter 7 Chapter 10 Chapter 11 Chapter 13
Give frequent, announced assessments. Return the assessments promptly and provided detailed feedback.	Frequent assessment is associated with increased learning, and the need for feedback is a principle of learning. This practice is consistent with both learning and motivation theory.	Chapter 8 Chapter 11 Chapter 13 Chapter 15
Use a criterion-referenced system and emphasize learning rather than performance. Put students' scores on the back page of their quizzes and tests as a symbol of this process.	Criterion referencing and emphasizing learning helps promote a learning-focused classroom environment.	Chapter 11 Chapter 15

SUGGESTED PROJECTS

The following are projects you might consider having your students complete as part of the course.

1. **Case Study:** You might have students complete a case study in which applications of the content of the chapters are utilized. Case studies from chapter opening pages could be used as models. The following are four possible classroom scenarios for which students could prepare case studies. The case studies would be intended to be applications of the content of the text.

2. **Class Presentations:** Since the way topics are represented is an essential factor in what and how much students learn, and research indicates that teachers with strong content backgrounds don't always possess adequate pedagogical content knowledge (discussed in Chapter 1), you might require that students select one or more topics and prepare representations for those topics. To help students understand the requirement, you might refer them to the case studies that begin and end the chapters as examples of the ways teachers represent their topics.

3. **Peer Taught Lessons:** Ask students to select a topic and teach that topic in a peer setting. You might require that the lesson focus on a particular aspect of the content you're emphasizing in your class, such as applications of constructivist approaches to instruction, teaching for transfer, promoting learner motivation, or learner-centered instruction. Students could critique one another's lessons using an observation guide similar to the guides in this manual in *Observing in Classrooms: Exercises and Activities.*

4. **Commercial Movies***:* Consider requiring students to watch one or more commercial movies and then discuss the relationships between the movies and their lead characters and the content of your class. Some possibilities might include: *Mr. Holland's Opus, Stand and Deliver, Dead Poet's Society*, or *Dangerous Minds*. They could be encouraged to select others with your approval.

5. **Research Articles:** You might require students search journals, such as the *Journal of Educational Psychology, Journal of Educational Research, Review of Educational Research*, and others, to summarize a selected number of articles and their implications for learning and teaching. You might require that the reference dates for articles be older than a particular year, such as 2000, for example. Suggest students share the results of their efforts with the whole class.

6. **Concept Mapping**: Concept maps provide opportunities for students to make connections among concepts. Request students to try constructing concept maps using only the key concepts listed at the end of individual chapters) or, ask students to link concepts from several chapters (e.g., 7 and 13, 7, 10 and 13, or 4, 12 and 13). Students should be able to verbally describe their concept maps in student groups or to the whole class by putting them on the board or a transparency.

7. **Item Writing:** To encourage a greater depth in the processing of information ask students to write several assessment items over the content they study. We've had good luck with asking students to write multiple-choice items, because writing good stems and distracters seems to encourage a deeper processing of content knowledge. The items students write can then be used in several ways: 1) as review items to be discussed in a whole class activity, 2) as homework review, or 3) as an opportunity to talk about the item writing process.

8. **Journals:** Encouraging students to keep journals and enter personal reflections and reactions to chapter content can be an effective learning tool.

10. **Field Work**: If you have a field component attached to your course, or you can arrange field experiences for your students, consider having students complete field assignments outlined in the section **Observing in Classrooms: Exercises and Activities**, which begins on the next page.

OBSERVING IN CLASSROOMS: EXERCISES AND ACTIVITIES

This section provides your students with exercises designed to help them in field service experiences. These exercises include suggestions for observing teachers as they work with their students, observing students in learning activities, and conducting interviews with teachers and primary, elementary, or secondary students.

Remind students before they begin any classroom visitations that professional courtesy should be extended to teachers and classrooms in which your students are guests.
The following are specific suggestions for students to use for their classroom observations.

Chapter 1: Educational Psychology: Developing a Professional Knowledge Base

Learning to Teach
Teacher Interview: This exercise is intended to gather information with respect to teachers' beliefs about learning to teach. The following are some suggested questions:
1. How important is knowledge of content in being an effective teacher? Is knowledge of content all that is necessary? Why do you think the way you do?
2. How important is experience in schools in learning to teach? Is experience all that is necessary? Explain.
3. If a person has a good command of their subject matter and they are able to acquire experience in schools, is that sufficient in learning to teach? Please explain.

Reflection
Teacher Interview: This exercise focuses on teachers as reflective practitioners. To begin the interview you may want to provide a brief overview of the topic of reflection (See text page 6). The following are some suggested questions:
1. Is reflection relatively important or relatively unimportant in a teacher's development? Why do you feel the way you do?
2. When do you find opportunities to reflect about your teaching?
3. Can you give me a specific example where you were involved in reflection in the last day or two?
4. Can you give me an example of how the process of reflection changed your teaching?
5. How do the following stimulate your thinking about teaching?
   - Interactions with students
   - Evaluations of student work
   - Interactions with parents or guardians
   - Conversations with other professionals
   - Research?
6. What changes in your professional life would give you greater opportunities to reflect?

Diversity
Student Observation: The purpose of this exercise is to gather basic information about the diversity found in the classroom. Seat yourself at the side of a room so that you can observe students during a lesson and as they enter and leave the room. Gather the following information:
1. Describe the students' physical development. How much do they differ in size? Who is the largest? Smallest?
2. How many males and females are there? How do they interact with each other?
3. Notice the students' clothes. Do they dress alike or is there considerable variation? Are the clothes new or do they appear well worn? Are they clean and in good repair? What do their shoes tell you?
4. How many different cultures appear to be represented? How can you tell? To what extent do students from different cultures interact?

Teacher interview: Explain to the teacher that the purpose of the interview is to gather information about diversity in classrooms. The following are some suggested questions.
1. How much do your students differ in ability?
2. What is the socioeconomic status of most students in your class? What is the range? How does this influence your teaching?

3. How many different cultures are represented in your classroom? For what percentage is English their first language? Is English spoken in the home? How does culture and language influence your teaching?
4. Do the boys and girls in your class do equally well in all subjects? Do they participate equally? Does student gender influence your teaching? If so, how?

Chapter 2: Development of Cognition and Language

Cognitive Development

Student Interview: The purpose of this exercise is to provide you with some experiences in conducting Piagetian tasks with students. If possible, conduct the interviews with a 5–6 year old, a 9–10 year old, and a 13–14 year old and compare their responses. If this isn't possible, interview several students at one grade level and compare their responses.

1. Conservation of Mass: Give the student two equal balls of clay. After the student confirms that they are equal, flatten one of the balls into a pancake shape. Ask: Are the amounts of clay in the two pieces the same or different? How do you know?
2. Conservation of Volume: Show the student two identical clear containers partially filled with water. Ask if the amounts are the same. Then pour the water from one of the containers into a larger clear container. Ask: Are the amounts of liquids in the two containers same or different? How do you know?
3. Conservation of Number: Arrange ten coins in two rows as they appear on page 40 of the text. Ask if the number of coins in the two rows is the same. Then rearrange them so the lower row is spread out. Ask: Are the number of coins in the two rows the same or different? How do you know?
4. Control of Variables. Present the following problem to the student: I have ten puppies and I want to find out which of two kinds of dog food will make the puppies grow faster. Ask: What kind of experiment could I do to answer the question? and Is there anything else I need to do?

Accommodating Developmental Diversity

Teacher Interview: Interview a teacher to determine how developmental diversity influences teaching. The following are some suggested questions:

1. How do the age and developmental level of your students influence your teaching? Can you give me specific examples?
2. How has your view of students changed as a result of working with them over time?
3. To what extent do you use the following strategies to accommodate diversity:
   - Design classroom experiences to specifically address background differences
   - Use concrete examples to illustrate abstract ideas
   - Use classroom interaction to encourage students to share their diverse experiences?

Chapter 3: Personal, Social and Emotional Development

Moral Development

Student Interview: As with the previous developmental exercises try to select several students at different age levels to interview. If this is not possible, interview several students at the same level and pose these hypothetical dilemmas:

1. Cheating. You may want to simplify it if you use it with younger students.
   Steve, a high school junior, is working at a night job to help support his mother, a single parent of three. Steve is a conscientious student who works hard in his classes, but he doesn't have enough time to study. History isn't Steve's favorite course, and with his night work, he has a marginal D average. If he fails the final exam, he will fail the course, won't receive credit, and will have to alter plans for working during his senior year. He arranged to be off work the night before the exam so he could study extra hard, but early in the evening his boss called, desperate to have Steve come in and replace another employee who called in ill at the last moment. His boss pressured him heavily, so reluctantly Steve went to work at 8:00 p.m. and came home exhausted at 2:00 a.m. He tried to study, but fell asleep on the couch with his book in his lap. His mother woke him for school at 6:30.
   Steve went to his history class, looked at the test, and went blank. Everything seemed like a jumble. However, Jill, one of the best students in the class, happened to have her answer sheet positioned so he could clearly see every answer by barely moving his eyes.

- Is it OK for Steve to cheat? Why do you think so?
- What information in the story influenced your decision?
- Is it ever alright to cheat? If yes, when and why? If not, why not?

2. Honesty: Share the following situation with the students.
   Kenny is walking to the store. It's his mother's birthday on Saturday. He's feeling bad because he hasn't been able to save up enough money to get her the present he'd like to give her. Then, on the sidewalk he finds a wallet with $10 in it--just what he needs to buy the present; but there's an identification card in the wallet telling the name and address of the owner.
   - What should Kenny do? Why?
   - What information in the story influenced your decision?
   - Is it ever alright to keep something that doesn't belong to you? If yes, when and why? If not, why not?

Chapter 4: Learner Differences

Students: Individual Differences

Student Observation: The purpose of this exercise is to begin exploring the individual differences found in students. Ideally, it should be done in at least two different classes or at two different grade levels. Observe students and describe the following:

Physical Differences:
1. Describe the physical differences in the students.
2. Do these differences seem to have any effect on the way the students interact with each other or the way they behave in class? If they do, explain, including specific examples.

Energy and Attention Span:
1. How capable are students of monitoring their own attention spans?
2. How much do they fidget, play, and doodle during class?
3. How often does the teacher have to remind students to attend? Is it the group as a whole or certain students?

Ability Differences

Teacher Interview: Interview a teacher to gather information about the differences in student ability. The following are some suggested questions:
1. How much does the ability of your students vary?
2. What kind of information do you gather to help you deal with ability differences?
3. How do you group your students to deal with ability differences? How does it work?
4. What other strategies do you use to deal with ability differences?

Student Observation: Ask the teacher to identify two high and two low-ability students to observe. As you observe them describe the following:
1. How do the two pairs of students differ in their ability to pay attention and stay on task?
2. Compare the participation of the two pairs. Specifically count the number of times students:
   - raise their hands to participate.
   - are called on.
   - answer questions correctly.
   - are given positive feedback about their answers.
3. How do the two pairs of students differ in terms of behavior problems?
   Student Interview: If possible, interview the students and ask the following questions:
   - How much do you like school?
   - What is your favorite part of school?
   - What is your best subject?
   - What is your hardest subject?

Culture

Teacher Interview: Interview a teacher and observe a classroom to examine how culture affects learning. The following are some suggested questions:

1. How many cultures are represented in your classroom?
2. How does culture affect learning in your classroom? Can you give me specific examples?
3. What modifications have you made in your teaching to accommodate cultural differences? How successful have they been? Can you give some specific examples?
4. What suggestions do you have for a beginning teacher working with students from different cultures?

Student Observation. Ask the teacher to provide you with a seating chart and identify students from different cultures. Observe the students and ask yourself the following:

1. Where do these students sit? (Is it by choice or assigned?)
2. Who do these students interact with?
3. How does the participation of these students compare to the participation of non-minorities?
4. How does their behavior (in terms of classroom management) compare to other students?

Students' Language Differences

Teacher Interview: The purpose of this exercise is to examine language development and its effect on classroom performance. Interview a teacher. The following are some suggested questions:

1. Do all students speak English fluently?
2. Describe the differences in your students' language development.
3. What do you do to accommodate those differences?
4. Are there any English dialects spoken in your classroom? Do these dialects have any effect on classroom performance, such as in oral reports? Do they have any effect on the way the students interact with each other? Can you describe the effects?
5. Do you do anything to work with the dialects? If so, what?

Student Interview: Ask the teacher to help you identify several students who differ in their verbal skills. The following are some suggested questions:

1. Do you like school? What's the best part? The worst part?
2. Do you have many friends at school? Who are they? What do you do with them? Do your friends like school?
3. What is your favorite subject? Why do you like it? What is the hardest subject? What makes it hard?
4. If you could change one thing about school, what would it be? Why?

English as a Second Language

Teacher Interview: The following are some suggested questions for gathering information about students who are not native English speakers.

1. How many students are there with English as a second language? What countries do they come from?
2. How are the students performing? Can you give some specific examples?
3. What programs exist for these students? How successful are they?
4. What do you do in the classroom to accommodate these language differences?

Student Observation: (Select several of these students and observe them during classroom instruction.) Try and answer the following questions:

1. How much do they participate in class? Do they volunteer?
2. Who do they talk to in class? Out of class? Who are their friends?
3. What special help are they given in the classroom? From the teacher? Other students? Special material? Pullout programs?

Gender Differences:

1. Do boys and girls participate equally? If not, who participates more? Is this in all classes or just certain ones?
2. Who do students sit next to? Talk to? Play with?
3. Are there differences in terms of behavioral problems?

Socioeconomic Status
Teacher Interview: This exercise involves interviewing a teacher to examine how SES influences learning. The following are some suggested questions:
1. Describe the socioeconomic status of your students. How much do they vary?
2. How many of your students qualify for free or reduced-cost meals?
3. How many of your students come from single-parent families?
4. Do the parents support their children's efforts? Are they supportive of the school?
5. What do you do to accommodate the differences in SES among your students?

Chapter 5: Learners with Exceptionalities

Individuals with Disabilities Education Act (IDEA)
Teacher Interview: Interview a teacher to discover how different components of IDEA are implemented in the classroom. The following are some suggested questions:

Due Process through Parental Involvement:
1. How are parents involved in the process?
2. What obstacles exist for greater parent involvement?
3. How are language barriers dealt with?

Protection against Discrimination in Testing:
1. What provisions are made for ESL students?
2. How are classroom performance and general adaptive behavior assessed?

Least Restrictive Environment:
1. How does the concept of least restrictive environment work in your school?
2. Besides mainstreaming, what other options exist?

Individualized Education Program (IEP):
1. What does an IEP look like?
2. From your perspective what are the most important parts of the program? How well do they work? How could they be improved?

Students with Learning Problems
Teacher Interview: This exercise is intended to give you some information about a student having an exceptionality. Talk with a teacher to gather background experience about the student. The following are some suggested questions:
1. What kind of learning problem does the student have?
2. How did you discover this problem?
3. What help did you have in diagnosing the problem?
4. How do you use the IEP (Ask to see it.) to adapt instruction to the needs of the student?
5. What kinds of approaches (e.g., strategy instruction, social skills training) are being used to help the student?
6. Is supplementary instruction integrated or pull out?
7. How well is the student integrated into the regular flow of the classroom?
8. How well is the student accepted by other students?

Students with Physical Impairments
Teacher Interview: Work with the regular classroom teacher to identify a student with a physical impairment. Interview the teacher. The following are some suggested questions:
1. What kind of physical impairment is it?
2. How does it affect the student's classroom performance?
3. How is instruction being adapted for the student?
4. How well is the student integrated into the regular flow of the classroom?
5. How well is the student accepted by other students?

Students Who are Gifted and Talented
Teacher Interview: Interview a teacher and observe a program for students who are gifted and talented. The following are some suggested questions:
1. How are students who are gifted and talented defined?
2. How are these students identified?
3. What percentage of the student population is identified as gifted and talented?
4. Does the program emphasize enrichment or acceleration?
5. How well are students who are gifted and talented accepted and integrated into the regular classroom?

Chapter 6: Behaviorism and Social Cognitive Theory

Classical Conditioning: Classroom Climate
Classroom Observation: Observe in a classroom to investigate how the physical and social environment interact to create the classroom climate. Ask yourself the following questions:

Physical Environment:
1. What kinds of things are on the wall (e.g., pictures, charts, diagrams)? Are there any plants? Does the room look like an inviting place in which to be?
2. What student work is displayed? (e.g., art work, projects, etc.)?
3. How are the desks arranged? What does this tell you about instruction?
4. Are there areas where students can go when their work is finished?
5. Are rules and procedures posted on the walls? Are these stated in a positive way?

Social Climate:
1. How do students enter the room? Do they seem glad to be there?
2. Do classes start in a positive, inviting way?
3. How does the teacher relate to students?
4. Is interaction in the classroom relaxed and easy?

Operant Conditioning
Classroom Observation: Observe a classroom and describe how the following are used:

Reinforcers:
1. Verbal reinforcers (e.g., praise, positive comments)
2. Tangible reinforcers (e.g., candy, pencils, etc.)
3. Token reinforcers (smiling faces, tickets, etc.)
4. Activity reinforcers (e.g., extra recess, time to work on the computer)

Punishers:
1. Verbal Reprimands (e.g., "Mary, be quiet." "Jared, turn around.")
2. Non-verbal Reprimands (e.g., stern look, hand to lips)
3. Time out (e.g., isolation in corner of room or hall)
4. Lost privileges (e.g., Decreased recess, lunch time).
5. Call to parents
6. Visit to principal's office

Reinforcement Schedules
Classroom Observation: Observe a classroom and describe how different reinforcement schedules are implemented in the following areas:

Verbal Interaction:
1. Are correct responses reinforced every time? If not, how often are they reinforced?
2. How are incorrect, incomplete, or no responses reacted to?

Homework:
1. How often is homework given and collected?
2. Is homework graded every time, periodically, or sporadically? Do students know when it will be collected and graded?

Tests and Quizzes:
1. Are tests and quizzes announced beforehand?
2. Are tests and quizzes given on a regular basis? Is it determined by time or work (units) completed?

Modeling
Classroom Observation: Talk to a teacher and find out when they'll be using modeling to teach some concept or skill. Observe the lesson in terms of the following processes:

Attention:
1. What did the teacher do to attract the class's attention?
2. How did the teacher introduce the new content? Was it linked to a previously learned concept?

Retention:
1. As the new skill was modeled did the teacher point out key characteristics or steps?
2. Did the teacher think out loud, modeling the cognitive process as he or she proceeded?

Reproduction:
1. Were students given opportunities to try the new skill?
2. Did the teacher provide feedback?

Motivation:
1. How was the skill introduced? Did the teacher explain how it would be useful later on?
2. Were students provided with reinforcement as they practiced the skill?

Types of Modeling:
1. What types of modeling do you see displayed in the classroom (e.g., direct, symbolic, synthesized,)? Provide specific examples.

Modeling Outcomes:
1. Describe the modeling outcomes you see (e.g., learning new behaviors, facilitating existing ones).

Chapter 7: Cognitive Views of Learning

Attention/Perception
Classroom Observation: Observe a classroom lesson and interview the teacher afterwards to clarify your observations. During the observation ask yourself the following questions:
1. How did the lesson begin? Were all students drawn into the lesson? Did the lesson maintain student attention?
2. How successful were these strategies?
3. What other strategies does the teacher use to gain and maintain student attention?
4. Was there a problem with student inattention? If so, describe the problem. What appears to be the reason for the problem?
5. What did the teacher do to check the students' perceptions? Did any of the students appear to be misperceiving the teacher's materials?

Working Memory
Classroom Observation: Observe a lesson to determine how the teacher accommodates limitations of working memory. As you observe, ask yourself the following questions:
1. How long does the teacher talk before pausing and asking questions to connect material? How does this relate to developmental characteristics of students?

2. What visual aids (e.g., chalkboard, overhead, charts) does the teacher use to supplement the oral presentation? How effective are these?
3. How does the teacher identify important points in the presentation?

Long-Term Memory and Encoding
Classroom Observation: Observe a lesson and interview the teacher to determine how the teacher insures that information is stored in long term memory. Ask yourself the following questions as you observe:
1. Did the teacher involve the students in rehearsal? Describe specifically what the teacher did.
2. How active were the students during the lesson? What did the teacher do to promote activity?
3. How did the teacher organize the information for the students? What did the teacher do that encouraged the students to organize their own information?
4. What kinds of questions did the teacher ask that encouraged the students to elaborate on what they already knew?

Metacognition
Student Interview: Interview four students (two high and two low achievers) to assess the development of their metacognitive abilities.

Meta-attention:
To determine how aware the students are of the role that attention plays in the learning process ask:
1. Where do you go when you study or have school work to do?
2. Does noise bother you when you're studying? What do you do if it does?
3. Do you ever drift off when your teacher is talking? What do you do when this happens?

Metamemory:
To determine how aware the students are of the process of memory and the role it plays in learning ask:
1. If you had a telephone number to remember to call five minutes later, what would you do? What if you had to remember it for tomorrow?
2. If I gave you a list of ten objects (like shoe, ball, tree, etc.) to study for a minute and then remember, how many do you think you could remember? How would you try to do this?
3. If you had a list of spelling (or foreign language vocabulary) words to remember for a quiz on Friday, what would you do? Why?

Diversity and Information Processing
Teacher Interview: Interview a teacher to determine the impact of student diversity on information processing in the classroom. The following are some suggested questions:
1. Can you describe the differences in background experiences that your students bring to school? Can you give me some specific examples? How does this influence their learning?
2. How often do you do the following to accommodate students' background diversity? Please offer a specific example of where you did each of the following:
   - Assessed their background knowledge prior to a lesson
   - Assessed student perceptions of new material through questioning
   - Provided background experiences when they are lacking
   - Used the background experiences of peers to augment the backgrounds of others

Chapter 8: Constructing Knowledge

Characteristics of Constructivism
Teacher Interview: Interview the teacher to determine the extent to which he or she understands constructivism and implements lessons based on constructivist views of learning. The following are some suggested questions:
1. What is your typical approach to instruction, i.e., when you teach a topic, how do you typically teach it? Explain.
2. How often do you do lessons that are discovery or guided-discovery in their orientation? Please explain how you decide to do the number that you do.

Constructivism in Classrooms

Classroom Observation: Observe a lesson to determine the extent to which the teacher bases the instruction on constructivist views of learning. As you observer ask yourself the following questions:

1. What examples and other representations did the teacher use to provide background knowledge for the students?
2. Did the teacher guide the students' developing understanding with questioning, or did the teacher rely on explanations?
3. To what extent did the teacher connect the content to the real world?

Concept Learning

Classroom Observation: Observe a lesson in which a concept is being taught, or examine a textbook and identify a section where a concept is presented. Ask yourself the following questions:

1. How complete was the definition? Was a superordinate concept identified in the definition? Were characteristics clearly specified?
2. Were positive and negative examples provided? Did they contain characteristics that enabled students to differentiate between the two? Were positive examples familiar to students? Did the negative examples help differentiate the target concept from coordinate concepts?
3. Was the concept linked to other, related concepts?
4. Was the concept presented in context, or was it presented in isolation?
5. What did the teacher do to accommodate differences in the students' background knowledge?
6. Was the concept or relationship among concepts applied in a real-world setting?
7. What did the teacher do to accommodate differences in the students' prior knowledge?

Chapter 9: Complex Cognitive Processes

Problem Solving

Classroom Observation: Observe a lesson in which problem solving is being taught. Ask yourself the following questions:

1. How was the lesson introduced? Had students been introduced to problem solving before? Were the problems well or ill-defined?
2. What did the teacher do to assist students' learning during the following stages?
   - Identify the problem
   - Represent the problem
   - Select a strategy
   - Implement the strategy
   - Evaluate the results
3. What types of practice and feedback were provided?
4. To what extent did the teacher implement the principles of instruction for helping students become better problem solvers?

Study Skills

Student Interview: Interview several students to determine their knowledge and use of different study strategies. If possible, select two high and two low-achieving students and compare their responses. Ask the following questions:

1. When you're studying a chapter (e.g., social studies, science) for the first time what do you usually do to help you learn the material? Why?
2. Have you ever used any of the following strategies? When do you use them and why? Do they help?
   - Underlining
   - Note taking
   - Summarizing
   - Spatial representations (e.g., concept maps, diagramming, hierarchies)
3. Have you ever been taught any study strategies? Do you ever use them? When and why?

Transfer of Learning
Teacher Interview: Interview a teacher to determine how the teacher teaches for transfer. The following are some suggested questions:
1. What specific things do you do to promote transfer? Can you give me some specific examples?
2. What are the biggest problems you have getting the students to transfer?

Chapter 10: Theories of Motivation

Perceptions of Motivation
Teacher Interview: Interview a teacher to gather information about their views of motivation. Based on the views, try to determine what aspects of their views are humanistic, behavioral, or cognitive in their orientation. The following are some suggested questions:

Motivation to Learn:
1. What do you believe is most important for the motivation of the students you teach? What do you do to capitalize on these motivators?
2. How much of the responsibility for student motivation is yours? How much is theirs?

Behavioral Approaches:
1. How important do you think it is to praise students? How much praise do you use? Why?
2. Do you use any other kinds of rewards to motivate your students to study? Can you give me some specific examples?

Humanistic Views:
1. How important do you think it is for you to try and help students develop their self-concepts? What do you do to help students develop their self-concepts? Can you give me a specific example?
2. How important do you think it is for students to believe that teachers care about them as people? Is this part of your job? Why or why not?

Cognitive Views:
1. What do you do to capitalize on students' curiosity? Can you give me some specific examples?
2. What can teachers do to make students feel responsible for their learning? What do you do? How well does it work?
3. What do you do to make the students feel that what their learning is important or worthwhile? Can you give me some specific examples?
4. How important do you think it is to challenge your students? Do they feel better about what they've learned when it has been challenging? Can you give a specific example to illustrate your point?

Maslow's Hierarchy of Needs
Teacher Interview: Make a copy of Maslow's Hierarchy of Needs, and interview a teacher. The following are some suggested questions:
1. Where on the hierarchy are most of your students? How can you tell (i.e., what specific behaviors do you observe that suggest this)?
2. How do you adapt your teaching to accommodate the needs of your students?

Attributions
Student Interview: Interview two high and two low-achieving students to investigate their views about success and failure. Ask the following questions:
1. How well do you usually do in school? Why do you think you are doing well (or not so well)?
2. Think about the last test that you took. What kind of grade did you get? Why do you think you got that grade?
3. Do you think your grades depend most on you, such as how hard you study, or do you think they depend on something else? If something else, what?

Chapter 11: Motivation in the Classroom

The Model for Promoting Student Motivation

Teacher Observation: The purpose of this observation is to see if teacher expectations influence interaction patterns in the classroom. Ask the teacher to identify four high and four low achieving students. Write these students' names on two sheets of paper and observe them during an interactive instructional segment. Then, answer the following questions for each student:

Teacher Expectations:
1. Where is the student seated with respect to the teacher?
2. How often does the teacher talk to or make eye contact with the student?
3. How often is the student called on during the lesson? How much time is the student given to answer?
4. What does the teacher do when the student is unable (or unwilling) to answer?
5. What kind of praise is given for correct responses?

Classroom Climate: Observation: Observe a classroom to determine how the following variables influence classroom climate. Ask yourself the following questions:
1. Are the students orderly when they enter and leave the classroom? Are the rights of all student guaranteed by the teacher?
2. During lessons are students free to respond without fear of being laughed at, ridiculed, or harassed?
3. Are students able to successfully answer most questions during learning activities? How successful are the students on their seatwork and homework?
4. Does the teacher tell the students why they are studying a particular topic?
5. Is the material challenging but learnable? How do you know? Cite a specific example to illustrate your point.

Classroom Instruction: Observation: Observe a classroom to determine how the following variables influence learner motivation. Ask yourself the following questions:
1. What did the teacher do to introduce the lesson? To what extent did it attract the students' attention?
2. How involved were the students in the lesson? What did the teacher do to promote involvement?
3. What did the teacher do to help students personally relate the information they were learning?
4. Describe the kind of feedback students are getting about their progress.

Chapter 12: Creating Productive Learning Environments: Classroom Management

Time

Teacher Interview: Interview a teacher to determine how he or she thinks about time. The following are some suggested questions:
1. How do you decide how much time to devote to a particular topic?
2. What do you do about the "dead time" periods in your classes?
3. What do you do when you see that students aren't paying attention?
4. How can you tell if students are "getting it" when you teach?

Teacher Observation: Now, observe the teacher. Ask yourself the following questions as you observe:
1. How much time does the teacher allocate to the topic?
2. How much of the allocated time is actually devoted to instruction?
3. How did the teacher begin the lesson? Did he or she purposely do something to attract the students' attention? If so, what? How well did it work?
4. Did the teacher review during the lesson? If so, when?
5. What does the teacher do when a student "drifts off?"

Student Observation: Observe four students during the course of a lesson (Ask the teacher to select two that are high achieving and two that are low achieving). Seat yourself so that you can observe their faces during the lesson. Focus on each student at fifteen-second intervals and decide whether the student was attending to the lesson. A "Y" indicates yes, an "N" indicates no, and a question mark indicates that you cannot tell. At the end of the twenty-minute observation period, compute averages for each student and the group as a whole. (Engagement Rate = # of times engaged/Total # of observations.)

	Student A	Student B	Student C	Student D
Minute 1				
Minute 2				
Minute 3				
.				
.				
.				
Minute 20				

Ask yourself the following questions:
1. Did the engagement rates vary during the course of the presentation? If so, why?
2. What did the teacher do differently when the students were paying attention compared to when they were inattentive?
3. How did the attentiveness of the high and low achievers compare?

Classroom Procedures and Rules
Teacher Interview: Interview a classroom teacher to find out about the classroom procedures and rules that the teacher is using. The following are some suggested questions:
1. How did you choose the rules and procedures you're using?
2. How did you teach the rules and procedures?
3. What procedures do you feel are most important in your class (e.g., the way papers are turned in, the way students enter and leave the room)?
4. What do you do when a student doesn't follow a procedure?
5. What do you do when a student breaks a rule?

Student Interview: Interview four students: Try to select students from different segments of the class (e,g., high and low achieving, students from different ethnic or cultural backgrounds). Ask the following questions:
1. How do you feel about the rules in this class? Are they fair? What does the teacher do if you break a rule?
2. Do you think rules are important to make learning easier for you? Why do you think so?

Classroom Observation: Observe the class and answer the following questions:
1. Can all the students see the chalkboard, overhead, and other displays?
2. Can all students hear the teacher and each other? If not, what is distracting the students?
3. What does the teacher do if the students are inattentive or if they break a rule?
4. How effective is the lesson in maintaining student attention? Cite specific evidence to support your assessment.

Communication with Parents
Teacher Interview: Interview a teacher to find out how the teacher and the school communicate with parents or guardians. The following are some suggested questions:
1. What does the school do to communicate with parents (e.g., back-to-school night, open house, school newsletters, packets of papers sent home)? How well do they work?
2. What do you personally do to communicate with parents? How well does it work?

Advice for New Teachers
Teacher Interview: Since classroom management is one of the most challenging problems new teachers face, what advice would you give them? Be as specific as possible.

Chapter 13: Creating Productive Learning Environments: Principles and Models of Instruction

Planning for Instruction

Teacher Interview: Interview an experienced teacher to find out how he or she plans for lessons, unit studies, etc. The following are some suggested questions:

1. When you're planning, how do you begin? What do you do second? Third? How does this vary with different topics?
2. Do you use state or district curriculum guides? Do they help you in your planning?
3. Do you use the teacher's edition of your text? If so, how?
4. Do you do any cooperative planning with other teachers? Why or why not?
5. When you plan, what and how much do you write down?
6. Describe your long-term plans. How are they different from daily plans?
7. Do you take affective factors, such as student motivation, into account when you plan?

Teacher Observation: Ask a teacher if you can look at some of his or her plans and then observe a lesson. As you study the plans and observe the lesson, ask yourself the following questions:

1. How detailed are the plans? What does the teacher write down?
2. How closely does the teacher follow the plan? If he or she deviates from it, why do they do so?

Essential Teaching Skills

Teacher Observation: Observe a second lesson, and devote your observation specifically to the teacher's application of the essential teaching skills. Describe the example of the teacher's implementation of an essential teaching skill when you see the teacher apply it in his or her instruction.

Questioning

Teacher Observation: For this observation focus specifically on the teacher's questioning patterns. Make a seating chart for the students. Sit in the room so you can see who is being called on. Every time the teacher asks a question, put a check mark by the student being called on. If the student is called on because of attempting to volunteer (such as raising a hand), put an X by the student's name. Observe the lesson and tally the teacher's questions. Then ask yourself the following questions:

1. Does the teacher call on students by name, or are students called on only when they volunteer?
2. Are all the students in the class called on?
3. Are students allowed to call out answers?
4. What does the teacher do when students are unable or unwilling to answer?
5. When the teacher asks a question, how long does he or she wait for the student to answer?
6. Does the teacher direct a similar number of questions to boys and girls? To cultural minorities and non-minorities?

Models of Instruction

Teacher Observation: As you observe the teacher's implementation of the essential teaching skills or questioning, describe the model of instruction that the teacher appears to be most nearly applying. Describe each phase of the model as you see the teacher implement it.

Cooperative Learning

Teacher Interview: This exercise focuses on cooperative learning activities. Interview the teacher to see how she organizes her groups. The following are some suggested questions:

1. How did you form the teams?
2. What did you do to be sure that the groups were about equal in ability, gender and cultural background?
3. What did you do to train the students to effectively interact with each other?

Classroom Observation: Now observe the class and answer the following questions:

1. Does everyone have meaningful tasks to perform during the activity?
2. Do tasks use a variety of skills and call on a variety of knowledge?
3. Do tasks provide opportunities for all students to make contributions?
4. How does the teacher monitor the groups as they work?

Chapter 14: Learning and Instruction and Technology

Instructional Applications of Technology

Teacher Interview: This exercise focuses on ways that teachers use technology to support their instruction. Interview a teacher as ask how he or she uses technology in their teaching. The following are some suggested questions:

1. In what ways do you use technology as part of the instructional process, such as using drill-and-practice software to help your students acquire basic skills?
2. To what extent do you use technology for routine tasks, such as recording attendance and communicating with parents?
3. To what extent do you use technology to support your instruction, such as storing examples that you use to illustrate the topics you teach, preparing and storing test items, and similar activities?
5. How important is technology in your teaching?
6. Do you believe that the benefits of using technology in your teaching justify the cost of the equipment? Why do you think so, or why do you think not?

Chapter 15: Assessing Classroom Learning

Teachers' Assessment Patterns

Teacher Interview: Interview a teacher about his or her attitudes toward testing and assessment patterns. The following are some suggested questions:

1. How important do you feel testing is in the assessment of your students? Can you explain?
2. Do you usually make out your own tests, or do you use tests that come with your textbook?
3. What kinds of performance assessments do you use? Can you give me some specific examples of some that you use in your class?

Test Construction

Observation: Obtain a teacher-made test, examine its contents, and ask yourself the following questions:

1. What format was used (e.g., multiple-choice)? Most of the questions were written at what level (e.g., knowledge, comprehension)?
2. To what extent were the items consistent with the guidelines provided in your text?

Teacher Interview: Interview the teacher to gather information about the way he or she prepared the test you examined. The following are some suggested questions:

1. What were your goals in constructing the test? How were the items designed to measure different types of knowledge?
2. What did you do to be sure that the content you wanted covered was covered?
3. Did you use any kind of chart or matrix in designing the test?
4. Did you utilize a computer in any way as you designed your test?
5. How will you grade the test? Will any part of it be machine scored?

Test Administration

Teacher Interview: Interview a teacher who has recently administered a test to gather some information about the ways students are prepared for tests. The following are some suggested questions:

1. Do you do anything to help your students deal with test anxiety? If so, what?
2. Do you, or have you, taught your students specific test-taking strategies? Can you describe specifically how you did this?
3. Did you have your students practice on some items similar to those that will be on the test?
4. How carefully do you supervise the students while they are taking tests?
5. Is cheating ever a problem? If so, what do you do about it?
6. When you hand tests back to the students, do you go over them? Why or why not?

Grading

Teacher Interview: Interview a teacher and get a copy of the course expectations (if available) and a copy of a sample report card. The following are some suggested questions:

1. How do tests and quizzes contribute to the final grade in your class?
2. How do you use homework and seatwork in your grading system?
3. Do you use a point or a percentage system for your grading? Why?
4. Do you use computers to help you in your grading? If so, how?

Diversity and Assessment

Teacher Interview: Interview a teacher to determine how student diversity influences the assessment process. The following are some suggested questions:

1. How does the diversity of student backgrounds in your class affect the assessment process?
2. Do you make any special provisions in preparing students for tests? If so, what are they?
3. Is language ever a problem for students as they take tests? If so, what do you do to accommodate the problem?

Chapter 16: Assessment Through Standardized Testing

Using Standardized Tests

Teacher Interview: Interview a teacher about his or her experiences with standardized testing. The following are some suggested questions:

1. Is the emphasis placed on standardized tests appropriate? Too much emphasis? Too little emphasis? Why do you think so?
2. What roles do you play in selecting and administering standardized tests?
3. Is high-stakes testing increasing, decreasing, or having no effect on learning? Why do you think so?

GUIDELINES FOR WORKING IN SCHOOLS

The following are some suggestions for students as they work in schools:

1. *Dress and behave professionally.* The way you dress and act will make a strong impression on the teachers and administrators in the school. Unprofessional dress, and particularly unprofessional behavior, is inexcusable.

2. *Try to be unobtrusive.* To the extent that you can, avoid interrupting classroom routines. It is a simple courtesy, and the information you gather will be more accurate if you aren't noticed.

3. *Maintain confidentiality.* In any reports you make, avoid using last names and don't identify specific persons. You want to prevent even the most remote possibility of embarrassing someone.

4. *Keep information factual.* The purpose of your classroom visits is to observe how the concepts you learn about in your text are applied in classrooms; it is not to assess a teacher's performance. While you will certainly have some reactions to what a teacher does, try to report your observations as objectively as possible, and avoid making premature judgements.

CHAPTER 1: EDUCATIONAL PSYCHOLOGY: DEVELOPING A PROFESSIONAL KNOWLEDGE BASE

CHAPTER OVERVIEW

Chapter 1 serves as the student's entry into the book and introduces them to the characteristics of professionalism and the role of research and theory in professional decision making. The student is introduced to the different kinds of knowledge–knowledge of content, pedagogical content knowledge, general pedagogical knowledge, and knowledge of learners and learning--in learning to teach. They then see the different kinds of research that lead to a professional knowledge base, how that research is evaluated, and the link between research and theory. The chapter closes with a description of the use of case studies in educational psychology.

CHAPTER OBJECTIVES

- Describe and explain the characteristics of professionalism, and identify examples of the characteristics in teachers' actions.
- Describe and illustrate the different kinds of knowledge professional teachers possess, and identify examples of professional knowledge in teachers' actions.
- Describe and explain different types of research, and analyze applications of these types.
- Explain how using case studies makes educational psychology more meaningful than it would be without the use of these case studies.

POWERPOINT SLIDES

PP 1.1 Characteristics of Professionalism
PP 1.2 Learning and Teaching Inventory
PP 1.3 Learning and Teaching Inventory: The Research Base
PP 1.4 Knowledge Needed for Expert Teaching
PP 1.5 The INTASC Principles
PP 1.6 Different Types of Research
PP 1.7 Evaluating Research Studies
PP 1.8 Praxis Practice: Feedback for Short-Answer Questions
PP 1.9 Feedback for Online Case Questions
PP 1.10 Classroom Exercises

VIDEO

DVD 1, Episode 1: "Demonstrating Knowledge in Classrooms"
This episode illustrates the different forms of knowledge required of teachers. It exists in four segments. The first involves a kindergarten teacher discussing planting a garden with her children; the second is a seventh-grade teacher illustrating the concept of symmetry; the third is a chemistry teacher discussing Charles' law; and the fourth is a history teacher presenting information about the Vietnam War.

It is also the closing case study for this chapter.

CHAPTER OUTLINE

I. Educational psychology and becoming a professional
   A. Characteristics of professionalism
      1. Commitment to learners
      2. Decision making
      3. Reflection
      4. Professional knowledge
II. Professional knowledge and learning to teach
   A. Knowledge of content
   B. Pedagogical content knowledge
   C. General pedagogical knowledge
      1. Instructional strategies
      2. Classroom management
   D. Knowledge of learners and learning
      1. Knowledge of learners
      2. Knowledge of learning
   E. The INTASC standards: States respond to the need for professional knowledge
   F. Changes in education: Reform and accountability
      1. The Praxis Exam
   G. Learning contexts: Teaching and learning in urban environments
III. The role of research in acquiring knowledge
   A. Descriptive research
      1. Evaluating descriptive studies
   B. Correlational research
      1. Evaluating correlational research
   C. Experimental research
      1. Evaluating experimental research
   D. Action research
   E. Conducting research in classrooms: Action research strategies
   F. Research and the development of theory
IV. The use of case studies in educational psychology

PRESENTATION OUTLINE

The suggested activities can be completed in small groups and discussed as a whole group, or they can be conducted as whole-class activities. We recommend that you promote as much discussion–both in small groups and with the whole class–as possible.

I. Educational psychology and becoming a professional
   A. Characteristics of professionalism
      1. Commitment to learners
      2. Decision making
      3. Reflection
      4. Professional knowledge
II. Professional knowledge and learning to teach
   A. Knowledge of content
   B. Pedagogical content knowledge
   C. General pedagogical knowledge
      1. Instructional strategies
      2. Classroom management
   D. Knowledge of learners and learning
      1. Knowledge of learners
      2. Knowledge of learning
   E. The INTASC standards: States respond to the need for professional knowledge
   F. Changes in education: Reform and accountability
      1. The Praxis Exam
   G. Learning contexts: Teaching and learning in urban environments

Teaching suggestions:

■ *The purpose of this activity is to help students understand the characteristics of professionalism.*

1. **Display PP 1.1 "*Characteristics of Professionalism.*" Have the class identify each of the characteristics in Jan Davis' and Keith Jackson's conversation in the case study at the beginning of the chapter. The feedback for the "Checking Your Understanding" questions 1.1-1.3, which are in Appendix B of the text provides some specific examples of the characteristics of professionalism in their conversation.**

■ *To help students understand the different kinds of knowledge required in learning to teach:*

1. **Display PP 1.2 "*Learning and Teaching Inventory*" and ask students to identify the statements as true or false. Some of the results will be intuitively sensible, while others will not.**

2. **For each item, ask students (or groups) to write a brief explanation as to why they think the statement is true or false.**

3. **To provide a brief explanation for each of the items together with a research citation that documents the results display PP 1.3 "*Learning and Teaching Inventory: The Research Base.*"**

4. **Display PP 1.4 "*Knowledge Needed for Expert Teaching.*" As you discuss each of the results, have the students identify the type of knowledge–knowledge of content, pedagogical content knowledge, general pedagogical knowledge, or knowledge of learners and learning–required to respond correctly to the item in the *Learning and Teaching Inventory*. (Point out that each of the items is discussed in detail in the chapter.)**

5. **To help students understand the different forms of knowledge that professional organizations expect of them–even as first year teachers, display PP 1.5 "*The INTASC Principles.*" Have**

them identify the type of knowledge addressed in each of the principles. For example, "Principle 1: Knowledge of Content" addresses both knowledge of content and pedagogical content knowledge, because it says, "Teachers understand the knowledge they teach and can make the content meaningful for students."

Here would be a good point to show or discuss **Episode 1 on DVD 1**: "Demonstrating Knowledge in Classrooms" if you should choose to do so.

III. The role of research in acquiring knowledge
  A. Descriptive research
    1. Evaluating descriptive studies
  B. Correlational research
    1. Evaluating correlational research
  C. Experimental research
    1. Evaluating experimental research
  D. Action research
  E. Conducting research in classrooms: Action research strategies
  F. Research and the development of theory

IV. The use of case studies in educational psychology

Teaching Suggestions:

■ ***The purpose of this activity is to help the students understand the differences between descriptive, correlational, and experimental research and how to evaluate each.***

1. **Display PP 1.6 "*Different Types of Research,*" and PP 1.7 "*Evaluating Research Studies.*" Give them some examples, such as the following:**
   - **Descriptive Research: Researchers found that teachers, after asking a question, often give students very little time to think about their answers before turning the question to someone else or providing a prompt to help the student.**
   - **Correlational Research: Researchers have found that a caring teachers are more successful with students placed at risk than teachers who are less warm.**
   - **Experimental Research: Researchers systematically manipulated the amount of time teachers waited for students to answer, and they found that the longer wait times caused an improvement in the quality of students' answers.**

2. **To further increase the students' understanding of the relationship between theory and research have the students decide whether or not the statement:**

   "Success is the primary factor that increases student motivation and self-esteem,"

   is true or false. After you've polled the students, point out that research indicates that the statement is false (Baron, 1998; Ryan & Deci, 1998). Then note that we can explain why the answer is false by using Expectancy x Value Theory (discussed in Chapter 10). This theory suggests that learners will be motivated to the extent that they expect to succeed on a task times the amount of value they place on the task, and learners value challenging tasks much more than they value trivial tasks. This allows us to predict that learners must be challenged if their motivation is to be increased. (You might want to point out that Expectancy *times* Value is important. This means if either is zero the product is zero. So, if learners don't value success, no amount of success will increase motivation to learn.)

V. The use of case studies in educational psychology

Teaching Suggestions:

■ *To help students understand the use of case studies in educational psychology:*

1. **Refer them to the case study at the beginning of the chapter and point out that every chapter begins and ends with a case study.**

2. **Point out that the "Short-Answer" questions that follow the end-of-chapter case parallel the kinds of items they will experience on the Praxis exam. Also, tell them that feedback for all the short-answer questions is available on the Companion Website at www.prenhall.com/eggen.**

ENRICHMENT MATERIALS

TEACHER PREP WEBSITE

The *Teacher Prep* website an online resource for students and instructors. Both you and students can access the *Teacher Prep* website by going to http://www.prenhall.com/teacherprep. Enter your user name and password and click on "Log In." The *Teacher Prep* website includes video episodes, student and teacher artifacts, teacher and research resources, and information about licensing and beginning a teaching career. The *Teacher Prep* website is described in detail in the Media Guide.

The following articles are recommended by the *Exploring Further* section titled "Increasing Your Professionalism" on page 6 of the chapter.

Once into the *Teacher Prep* website access the articles by completing the following steps:

1. Click on "Research Resources" on the left panel of the screen, scroll down the middle of the page and again click on "Research Resources."
2. Go to "Classroom Processes" and click on "Refining Your Practice."
3. Click on the following article:
   Practicing Professional Responsibilities: Professional Development, by B. Hurst and G. Reding (2000), Ref. No. 729,
   Practicing Professional Responsibilities: School Responsibilities, by B. Hurst and G. Reding (2000), Ref. No. 730,
   Professionalism at Its Best: Effective Social Skills, by B. Hurst and G. Reding (2000), Ref. No. 734, and
   Professionalism at Its Best: Personal Attire, by B. Hurst and G. Reding (2000), Ref. No. 735,.

These excerpts offer pre-service teachers practical suggestions for increasing their professionalism and tips for creating a positive impression when beginning their first jobs.

ADDITIONAL EXPLORING FURTHER SUGGESTIONS

Page 5 of the chapter suggests that students to go the *Exploring Further* module of Chapter 1 to see the National Education Association code of ethics.

Page 13 of the chapter suggests that students to go the *Exploring Further* module of Chapter 1 to see more information about the INTASC standards.

Page 14 of the chapter suggests that students to go the *Exploring Further* module of Chapter 1 to see information about the Praxis Principles of Learning and Teaching Exams.

DISCUSSION STARTERS

You may choose to have your students discuss one or more of the following questions to further enrich their understanding of your learning activities.

1. Of the different roles that teachers perform—manager, motivator, instructor, and evaluator—which is most important to your grade level or content area? Least? How does the context of your teaching situation influence your answer?

2. In the future which side of teaching—artistic or scientific—is likely to become more important? Why?

3. What is the role of research in teacher decision making? How does knowledge of classrooms help in this process?

4. How can research make teachers more reflective? Besides a thorough knowledge of the research base, what else can teachers do to make themselves more reflective?

5. What are some personal characteristics that make teachers effective? Can these be taught or developed?

6. What are some of the reasons for the increased diversity in our schools? What kinds of things can teachers do to make themselves more effective teachers of students whose backgrounds are diverse?

BACKGROUND READINGS

Berliner, D. (1994). Expertise: The wonder of exemplary performances. In J. Mangieri & C. Collins (Eds.), *Creating powerful thinking in teachers and students* (pp. 161–186). Fort Worth, TX: Harcourt Brace.
This chapter describes the continuum from novice to expert that has become popular in descriptions of professional development.

Borko, H., & Putnam, R. (1996). Learning to teach. In D. Berliner & R. Calfee (Eds.), *Handbook of educational psychology* (pp. 673–708). New York: Simon & Schuster Macmillan.
This chapter provides an excellent overview of the processes involved in learning to teach.

Darling-Hammond, L., & Baratz-Snowdon, J. (Eds.).(2005). *A good teacher in every classroom: Preparing the highly qualified teachers our children deserve.* San Francisco: Jossey-Bass/Wiley.
This short book provides a succinct overview of the knowledge teachers need to be successful.

Darling-Hammond, L. & J. Bransford (Eds). (2005). *Preparing teachers for a changing world.* San Francisco: Jossey-Bass.
This book is dense, but it covers topics ranging from learning theory to teacher development, including discussions of learner diversity, assessment, classroom management and others relevant to teachers.

Educational Testing Service. (2005). *The Praxis Series 2005–2006: Information and Registration Bulletin.* Available online at http://www.ets.org/praxis/prxtest.html
This bulletin provides detailed information on the Praxis exam.

Gage N. (1991). The obviousness of social and educational research results. *Educational Researcher 20*(1) 10–16.
Gage makes a convincing case that educational research is not just reinventing the wheel.

FEEDBACK

Developing as a Professional: Praxis Practice: Feedback for Short-Answer Questions

The feedback that appears here is for the short-answer questions that follow the case study on pages 25 and 26 of the text. The feedback is also available to students on the companion website.

1. What type or types of knowledge did Rebecca Atkins primarily demonstrate? Explain.
   Rebecca most explicitly demonstrated general pedagogical knowledge in her lesson. The children were orderly, and she used questioning to involve several of the children in the lesson.

2. What type or types of knowledge did Richard Nelms demonstrate in his lesson? Explain.
   Richard demonstrated each of the forms of knowledge, but pedagogical content knowledge and knowledge of learners and learning were most prominent. Using concrete examples such as a starfish and Jason to illustrate different types of symmetry demonstrated his ability to represent abstract concepts in ways that make sense to learners demonstrated his pedagogical content knowledge.
   Richard demonstrated knowledge of learners and learning by having Jason go to the front of the room. He understood, for instance, that using a personalized example, such as Jason, increases motivation to learn.

3. What type or types of knowledge did Didi Johnson primarily demonstrate? Identify at least two decisions that Didi made in an attempt to help her lesson progress smoothly.
   Didi primarily demonstrated pedagogical content knowledge in her lesson. Her ability to represent the relationship between temperature and pressure in a way that made sense to students demonstrated this type of knowledge.

4. What type or types of knowledge did Bob Duchaine primarily demonstrate?
   Bob Duchaine primarily demonstrated knowledge of content. He obviously understood the factors surrounding the Vietnam War. However, the fact that he only used lecture as a way of delivering the content suggests that he might not be as knowledgeable about other types of teacher knowledge.

Feedback for Online Case Questions:

The feedback below is for the *Online Case Book* for Chapter 1 (referenced on page 19 of the chapter). Both you and the students can access the case study by going to www.prenhall.com/eggen, selecting Chapter 1, and clicking on *Online Case Book.*

You may choose to assign the online case as homework or you may want to discuss the case in class. Answers to these questions *do not* appear on the companion website, so students *do not* have access to the feedback.

Multiple-Choice Items:

1. Which of the types of professional knowledge is Tony best demonstrating in paragraph 2?
   a. Knowledge of content
   b. Pedagogical content knowledge
   c. General pedagogical knowledge
   d. Knowledge of learners and learning
   d. In recognizing that the students may think the topic is boring, and making an effort to increase their interest by involving them, Tony is demonstrating a knowledge of learners and learning.

2. Which type of research is best illustrated in Tony's comment in paragraph 2 in reference to the article he read?

a. Descriptive research
b. Correlational research
c. Experimental research
d. Action research

c. An article reporting" that kids were more interested in classes when they gathered the information themselves than they were in classes where the information was presented to them" is describing a relationship between interest and involvement, which describes correlational research.

3. Which of the types of professional knowledge is Tony best demonstrating in paragraph 8?

a. Knowledge of content
b. Pedagogical content knowledge
c. General pedagogical knowledge
d. Knowledge of learners and learning

c. Tony's ability to organize his groups efficiently demonstrates general pedagogical knowledge.

Short-Answer Item:

4. Assess the extent to which Tony demonstrated the characteristics of professionalism in his planning and in the conduct of the lesson. Include as many of the characteristics of professionalism as apply.

Tony demonstrated each of the characteristics of professionalism in planning and conducting his lesson. He demonstrated commitment to learners, reflection, and decision making by being concerned about whether or not the students would be bored, and then making decisions about the steps necessary to involve them. And, he made his decisions about planning and conducting he lesson based on professional knowledge.

CLASSROOM EXERCISES

The classroom exercises that follow appear *only here* in the instructor's manual. Students do not have access to *either the questions or the answers*.

The purpose of keeping the exercises only in the instructor's manual is to allow you to use them as class discussion items, or for homework, if you should choose to do so.

Feedback for the exercises follows immediately.

1. Misha Pauley stood at the front of his classroom and smiled broadly as his students filed in for their first meeting. He was excited about his first day. He had his notes, motivation plan, and management system ready. He was confident that his double-major in history and English would make him a stellar teacher. He was especially lucky in that he'd obtained an emergency certificate and hadn't been forced to waste all that time in teacher education classes. If Misha's experience is consistent with patterns identified by research, is Misha likely to be relatively successful or relatively unsuccessful in his first year of teaching? Explain.

2. A sixth grade teacher presents an introductory math lesson on multiplying fractions. During the lesson, she notices that several of the students ask for clarification of the terms "numerator," "denominator," and "reduce." She reflects that evening after school, and plans to go back and review the basics of fractions by using concrete materials (manipulatives) that will allow her students to understand these abstract concepts. What concept from the chapter is the teacher best illustrating by using the manipulatives to illustrate multiplication of fractions.

3. In general, biology teachers carefully and accurately explain the process of photosynthesis in green plants. Yet many learners mistakenly believe that we "feed" green plants, much as we feed animals, instead of understanding that green plants manufacture their own food. Explain how each of the types of knowledge described in the chapter is required to deal with this problem.

4. We see a person struggle to solve a brain teaser, simply for the experience of solving it. We conclude, "People have an innate desire to understand how the world works. When they don't, they struggle until they do." Of the Important Concepts that are listed at the end of the chapter, which two are best illustrated by our conclusion? Explain.

5. The process of making decisions is essential in teaching. Assuming teachers are reflective, which two of the Important Concepts at the end of the chapter are most important in the process of making decisions? Explain.

FEEDBACK FOR CLASSROOM EXERCISES

1. If Misha's experience fits patterns identified by research, he is likely to be somewhat unsuccessful. His double major doesn't ensure that he has the pedagogical content knowledge to be an effective history or English teacher, and his lack of knowledge of learners and learning is likely to detract from his effectiveness. His thinking illustrates the misconception that majoring in a subject provides all the knowledge needed to teach the subject.

2. Knowing that concrete examples are necessary to understand abstract ideas and being able to prepare the concrete examples illustrates pedagogical content knowledge.

3. Knowledge of content is required to understand the process of photosynthesis. Pedagogical content knowledge is required to enable teachers to represent the process of photosynthesis in such as way that students don't confuse it with the intake of food–as occurs with animals. General pedagogical knowledge is needed to have the questioning skills, for example, to guide learners' understanding, and knowledge of

learners and learning is required to understand why learners are likely to have the misconception in the first place and what can be done to help eliminate it.

4. The two concepts best illustrated by the comment are principle and theory. A theory is a set of related principles that is used to explain observations. We explain the person's efforts based on the theory that people have a need for order, predictability, and understanding. This is the basic premise on which cognitive theories of motivation are based. The principles are, "People have an innate desire to understand how the world works," and "When people don't understand how the world works, they struggle until they do."

5. The two concepts are research and theory. Research and theory make up the knowledge base teachers use for making decisions. (Since theories are based on principles, they are also important.)

CHAPTER 2: DEVELOPMENT OF COGNITION AND LANGUAGE

CHAPTER OVERVIEW

In this chapter students examine the development of cognition and language. The chapter begins with a definition and description of principles that apply to all forms of development. Within this framework, Piaget's theory of intellectual development is then discussed, followed by an examination of Vygotsky's description of development. Piaget's and Vygotsky's views are then compared in the context of constructivism. The chapter closes with a discussion of language development, language diversity, and English as a second language.

CHAPTER OBJECTIVES

- Describe the principles of development, and identify examples of the principles in children's behaviors.
- Use concepts from Piaget's theory of intellectual development to explain both classroom and everyday events.
- Use Vygotsky's sociocultural theory to explain how language, culture and instructional support can influence learner development.
- Explain language development using different theories of language acquisition.

POWERPOINT SLIDES

PP 2.1 Factors Influencing Human Intellectual Development
PP 2.2 Principles of Development and Examples
PP 2.3 The Drive for Equilibrium
PP 2.4 Maintaining Equilibrium Through the Process of Adaptation
PP 2.5 An Example of Development in the Real World
PP 2.6 Piaget's Stages and Characteristics
PP 2.7 An Example of Centering
PP 2.8 An Example of Egocentrism
PP 2.9 Measuring Thinking
PP 2.10 Preoperational Characteristics in Adults' Thinking
PP 2.11 Principles of Instruction for Applying Piaget's Work in Classrooms
PP 2.12 Learning and Development in a Cultural Context
PP 2.13 The Zone of Proximal Development
PP 2.14 Scaffolding in Three Zones of Proximal Development
PP 2.15 A Comparison of Piaget's and Vygotsky's Views of Knowledge Construction
PP 2.16 Principles of Instruction for Applying Vygotsky's Theory in the Classroom
PP 2.17 Promoting Language Development: Suggestions for Teachers
PP 2.18 Praxis Practice: Feedback for Short-Answer Questions
PP 2.19 Feedback for Online Case Questions
PP 2.20 Classroom Exercises

VIDEOS

DVD 1, Episode 2: "Examining Learner Thinking: Piaget's Conservation Tasks"
This episode illustrates the thinking of students at different ages in response to Piaget's conservation tasks. It illustrates differences in preoperational and concrete operational thinking.

DVD 1, Episode 3: "Developmental Differences: Studying Properties of Air in First Grade"
This video episode illustrates the thinking of first graders as they try to explain why water doesn't go into a glass that is inverted and immersed in a fishbowl of water. It illustrates preoperational thinking, and it is also the closing case study for this chapter.

CHAPTER OUTLINE

- I. What is development?
    - A. Principles of development
    - B. The human brain and cognitive development
        - 1. The learning physiology of the brain
        - 2. Putting brain research into perspective
- II. Piaget's theory of intellectual development
    - A. The drive for equilibrium
    - B. Organization and adaptation: The development of schemes
        - 1. Achieving equilibrium: The process of organization
        - 2. Maintaining equilibrium: The process of adaptation
    - C. Factors influencing development
        - 1. Experience with the physical world
        - 2. Social experience
    - D. Stages of development
        - 1. Sensorimotor (0 to 2 years)
        - 2. Preoperations (2 to 7 years)
            - a. Conservation
            - b. Egocentrism
        - 3. Concrete operations (7 to 11 years)
            - a. Classification and seriation
        - 4. Formal operations (11 to adult)
            - a. Characteristics of formal thought
            - b. Adolescent egocentrism
            - c. Formal operations: Research results
    - E. Applying Piaget's work in classrooms: Instructional principles
    - F. Putting Piaget's theory into perspective
- III. A sociocultural view of development: The work of Lev Vygotsky
    - A. Social interaction and development
    - B. Language and development
    - C. Culture and development
    - D. The relationship between learning and development
    - E. Vygotsky's work: Instructional principles
        - 1. Zone of proximal development
        - 2. Scaffolding: Interactive instructional support
    - F. Piaget's and Vygotsky's views of knowledge construction
- IV. Language development
    - A. Theories of language acquisition
        - 1. Behaviorist views
        - 2. Social cognitive perspectives
        - 3. Nativist theory
        - 4. Sociocultural theory
    - B. Stages of language acquisition
        - 1. Early language: Building the foundation
        - 2. Fine-tuning language
        - 3. Increasing language complexity
    - C. Promoting language development: Suggestions for teachers

PRESENTATION OUTLINE

The suggested activities can be completed in small groups and discussed as a whole group, or they can be conducted as whole-class activities. We recommend that you promote as much discussion—both in small groups and with the whole class—as possible.

I. What is development?
   A. Principles of development
   B. The human brain and cognitive development
      1. The learning physiology of the brain
      2. Putting brain research into perspective

Teaching Suggestions:

■ ***These activities are designed to help students understand the concept "development" and principles that influence all forms of development.***

1. Ask the students to describe what the term "cognitive development" means to them. Guide them to conclude that it describes changes in thinking that result from learning, experience, and maturation. Ask them if they, as adults, also develop. They will likely conclude that they do, and you can then emphasize the role of learning and experience in their development.

2. Describe ways that the term development is commonly used, such as developmental approaches to curriculum and instruction, and topics, problems, or issues that are developmental. Point out that when someone says they use a developmental approach it usually means that they begin with concrete experiences and gradually move to more abstract experiences.
Even university students approach topics "developmentally," meaning they first look at the topics concretely before they're able to deal with the topics in the abstract.

3. Display PP 2.1 "*Factors Influencing Human Intellectual Development.*" Ask students for some examples from their personal lives that illustrate each of the three factors.

4. Display PP 2.2 "*Principles of Development and Examples,*" which includes the principles and an example of each. Have the students identify other examples from their own experiences.

5. Have the students suggest implications that brain development has for education. Some possibilities include:
- **Teaching foreign languages to young children, rather than waiting until they're in middle school, as is present practice.**
- **Creating stimulating environments for infants and young children.**
- **Placing even more emphasis on language and reading with young children than presently exists.**

Remind students that brain research is still in its infancy, and applying the research in classrooms should be approached with caution.

II. Piaget's theory of intellectual development
   A. The drive for equilibrium
   B. Organization and adaption: The creation of schemes
      1. Achieving equilibrium: The process of organization
      2. Maintaining equilibrium: The process of adaptation
   C. Factors influencing development
      1. Experience with the physical world
      2. Social experience
   D. Stages of development
      1. Sensorimotor (0 to 2 years)

2. Preoperations (2 to 7 years)
    1. Conservation
    2. Egocentrism
3. Concrete operations (7 to 11 years)
    1. Classification and seriation
4. Formal operations (11 to adult)
    1. Characteristics of formal thought
    2. Adolescent egocentrism
    3. Formal operations: Research results

E. Applying Piaget's work in classrooms: Instructional principles
F. Putting Piaget's work into perspective

Teaching Suggestions:

■ *The following activities are intended to help students understand the concept of equilibrium and why it is the cornerstone of Piaget's theory:*

1. **Ask the following question: "How many of you in this class are married or living with someone?" You will have a sprinkling of hands. Then ask, "For those of you who are, do you have your side of the bed that you sleep on every night, and does your husband/wife have his/her side?" Since people almost always have their own side of the bed, this usually results in some laughter. Tell them to keep the question in mind, and that the point in it will be clear in a moment.**

2. **Display PP 2.3 "*The Drive for Equilibrium*" (keeping the title covered) and have the students identify what the examples have in common. After a series of responses, use both the examples on PP 2.3 and the question about their side of the bed to introduce the idea of equilibrium. Point out that this concept is the cornerstone of Piaget's Theory of Intellectual Development.**

3. **Ask students to cite additional examples of people's need for equilibrium. (During the discussion, point out that most of them tend to sit in the same seat each time they come to class, which is a personal example.)**

■ *To help the students understand the relationships among the concepts* equilibrium, organization, scheme, adaptation, assimilation, accommodation, experience, *and* development.

1. **Display PP 2.4 "*Maintaining Equilibrium Through the Process of Adaptation.*" Students commonly have difficulty with the concepts assimilation and accommodation, often confusing the two. Emphasize that accommodation involves modifying the original scheme and creating a new scheme.**

2. **To help students understand how forming schemes helps us function in the world, display PP 2.5 "*An Example of Development in the Real World.*" Have them complete the activity as suggested in the directions. Discuss their products, and display the feedback.**

3. **Have students identify other examples of development using the same concepts.**

■ *To help the students understand the characteristics of thinking at each stage of development:*

1. **Display PP 2.6 "*Piaget's Stages and Characteristics.*" Review the information.**

Here would be a good point to show or discuss **Episode 2**: "Examining Learner Thinking: Piaget's Conservation Tasks," and **Episode 3**: "Developmental Differences: Studying Properties of Air in First Grade." Both are on **DVD 1.**

2. Display PP 2.7 "*An Example of Centering*" and PP 2.8 "*An Example of Egocentrism*" to illustrate the concepts *centering* (centration) and *egocentrism* in the thinking of young children.

3. Display PP 2.9 "*Measuring Thinking*." Emphasize that the objects are solids and cubes. Point out that solids are treated as non-compressible, and remind them that this information is relevant for their responses. Have them decide what stage of development would be required to answer correctly, and discuss the results.

The answers are as follows:

1. ***True.* We can see that A is bigger than B. A preoperational thinker would be able to respond correctly to this item, since it is perceptual.**
2. ***False.* The balance is balanced, so they have the same weight. This requires concrete operational thinking. Young children center on the size and conclude that A is heavier. (Technically the balance measures mass, but using weight is acceptable for this discussion.)**
3. ***False.* Since their weights (masses) are the same and A is larger, it is less dense than B. Again many students center on the size and conclude that A is more dense. Your students are likely to conclude that this is a formal operational task. However, they can see that block A is larger than block B, and they can readily conclude (based on the concrete materials) that the blocks are the same weight, so it is a concrete operational task. (Point out that curriculum writers often present the concept of density in 5th grade science books, which is evidence that the curriculum writers view concrete thinkers as capable of understanding the concept.)**
4. ***True.* If the two objects have the same weight, they cannot be made of the same substance. This is an abstract idea, and requires hypothetical thinking. This is a formal operational task.**
5. ***True.* In order to make the balloons the sizes of the blocks, more air would have to be put into balloon 1, so it would be heavier. This is also abstract and hypothetical–a formal operational task.**
6. **Emphasize that research indicates that few people are formal operational outside their own areas of expertise. Point out that you use as many concrete examples in your instruction as possible, because they are likely to be concrete operational with respect the many of the topics you cover in this class. Note that you are also concrete operational in areas where you lack experience.**

4. To demonstrate that adults sometimes demonstrate preoperational thought display PP 2.10 "*Preoperational Characteristics in Adults' Thinking*." Have the students identify egocentrism and centration in the examples (the same two concepts in each example). (These are real-world examples, so you can point out that fact to the students.)

■ *To help the students understand how Piaget's work can be applied in classrooms:*

1. Display PP 2.11 "*Principles of Instruction for Applying Piaget's Work in Classrooms*." Have the students offer examples of each principle. Have the students identify where Kristen Michler (in the case study beginning on page 41 of the chapter) applied each of the principles in her teaching.

2. Have the students identify examples of how Piaget's work has influenced instruction and curriculum development. Some examples include:

- **Hands-on science**
- **The use of manipulatives in math**

- **Language experience and whole language in reading and writing**
- **Project methods in social studies**

The focus in each of these is beginning instruction with direct experiences and moving from the concrete to the abstract.

III. A sociocultural view of development: The work of Lev Vygotsky
  A. Social interaction and development
  B. Language and development
  C. Culture and development
  D. The relationship between learning and development
  E. Vygotsky's work: Instructional principles
    1. Zone of proximal development
    2. Scaffolding: Interactive instructional support
  F. Piaget's and Vygotsky's views of knowledge construction

Teaching Suggestions:

■ ***The following suggestions are designed to help the students understand the concepts involved in Vygotsky's theory, how they can be applied in classrooms, and how they compare to Piaget's work.***

1. **Display PP 2.12 "*Learning and Development in a Cultural Context.*" Then, refer to your own teaching in this chapter. Have the students state specifically what you ask them to do with the examples, such as those in PP 2.3 "*The Drive For Equilibrium,*" and PP 2.5 "*An Example of Development in the Real World.*" Guide them to notice that they:**
   - **were involved in social interaction through the discussions (and perhaps worked in groups).**
   - **worked collaboratively on the solution to problems—to identify the common characteristics in the examples.**
   - **used language, as you encouraged them to put their understanding into words.**

2. **Ask them what your role was in the activities. (You provided enough, but not too much, guidance to help them make their own progress—this is the essence of scaffolding, and students often miss the distinction. You arranged the learning activity to be in their zones of proximal development, and you provided the scaffolding.) Display PP 2.13 "*The Zone of Proximal Development*" and PP 2.14 "*Scaffolding in Three Zones of Proximal Development*" to further emphasize your points.**

3. **Display PP 2.15 "*A Comparison of Piaget's and Vygotsky's Views of Knowledge Construction,*" and discuss the information included on it.**

4. **Remind students that constructivism will be discussed in depth in Chapter 8.**

5. **To summarize and relate Piaget's and Vygotsky's theories to constructivism, display PP 2.16 "*Principles of Instruction for Applying Vygotsky's Theory in the Classroom*" and have the students identify where Jeff Malone (in the case study on page 48 of the chapter) applied the principles in his teaching.**

6. **Compare the principles to those in PP 2.11 "*Principles of Instruction for Applying Piaget's Work in Classrooms.*" Note that Piaget and Vygotsky are both constructivist in their orientation, but they differ in their views.**

V. Language development
   A. Theories of language acquisition
      1. Behaviorist views
      2. Social cognitive perspectives
      3. Nativist theory
      4. A sociocultural view of language development
   B. Stages of language acquisition
      1. Early language: Building the foundation
      2. Fine-tuning language
      3. Increasing language complexity
   C. Promoting language development: Suggestions for teachers

Teaching Suggestions:

■ ***The following suggestions are designed to help the students understand the importance of language development and how teachers can promote this development in their students.***

1. **Point out that research indicates that early language experience is one of the strongest determiners of success in school.**

2. **Have them decide which of the theories of language acquisition tends to offer strong support for these results, and which of the theories tends to offer limited support for these results. Share the groups' results in a whole-class discussion.**

3. **Display PP 2.17 "*Promoting Language Development: Suggestions for Teachers.*" Point out that this is the reason you encourage them to put their understanding of the topics you're studying into their own words.**

ENRICHMENT MATERIALS

TEACHER PREP WEBSITE

The *Teacher Prep* website an online resource for students and instructors. Both you and students can access the *Teacher Prep* website by going to http://www.prenhall.com/teacherprep. Enter your user name and password and click on "Log In." The *Teacher Prep* website includes video episodes, student and teacher artifacts, teacher and research resources, and information about licensing and beginning a teaching career. The *Teacher Prep* website is described in detail in the Media Guide.

The following articles are recommended by the *Exploring Further* section titled "Brain-Based Education" on page 33 of the chapter.

Once into the *Teacher Prep* website access the articles by completing the following steps:

1. Click on "Research Resources" on the left panel of the screen, scroll down the middle of the page and again click on "Research Resources."
2. Go to "Classroom Processes" and click on "Instructional Methods."
3. Click on the following articles:
   Brain Science, Brain Fiction, by J. Bruer (1998), Ref. No. 2227, and
   Brain-Based Learning; A Reality Check by E. Jensen (2000), Ref. No. 2238.

The first article provides an overview of "brain science" and then offers a critical analysis of its implications for classroom practice. The author then offers a skeptical view of brain-based education and what it offers for increasing student learning.

The second article describes a number of common criticisms of brain-based education but offers a more optimistic view of its potential for increasing student learning.

ADDITIONAL EXPLORING FURTHER SUGGESTIONS

Page 34 of the chapter suggests that students go to the *Exploring Further* module of Chapter 2 to read a biography of Jean Piaget.

Page 41 of the chapter suggests that students go to the *Exploring Further* module of Chapter 2 to examine some ways of assessing learners' thinking with respect to Piaget's stages of development.

DISCUSSION STARTERS

You may choose to have your students discuss one or more of the following questions to further enrich their understanding of your learning activities.

1. Should age-driven grade levels be abolished and replaced by developmentally-driven groupings? What implications would this have for the curriculum? For instruction? What does "developmentally-driven groupings" mean?

2. Can maturation take place without experience? Offer a concrete example to support your point.

3. Can experience contribute to development without maturation? Offer a concrete example to support your point.

4. Should teachers and schools attempt to accelerate cognitive development? If so, how? If not, why not?

5. Which of the following concepts from Piaget's theory are most useful to teachers? Why are they useful? Which of the concepts are least useful? Why aren't they?
   - Equilibrium
   - Organization
   - Adaptation
   - Centration
   - Conservation
   - Developmental Stages

6. Do Piaget's descriptions of development have more or fewer implications for curriculum and instruction than do Vygotsky's descriptions? Explain.

7. Is the link between language development and Piaget's work stronger or weaker than the link between language development and Vygotsky's work? Explain.

8. If a teacher uses lecture as a primary method, do students still construct their own understanding of the topics they study? Explain.

BACKGROUND READINGS

Abbeduto, L. (Ed.). (2004). *Taking sides: Clashing views on controversial issues in educational psychology*. Guilford, CT: McGraw-Hill/Dushkin.
This edited work presents contrasting views on some of the prominent issues in learning and teaching, such as whether or not brain research has implications for classroom instruction, and whether or not English immersion should replace bilingual education.

Bredo, E. (1997). The social construction of learning. In G. Phye (Ed.), *Handbook of academic learning: Construction of knowledge* (pp. 3–45). San Diego: Academic Press.
This chapter provides a succinct view of Vygotsky's theory of development including a clear description of the relationship between development and learning.

Craig, D. I. (2003). Brain-compatible learning: Principles and applications in athletic training. *Journal of Athletic Training, 38*(4), 342–350.
This article provides an overview of the learning physiology of the brain, and though the focus is on athletic training, it applies the ideas to a variety of fields.

Fowler, R. (1994, April). *Piagetian versus Vygotskian perspectives on development and education.* Paper presented at the Annual Meeting of the American Educational Research Association, New Orleans.
Even though this paper was written in the middle 1990s, it provides an excellent in-depth comparison of Piaget's and Vygotsky's views of development. It is a very good resource for students who have some background in Piaget's and Vygotsky's work.

Gauvain, M. (2001). *The social context of cognitive development.* New York: Guilford Press. This book places Vygotsky's work into the larger context of social constructivism and sociocultural views of learning.

Glassman, M., & Wang, Y. (2004). On the interconnected nature of interpreting Vygotsky: Rejoinder to Gredler and Shields Does no one read Vygotsky's words. *Educational Researcher, 33*(6), 19–22.
This article and the one that follows examines some of the issues involved in Vygotsky's theory.

Gredler, M., & Shields, C. (2004). Does no one read Vygotsky's words? Commentary on Glassman. *Educational Researcher, 33*(2), 21–25.
This article and the one that precedes it examines some of the issues involved in Vygotsky's theory.

Paris, S., & Cunningham, A. (1996). Children becoming students. In D. Berliner, & R. Calfee (Eds.), *Handbook of educational psychology* (pp. 117–147). New York: Macmillan.
This chapter focuses on development during the preschool and primary years.

Puntambekar, S., & Hübscher, R. (2005). Tools for scaffolding students in a complex learning environment: What have we gained and what have we missed? *Educational Psychologist, 40*(1), 1–12.
This article provides an in-depth discussion of Vygtotsky's concept of scaffolding.

Wadsworth, B. J. (2004). *Piaget's theory of cognitive and affective development* (5th ed.). Boston: Pearson Education.
The author presents a comprehensive and conceptual account of Piaget's work in an understandable way. A good beginning point for anyone interested in further study of Piaget's theory.

Wigfield, A., Eccles, J., & Pintrich, P. (1996). Development between the ages of 11 and 25. In D. Berliner, & R. Calfee (Eds.), *Handbook of educational psychology* (pp. 148–185). New York: Macmillan.
This chapter examines development during early adolescence, adolescence and young adulthood.

FEEDBACK

Developing as a Professional: Praxis Practice: Feedback for Short-Answer Questions

The feedback that appears here is for the short-answer questions that follow the case study on pages 57 and 58 of the text. The feedback is also available to students on the companion website.

1. At what level of cognitive development were Jenny's students likely to be? Was her instruction effective for that level? Explain.

Jenny's students demonstrated characteristics of preoperational learners. For instance, Jessica's reason for the towel staying dry was, "Cause it's inside and the rest is outside," and Anthony concluded that "A water seal," had kept the towel dry. This is perceptually based reasoning, which is characteristic of preoperational learners.

Jenny's instruction was quite effective, because she provided direct and concrete experiences for the students. For example, to demonstrate that air was in the glass, she tipped it sideways to allow a bubble to escape. She also allowed her students to experiment with the materials in a follow-up hands-on activity, which provided even more direct experience.

2. Why was the medium of water important for Jenny's lesson? How does this relate to Piaget's levels of development?

The water was concrete and perceptual. Without the water, for example, the students wouldn't have been able to see air bubbles escape from the glass, so they wouldn't have had any direct experience with air being in the glass. Preoperational students need direct experiences to provide a foundation for logical thought, which marks the next step in development.

3. When Samantha and Terry disagreed about the condition of the inside of the glass, how did Jenny respond? What other alternatives might she have pursued? What are the advantages and disadvantages of these alternatives?

Jenny described the disagreement as a problem to be solved by the class. This is a desirable approach from a constructivist perspective because it places responsibility for making sense of the world on students.

She could simply have told the students that the inside of the glass was dry. She could also have asked other students to come up and check on the glass. The disadvantage of telling the students is that it wouldn't be convincing for those who believed that it was wet. The disadvantage of having other students come up is simply time and management. The advantage in having others check the glass is that more students would have directly experienced feeling the inside of the glass.

4. Did Jenny conduct the lesson in the students' zones of proximal development? Explain why you do or do not think so. What forms of scaffolding did Jenny provide? How effective was the scaffolding?

While we don't have enough evidence to determine if the lesson was conducted in all the students' zones of proximal development, the comments of several indicated that, with Jenny's guidance, they understood the topic. This suggests that the lesson was conducted in their zones.

Jenny provided effective scaffolding in the form of questions, prompts, and altering materials (e.g., tipping the glass to allow the air bubbles to escape, and having the students try the activities themselves).

Feedback for Online Case Questions

The feedback below is for the *Online Case Book* for Chapter 2 (referenced on page 55 of the chapter). Both you and the students can access the case study by going to www.prenhall.com/eggen, selecting Chapter 2, and clicking on *Online Case Book.*

You may choose to assign the online case as homework or you may want to discuss the case in class. Answers to these questions *do not* appear on the companion website, so students *do not* have access to the feedback.

Multiple-Choice Items:

1 . Based on what you saw in the lesson, at which of Piaget's stages of development did Robin assume her students were thinking?

a. Sensorimotor
b. Preoperations
c. Concrete operations
d. Formal operations
c. Robin represented each of the abstract ideas with a concrete example and she linked the example to the abstraction.

2. Early in their conversation Mary asked, "Can you help me out with anything on graphing? . . . The kids just see graphs as some meaningless lines. I explain the heck out of them, but it doesn't seem to help all that much." Based on Piaget's work, which of the following is the best explanation for the fact that the kids "see graphs as some meaningless lines"?

a. The students aren't chronologically at the age where they are able to deal with abstract ideas such as the information represented by the graphs.
b. The students didn't see how the information related to their daily lives, so they lacked the motivation to understand the math and science related topics that Robin had them studying.
c. The students were at a state of equilibrium, and they were reluctant to have their equilibrium disrupted.
d. The students lacked the concrete experiences they needed to make the abstract ideas represented by the graphs meaningful.
d. When students are unable to understand abstract ideas, it is usually because they lack the concrete experiences necessary to understand those ideas. The students were eighth graders, so they were chronologically at an age where they should have been able to deal with abstract ideas (choice a), and we have no evidence that they lacked motivation (choice b), or were reluctant to change an idea because changing the idea would disrupt their equilibrium (choice c).

3. Based on what you saw in the lesson, which of the following is the best assessment of Robin's lesson for promoting language development?

a. It was effective because she provided the students with a great deal of practice in using language.
b. It was ineffective, because Todd didn't understand the idea, and she had Lonnie explain it instead of explaining it herself.
c. It was effective, because she had the students work in groups.
d. It was ineffective because she told the students that struggling to put their understanding into words was acceptable, which might impair their correct use of language.
a. Robin gave the students many opportunities to practice language. Having a student explain an idea is effective rather than ineffective, because it gives the student additional practice with language (choice b), and putting students in groups, per se, may or may not be effective depending on how much topic-related language they use in the groups (choice c). In addition, she reminded them that struggling to put their understanding into words was a normal part of

learning, which is a positive, instead of a negative factor in promoting language development (choice d).

Short-Answer Items:

4. Using the principles of instruction for applying Piaget's work in classrooms, write an assessment of Robin's work with her students. Address each of the principles in your assessment.

Robin applied the principles quite effectively. She applied the first: "Provide concrete experiences that represent abstract concepts and principles" by using a concrete demonstration to illustrate each of the graphs, and she applied the second "Help students link the concrete representations to the abstract idea" and third "Use social interaction to help students verbalize their developing understanding" when she presented the graphs, had the students observe and describe them, and then identify the demonstration that corresponded to each of the graphs. Throughout this process, the students were involved in a great deal of social interaction. In identifying the demonstrations that corresponded to each of the graphs, she helped the students move to more advanced thinking, which applied the fourth principle: "Design learning experiences as developmental bridges to more advanced stages of development."

5. Using the principles of instruction for applying Vygotsky's work in classrooms, write an assessment of Robin's work with her students. Address each of the principles in your assessment.

Robin also applied the instructional principles for Vygotsky's work quite well. Each of her demonstrations was consistent with the cultural context in which the students were studying, which applied the first, "Embed learning activities in a context that is culturally authentic." She applied the second, "Create learning activities that involve students in social interactions," and the third "Encourage students to use language to describe their developing understandings," throughout the lesson. A great deal of social interaction took place, and she encouraged their use of language. The students being able to succeed with her support applied the fourth principle, "Create learning activities that are in learners' zones of proximal development," and she provided assistance whenever students struggled, which applied the fifth principle, "Provide instructional assistance to promote learning and development."

CLASSROOM EXERCISES

The classroom exercises that follow appear *only here* in the instructor's manual. Students do not have access to *either the questions or the answers.*

The purpose of keeping the exercises only in the instructor's manual is to allow you to use them as class discussion items, or for homework, if you should choose to do so.

Feedback for the exercises follows immediately.

1. In our everyday life, we commonly see prices written as $\$2.49^9$ for gas, for example, and an article of clothing for $39.95, as another example. What concept from Piaget's theory best explains why retailers present prices in this way? Why wouldn't they simply price the gasoline at $2.50 and the clothing at $40, for instance?

2. We periodically get frustrated when we want to change a procedure or something else in a business, and the people in charge want to continue doing business the way it's been done in the past, offering the rationale, "This is the way we've always done it." Using Piaget's work as a basis, explain why they would offer such a rationale.

3. One of the most basic principles in science is: "All objects in the universe want to be at their lowest energy level." Explain how this principle relates to Piaget's concept of equilibrium.

4. Consider the aphorisms, "Still water runs deep," and "Make hay while the sun shines." Describe the meaning that a concrete operational thinking would give to each. Then, describe the meaning a formal operational thinker would give to each.

5. Look again at the cartoon on page 21 of your text. Using Piaget's theory as a basis, explain specifically why the child responds as he does. What stage of development is best illustrated in the cartoon?

6. Trudge (1990) found that when pairing a student who was a conserver in the "conservation of volume" task with a nonconserver, and asking the pairs to try and explain the differences in the water level, 80% of the nonconservers in the pairs reached conservation, whereas only 50% reached conservation in regular classroom instruction. Does Piaget's or Vygotsky's theory better explain these experimental results? Defend your conclusion based on your understanding of the two theories.

7. Andrew, a fourth grader in private school, visits a classmate at his home for the first time. Andrew is struck by the obvious opulence of his friends home compared to his own. He is particularly impressed that his friend has such a big bedroom, and he is quick to notice the computer and television in it.

Andrew's mom picks him up after his afternoon of playing and on the way home Andrew asks his mom why his friend doesn't attend private school since his family is so rich. What concept from Piaget's theory best accounts for Andrew thinking that his classmate should attend private school? Explain.

8. Sandy and Shirley host a trip to Las Vegas each fall including their various friends, neighbors, and relatives. It's a women-only trip that they have arranged for several years. Sandy loves to play blackjack and usually budgets $300 to play. Shirley prefers slot machines and she budgets $200. On their return Sandy's husband, Lou, picks both of the women up at the airport and quizzes them about their success. Shirley says with a grin that she won $100; Sandy reports that she shot her wad and lost it all. When Lou asks Sandy if that was a good use of money, Sandy shakes her head at Lou and tells him,"You can't look at it that way." What concept from Piaget's theory of cognitive development best explains Sandy's view of winning? Provide the explanation.

9. Sydney, age 5, responds that she still only has two feet when her grandmother tells her that she's grown another foot since the last time she visited Sydney.

Bart, age 8, asks his mom, "What's for dinner?" Affectionately and laughing, she suggests having his baby back ribs and his sister's ham hocks–referring to a running family joke about the size of his baby sister's legs. The next morning Bart quizzes his mom, "Mom, I was thinking, if you love us why would you want to eat us?"

Joan, an adult, listens as her friend, Shasta, tells a first-person joke. After the punch line she asks–with concern–if Shasta's story is really true.

What major topic from the chapter best explains Sydney's, Bart's, and Joan's thinking in these cases?

FEEDBACK FOR CLASSROOM EXERCISES

1. We tend to center on the $2.49 and the 39, making it look like the price is less than it actually is. The perception of $2.50 and $40 is quite different from the perception of $2.49[9] and $39.95.

2. Doing it the way we've always done it allows us to remain at equilibrium. Any change disrupts our equilibrium, at least to a certain extent.

3. Being at equilibrium is a lower energy state than being at disequilibrium. Research indicates that when we're at disequilibrium, we're motivated to re-establish equilibrium. Our motivation can be explained by suggesting that we want to return to our lower energy state.

4. Concrete operational thinkers tend to describe the aphorisms literally, such as, "When the water isn't moving fast it is deep." Formal operational thinkers describe it metaphorically, such as "Reflective thinkers are likely to remain quiet about their thoughts until they've carefully considered the ideas."

5. The child is demonstrating preoperational thought. All he can see is the water and the faucet, he responds perceptually, and he concludes that all the water is in the faucet.

6. Vygotsky's work better explains the results. When the learners work in pairs, the level of social interaction is higher than in regular class instruction. Vygotsky places greater emphasis on social interaction than does Piaget.
The citation for the study is:

Trudge, J. (1990). Vygotsky, the zone of proximal development. In L. Moll (Ed.), *Vygotsky and education* (pp. 155–174). Cambridge: Cambridge University Press.

7. Centration is the concept best illustrated. Andrew is centering on the perceived wealth of his friend's family and assumes that private school is a logical choice for people with money.

8. Egocentrism is the concept best illustrated. Sandy's comment, "You can't look at it that way," indicates that she is not inclined to consider the incident from someone else's point of view. Adults are susceptible to barriers of logical thought. In this case Sandy is focusing on her enjoyment and views this as an appropriate expense.

9. Their thinking can best be explained on the basis of constructivism. Sydney, Bart and Joan are constructing their own understanding of the incidents based on their background experiences and the interaction involved.

CHAPTER 3: PERSONAL, SOCIAL, AND EMOTIONAL DEVELOPMENT

CHAPTER OVERVIEW

In this chapter we continue the discussion of learner development by examining learners' personal, social, and moral development. The chapter begins with an examination of the general characteristics of personal and social growth, followed by a description of Erikson's theory of psychosocial development. Self-concept and factors that influence it are then discussed. The chapter continues with a discussion of moral development, reviewing first Piaget's views on moral development and then Kohlberg's descriptions of moral reasoning.

CHAPTER OBJECTIVES

- Describe the factors influencing personal development, and explain how differences in parenting and peer interactions can influence this development.
- Describe characteristics that indicate advancing social development, and explain how social development relates to school violence and aggression.
- Use descriptions of psychosocial, identity, and self-concept development to explain learners' behaviors.
- Use descriptions of moral reasoning to explain differences in people's responses to ethical issues.

POWERPOINT SLIDES

PP 3.1 Influences on Personal Development
PP 3.2 Parenting Styles: An Application
PP 3.3 Parenting Styles and Patterns of Personal Development
PP 3.4 Principles of Instruction for Promoting Social Development
PP 3.5 Identity, Self-Concept, and Erikson's work
PP 3.6 Erikson's Stages of Psychosocial Development
PP 3.7 Assumptions and Corollaries Involved in Erikson's Theory
PP 3.8 Positive and Negative Resolutions of Crises
PP 3.9 Erikson's Theory in the Classroom
PP 3.10 States in identity development
PP 3.11 Self-Esteem in Our Popular Culture
PP 3.12 The Relationships Among the Dimensions of Self-Concept and Achievement
PP 3.13 Principles of Instruction for Promoting Psychosocial and Self-Concept Development
PP 3.14 Moral Reasoning on the Interstate
PP 3.15 An Application of Piaget's Description of Moral Development
PP 3.16 Kohlberg's Stages of Moral Development
PP 3.17 Stages of Moral Reasoning: An Application
PP 3.18 Emotional Factors in Moral Development: An Application
PP 3.19 Principles of Instruction for Promoting Moral Development
PP 3.20 Praxis Practice: Feedback for Short-Answer Questions
PP 3.21 Feedback for Online Case Questions
PP 3.22 Classroom Exercises

VIDEO

DVD 1, Episode 4: "Moral Reasoning: Examining a Moral Dilemma."
This episode examines the thinking of students at different ages in response to a moral issue. It illustrates differences between preconventional and conventional levels of moral reasoning as described in Kohlberg's theory of moral development.

CHAPTER OUTLINE

I. Personal development
   A. Heredity
   B. Parents and other adults
   C. Peers
II. Social development
   A. Perspective taking: Understanding others' thoughts and feelings
   B. Social problem solving
   C. Violence and aggression in schools
   D. Promoting social development: Instructional principles
III. The development of identity and self-concept
   A. Erikson's theory of psychosocial development
      1. Putting Erikson's work into perspective
      2. Supporting psychosocial development
         a. Early childhood
         b. The elementary years
         c. Adolescence
   B. The development of identity
      1. Patterns in identity development
      2. Sexual identity
   C. The development of self-concept
      1. Self-concept and self-esteem
      2. Self-concept and achievement
   D. Promoting psychosocial, identity and self-concept development: Instructional principles
   E. Ethnic pride: Promoting ethnic identity and positive self-esteem
      1. Ethnicity and self-esteem
      2. Ethnic pride and identity formation
IV. Development of morality, social responsibility, and self-control
   A. Increased interest in moral education and development
   B. Piaget's description of moral development
   C. Kohlberg's theory of moral development
      1. Level I: Preconventional ethics
         a. Stage 1: Punishment-obedience
         b. Stage 2: Market exchange
      2. Level II: Conventional ethics
         a. Stage 3: Interpersonal harmony
         b. Stage 4: Law and order
      3. Level III: Postconventional ethics
         a. Stage 5: Social contract
         b. Stage 6: Universal principles
      4. Putting Kohlberg's theory into perspective
         a. Gender differences: The morality of caring
   D. Emotional factors in moral development
   E. Promoting moral development: Instructional principles
   F. Learning contexts: Promoting personal, social, and moral development in urban environments

PRESENTATION OUTLINE

The suggested activities can be completed in small groups and discussed as a whole group, or they can be conducted as whole-class activities. We recommend that you promote as much discussion—both in small groups and with the whole class—as possible.

I. Personal development
   A. Heredity
   B. Parents and other adults
   C. Peers

Teaching Suggestions:

■ ***The purpose in the following suggestions is to help students understand factors that influence personal development.***

1. **To introduce the factors that influence personal development display PP 3.1 "*Influences on Personal Development.*"**

2. **Display PP 3.2 "*Parenting Styles: An Application*" and have the students discuss which of the three they believe is most effective. Ask them to provide specific evidence from the examples to support their conclusions.**

3. **Display PP 3.3 "*Parenting Styles and Patterns of Personal Development.*" Lead the students to conclude that the first example in PP 3.3 (Ellen) illustrates an authoritarian parenting style, the second (Tanya) an autoritative style, and the third (Jan) a permissive style.**

4. **Have the students offer specific examples of teacher actions or behaviors that would parallel each of the styles.**

II Social Development
   A. Perspective taking: Understanding others' thoughts and feelings
   B. Social problem solving
   C. Violence and aggression in the schools
   D. Promoting social development: Instructional principles

Teaching Suggestions:

■ ***The following suggestions are intended to help students understand what teachers can do to promote social development.***

1. **Have the students explain why young children typically are not good at perspective taking. Remind them that Piaget's theory helps us understand that young children tend to be egocentric.**

2. **Display PP 3.4 "*Principles of Instruction for Promoting Social Development.*" Have them identify where Teresa Manteras (in the case study on page 68 of the chapter) applied each of the principles in her work with her students. (Encourage the students to first look for the principles before reading the paragraphs that follow the case.)**

III. The development of identity and self concept
   A. Erikson's stages of psychosocial development
      1. Putting Erikson's work into perspective
      2. Supporting psychosocial development
         a. Early childhood
         b. The elementary years

        c. Adolescence
    B. The development of identity
        1. Patterns in identity development
        2. Sexual identity
    C. The development of self-concept
        1. Self-concept and self-esteem
        2. Self-concept and achievement
    D. Promoting psychosocial, identity, and self-concept development: Instructional principles
    E. Ethnic pride: Promoting positive self-esteem and ethnic identity
        1. Ethnicity and self-esteem
        2. Ethnic pride and identity formation

Teaching Suggestions:

■ *The following suggestions are designed to help the students understand Erikson's theory and how it relates to the development of identity.*

1. Introduce this section with PP 3.5 "*Identity, Self-Concept, and Erikson's work*" which describes the relationships between identity and Erikson's theory of psychosocial development.

2. Ask the students if they know people who seem to be somewhat "paranoid," or always feel that someone is out to take advantage of them. Also ask them if they know others who are inclined to take people at face value unless they get evidence to the contrary. (Erikson's theory helps us understand these people by suggesting that those in the first category didn't effectively resolve the trust-mistrust crisis.)

3. To provide some background and to put Erikson's work into context, display PP 3.6 "*Erikson's Stages of Psychosocial Development*" and PP 3.7 "*Assumptions and Corollaries Involved in Erikson's Theory.*" They identify Erikson's stages and summarize the assumptions on which his work is based.

4. Ask the students to describe what they believe positive and negative resolutions of the psychosocial challenges (crises) at each stage would be. Then, provide feedback for the discussion by displaying PP 3.8 "*Positive and Negative Resolutions of Crises.*" PP 3.8 describes the characteristics of a positive and negative resolution of each stage in adults.

5. Display PP 3.9 "*Erikson's Theory in the Classroom,*" have the students respond to the questions, and discuss their results.

6. As a way of helping your students visualize Erikson's work, tell them to imagine a circle, and think of the circle as representing the perfectly formed personality. This means that all the crises have been and remain resolved to this point in an individual's life. Now tell them to visualize an imperfect circle–one with indentations at various points. It remains approximately circular, but it is less than perfect. We all have personality imperfections, and the indentations in the circle help us visualize those imperfections. The imperfections don't mean that we can't cope with life, or that we remain stuck at a particular stage. Depending on the situation we're in, they might prevent us from functioning as effectively as we would if the imperfections didn't exist, but this is typical of most people. This is another way of thinking about Erikson's descriptions of the personality and their implications for the way we operate in the world.

■ *To help students understand identity development and relationships between self-concept, self-esteem and school achievement:*

1. Ask them for a definition of identity development. Then, display PP 3.10 "*States in identity development.*" Ask them to offer some perceptions about their own identity development.

2. Remind students of the differences between self-concept and self-esteem, and then, to promote some discussion related to issues involved in the development of self-concept and self-esteem, pose the following question:

"Is the improvement of self-esteem an appropriate and worthwhile goal for schools?"

Most students will say it is, and you can then ask, "How do we go about improving self-esteem?"

3. Point out that distinctions between self-concept and self-esteem are sometimes missed and what implications missing these distinctions has for schools and schooling. PP 3.11 "*Self-Esteem in Our Popular Culture*," includes a quote from Pintrich & Schunk (1996) that directly addresses this issue.

4. Display PP 3.12 "*The Relationships Among the Dimensions of Self-Concept and Achievement.*" Then, summarize the information in this section by displaying PP 3.13 "*Principles of Instruction for Promoting Psychosocial and Self-Concept Development.*" Have them identify where John Adler in the section, "Promoting Psychosocial, Identity, and Self-Concept Development: Instructional Principles" applied the principles with his students. (Encourage them to look for the principles in the case study before they read the paragraphs that follow it.)

5. To examine issues involved in ethnic pride and self esteem, read or display the following statement:

"Minority students need to know that their cultures are valued and that the languages they bring to school are assets rather than obstacles or liabilities. Teachers play a crucial role in making every student feel wanted and loved by the overt and implicit messages they send through their teaching."

6. Refer students to this statement and then ask them to identify ways that they can communicate these messages to their students. Require that they give specific and concrete responses.

IV. Development of morality, social responsibility, and self-control
- A. Increased interest in moral education and development
- B. Piaget's description of moral development
- C. Kohlberg's theory of moral development
  1. Level I: Preconventional ethics
     - a. Stage 1: Punishment-obedience
     - b. Stage 2: Market exchange
  2. Level II: Conventional ethics
     - a. Stage 3: Interpersonal harmony
     - b. Stage 4: Law and order
  3. Level III: Postconventional ethics
     - a. Stage 5: Social contract
     - b. Stage 6: Universal principles
  4. Putting Kohlberg's theory into perspective
     - a. Gender differences: The morality of caring
- D. Emotional factors in moral development
- E. Promoting moral development: Instructional principles
- F. Learning contexts: Promoting personal, social, and moral development in urban environments

Teaching Suggestions:

■ *The following suggestions are intended to help students understand Piaget's and Kohlberg's theories of moral development and Gilligan's criticisms of Kohlberg's work.*

1. **Display PP 3.14 "*Moral Reasoning on the Interstate.*" It is an example that some of the students may have experienced and all can relate to. Ask students why they think you are or are not justified in feeling you are being treated unfairly and why the highway patrol's position is more or less justified than yours.**

2. **Have students identify some examples of moral issues that exist today, at both the national and local levels. Among those they identify some might include:**
   - **abortion.**
   - **sex education.**
   - **affirmative action.**
   - **gun control.**
   - **the influence of political action committees.**
   - **censorship.**
   - **product liability.**

3. **Display PP 3.15 "*An Application of Piaget's Description of Moral Development.*" Have the students describe the reasoning of each of the three students in the example. Lead them to conclude that Talitha and Dwain each displayed external morality, whereas Krystal demonstrated thinking that reflected internal morality. Also point out that authoritarian parenting and teaching styles (as opposed to authoritative styles) tend to retard the development of autonomous morality.**

4. **Describe the grading system for your class. As an example, suppose your system has the criterion of 90-100% = A. Then, tell them to suppose that they have a friend in the class with an 89% average. Should you give the person an A? Many will say yes, and so then ask if you should give the person an A if they have an 88% average. Because the issue is personal, it generates considerable discussion, and many students will suggest that you should. Ask them for their reasons and write the reasons on the board.**

5. **Display PP 3.16 "*Kohlberg's Stages of Moral Development*" and have students classify some of the reasons they've offered into one of the stages. (At this point you might again display PP 3.14 "*Moral Reasoning on the Interstate*" and have them decide which stage is best represented by your reasoning and which stage is represented by the highway patrol's reasoning.)**

6. **Display PP 3.17 "*Stages of Moral Reasoning: An Application*" and have the students classify each of the reasons into one of Kohlberg's stages.**

> Here would be a good point to show **Episode 4 on DVD 1**: "Moral Reasoning: Examining a Moral Dilemma."

7. **From the students' responses to your question about whether or not you should give the student with an 89% an A, do an informal study to see if the women in your class are more inclined than the men to offer rationales for giving or not giving the A that would be classified into Kohlberg's stage 3, and also see if the men were more inclined than the women to offer reasons that would be classified into stage 4. (Most of the reasons students offer for giving or not giving the A fall into stage 3 or stage 4.) Discuss the results with the class, and refer the students to Gilligan's work, describing her criticisms of Kohlberg's theory.**

8. Display PP 3.18 "*Emotional Factors in Moral Development: An Application*" and have them respond to the items at the bottom. Note that experiencing the emotions Melissa felt represent an advance in moral development.

9. Display PP 3.19 "*Principles of Instruction for Promoting Moral Development.*" Have the students identify where in the case study illustrating Rod Leist's work with his students (in the case study on page 87 of the chapter) that Rod applied each of the principles.

ENRICHMENT MATERIALS

TEACHER PREP WEBSITE

The *Teacher Prep* website an online resource for students and instructors. Both you and students can access the *Teacher Prep* website by going to http://www.prenhall.com/teacherprep. Enter your user name and password and click on "Log In." The *Teacher Prep* website includes video episodes, student and teacher artifacts, teacher and research resources, and information about licensing and beginning a teaching career. The *Teacher Prep* website is described in detail in the Media Guide.

The following articles are recommended by the *Exploring Further* section titled "Teaching Social Problem Solving Skills" on page 69 of the chapter.

Once into the *Teacher Prep* website access the articles by completing the following steps:
1. Click on "Research Resources" on the left panel of the screen, scroll down the middle of the page and again click on "Research Resources."
2. Go to "Classroom Processes" and click on "Classroom Management."
3. Click on the following articles:
   Changing the Way Kids Settle Conflicts, by G. Holden (1997), Ref. No. 219, and
   Teaching Students to Be Peer Mediators by D. W. Johnson, R. T. Johnson, B. Dudley, and R. Burnett (1992), Ref. No. 2236.

These articles offer different strategies for developing students' perspective taking and social problem solving skills.

The following articles are recommended by the *Exploring Further* section titled "Developing Emotional Awareness" on page 86 of the chapter.

Once into the *Teacher Prep* website access the articles by completing the following steps:
1. Click on "Research Resources" on the left panel of the screen, scroll down the middle of the page and again click on "Research Resources."
2. Go to "Classroom Processes" and click on "Classroom Management."
3. Click on the following articles:
   Portraits in Emotional Awareness by C. M. Shelton (2000), Ref. No. 348,
   Reaching Out to Grieving Students by N. Naierman (1997), Ref. No. 357,
   Down with Put-Downs! by M. A. Lundeberg, J. Emmett, P. A. Osland and N. Lindquist (1997), Ref. No. 2297.

These articles describe strategies for helping students become aware of the ways that they can hurt one another's feelings and additional strategies for developing students' emotional awareness.

The following articles are recommended by the *Exploring Further* section titled "Different Instructional Approaches to Moral Education" on page 88 of the chapter.

Once into the *Teacher Prep* website access the articles by completing the following steps:
1. Click on "Research Resources" on the left panel of the screen, scroll down the middle of the page and again click on "Research Resources."
2. Go to "Grade Levels" click on "Primary" and then "Instructional Methods."
3. Click on the following articles:
   The Socratic Approach to Character Education, by D. H. Elkind and F. Sweet (1997), Ref. No. 786, and
   Teaching for Character and Community, by S. Kagan (2001), Ref. No. 1775.

These articles describe strategies for developing students' perspective taking and ways of promoting students' caring for one another.

DISCUSSION STARTERS

You may choose to have your students discuss one or more of the following questions to further enrich their understanding of your learning activities.

1. How would Erikson respond to the following educational practices?
   - Retention in grade
   - Ability grouping
   - Competitive grading systems
   - Failing grades
   - Competitive sports
   - Vocational education

   (When we have introduced these to our students we have found the issues are much more complex than they appear at first glance.)

2. Ask students if they agree or disagree with the following statement: "Differences between religions as well as differences between people who are and are not religious are so great that there would be little agreement on the application of Kohlberg's theory in the classroom."

3. How much of instruction should be targeted toward the development of self-concept? What specific things can teachers do to help develop positive self concepts?

4. What should be the school's role in helping students in the process of identity development? How would Erikson respond to this question? How would Kohlberg respond? How would Gilligan respond? What specific things can teachers do to aid in this process?

5. This text takes the position that moral issues cannot be avoided, and the most appropriate approach is for schools and teachers to deal with the issues openly and honestly. Do you agree or disagree with that position? Why do you feel the way you do?

6. Erikson studied under the famous Sigmund Freud's daughter Anna. How were his views of personality development influenced by these experiences? Explain.

7. Some prominent thinkers believe that schools' concerns for children's self-concepts and their self-esteem are misplaced, and the business of the school is to teach knowledge and cognitive skills. What is your position regarding this issue? Explain.

BACKGROUND READINGS

Bracey, G. W. (2005). A nation of cheats. *Phi Delta Kappan, 86*(5), 412–413.
This short article provides data on the prevalence of cheating in our nations schools and links it to the larger issue of cheating as a cultural trend.

Brown, R., & Evans, W. (2002). Extracurricular activity and ethnicity: Creating greater school connections among diverse student populations. *Urban Education, 37*(1), 41–58.
This article illustrates the benefits of extracurricular activities in students' general education.

Cooper, D., & Snell, J. (2003). Bullying—not just a kid thing. *Educational Leadership, 60*(6), 22–25.
The authors provide information on the destructive aspects of bullying in schools.

Forgas, J. P. (Ed.) (2001). *Handbook of affect and social cognition.* Mahwah, NJ: Erlbaum.
This edited work provides current perspectives on personal, social, and emotional development.

Gillies, R. M. (2003). The behaviors, interactions, and perceptions of junior high school students during small-group learning. *Journal of Educational Psychology, 95,* 137–147.
This study examines interaction in small-group learning and learners' perceptions of those interactions.

Gilligan, C. (1982). *In a different voice: Psychological theory and women's development.* Cambridge, MA: Harvard University Press.
Gilligan critiques Kohlberg's theory from a feminist perspective.

Grolnick, W., Kurowski, C., & Gurland, S. (1999). Family processes and the development of children's self-regulation. *Educational Psychologist, 34*(1), 3–14.
This article examines the influence of families on children's personal and social development.

Guerra, N. G., Huesmann, L. R., & Spendler, A. (2003). Community violence exposure, social cognition, and aggression among urban elementary school children. *Child Development, 74,* 1561–1576.
This article examines the relationships between exposure to violence and students' aggressive behaviors.

Koc, K., & Buzzelli, C. A. (2004). The moral of the story is . . . Using children's literature in moral education. *Young Children, 59*(1), 92–97.
This article offers a literature-based approach to moral education.

Murdock, T. B., Miller, A., & Kohlhardt, J. (2004). Effects of classroom context variables in high school students' judgments of the acceptability and likelihood of cheating. *Journal of Educational Psychology, 96*(4), 765–777.
This article examines some the role of classroom context on the likelihood of students cheating.

Osterman, K. F. (2000). Students' need for belonging in the school community. *Review of Educational Research, 70,* 323–367.
The author provides a summary of evidence that describes students' needs for belonging.

Skaalvik, E., & Valas, H. (1999). Relations among achievement, self-concept, and motivation in mathematics and language arts: A longitudinal study. *Journal of Experimental Education, 67*(2), 135–149.
This article discusses the relationships between achievement and self-concept and examines the implications of these relationships for learner motivation.

Wigfield, A., Eccles, J., & Pintrich, P. (1996). Development between the ages of 11 and 25. In D. Berliner & R. Calfee (Eds.), *Handbook of Educational Psychology* (pp. 148–185). New York: Macmillan.
This chapter examines several dimensions of learner development, including the development of self-concept.

FEEDBACK

Developing as a Professional: Praxis Practice: Feedback for Short-Answer Questions

The feedback that appears here is for the short-answer questions that follow the case study on pages 91 and 92 of the text. The feedback is also available to students on the companion website.

1. How might Erikson explain Karl's behavior in Helen's class?

   Based on Erikson's work we might conclude that Karl hasn't positively resolved the industry/inferiority crisis with respect to English. He says, "I'm no good at English," for example. On the other hand, he presumably feels a sense of accomplishment with respect to basketball, since Helen described him as "poetry in motion."

2. Using findings from the research on self-concept, explain Karl's behavior.

   Research indicates that the strongest correlations exist between specific academic self-concepts and achievement. This is corroborated in Karl's case. His self-concept in English is low, but in math and science it appears to be better. Also, his physical self-concept is probably quite high, since, according to Helen, he's very good at basketball.

3. Using concepts from Kohlberg's theory, analyze Helen's cheating problem. From Kohlberg's perspective, how well did she handle this problem?

   Helen's handling of the cheating problem was ineffective. First, her classroom structure promoted a form of external morality; for example, her comment to Nathan was, "Nathan, remember my first rule?"

   Second, her comment, "If I catch anyone cheating on Thursday, I'll tear up your quiz and give you a failing grade," was again consistent with external morality. A more effective approach would have been to try to promote autonomous morality by discussing the issue of cheating, and by describing teaching and learning as social contracts. When students take tests they are in a contract that requires them to do the work on their own. While this orientation won't stop all cheating, it creates a more mature and effective climate than the one in which Helen was operating.

4. If you think Helen's teaching could have been improved on the basis of the information in Chapter 3, what suggestions would you make? Again, be specific.

   Several things in Helen's approach to her classroom and her instruction could have been improved. In addition to the emotional climate, as indicated by her response to Nathan and her threat to tear up papers if others were caught cheating, her expectations for students were negative. For example, she commented to them, "You did so poorly on the quiz, and I explained everything so carefully. You must not have studied very hard." While we can't be completely sure, it appears that her instruction is very teacher centered, and built around abstract rules rather than dealing with the rules in the context of written work and developing an understanding of the rules based on interaction between the teacher and the students and the students with each other.

Feedback for Online Case Questions

The feedback below is for the *Online Case Book* for Chapter 3 (referenced on page 89 of the chapter). Both you and the students can access the case study by going to www.prenhall.com/eggen, selecting Chapter 3, and clicking on *Online Case Book.*

You may choose to assign the online case as homework or you may want to discuss the case in class. Answers to these questions *do not* appear on the companion website, so students *do not* have access to the feedback.

Multiple-Choice Items

1. Kyle and Carlos had a disagreement about a seat in the cafeteria, and neither seemed capable of considering the other's point of view. Of the following which is the best explanation for the boys' difficulty.

a. Both have an under-developed sense of identity, so they behaved in an egocentric way.
b. Both had poor self concepts, so they reacted to each other defensively.
c. Neither had developed social problem solving skills, so they were unable to resolve the issue.
d. Neither had developed their perspective taking,
d. The inability to interpret an incident from someone else's point of view suggests that an individual's perspective taking is underdeveloped.

Karl observed that students responded to his advice about copying other students' papers in two ways. One was to view the problem as "just another rule to follow" and others thought "that if I didn't catch them it wouldn't matter."

2. Suggesting that students view homework as "just another rule to follow" implies moral reasoning at which stage of development according to Kohlberg's theory?

a. Punishment and obedience
b. Market exchange
c. Interpersonal harmony
d. Law and order
d. Following a rule because it exists suggests moral reasoning at Stage 4: Law and Order.

3. Suggesting "that if I didn't catch them it wouldn't matter" implies moral reasoning at which stage of development according to Kohlberg's theory?

a. Punishment and obedience
b. Market exchange
c. Interpersonal harmony
d. Law and order
a. Believing an act is morally acceptable if an individual is unlikely to get caught suggests moral reasoning at Stage 1: Punishment and Obedience.

Short-Answer Questions:

4. As the teachers were discussing missing homework, Selena commented, "...if it weren't so sad, it would be funny. Some of them feel really bad about messing up so badly." How would Erikson explain this problem?

Erikson views psychosocial development as a series of stages in which individuals respond – either successfully or unsuccessfully – to challenges. In the approximate time period from 6 to 12 years, the challenge is developing a feeling of industry versus inferiority. When Selena's students continually fail to do their homework successfully, they may be developing feelings of inferiority rather than personal feelings of industry.

5. Using research on self-concept and self-esteem, comment on the advisability of Frank's suggestion to give students a boost by creating an award for doing their homework.

The research on self-concept and self-esteem is clear that focusing on these without changing student achievements won't be productive. For self-concept to change, students' accomplishments need to change. If rewarding homework completions results in changed behaviors and subsequently learning and achievement, then the idea might work. To just give rewards without thought of changing student behaviors and accomplishment would not work.

CLASSROOM EXERCISES

The classroom exercises that follow appear *only here* in the instructor's manual. Students do not have access to *either the questions or the answers*.

The purpose of keeping the exercises only in the instructor's manual is to allow you to use them as class discussion items, or for homework, if you should choose to do so.

Feedback for the exercises follows immediately.

Four generations were gathered together at a recent family reunion. During an after-dinner discussion the subject of continuing education came up among Bridget, the 40-year-old mother of two; Barbara, her mother; Mary, her grandmother; Severn, Bridget's son; and little Terese, Bridget's four-year-old daughter.

Mary shared her criticism of art she saw at an antique gallery, commenting, "The prices of the watercolors I saw were obscene, and the quality wasn't as exacting as the art we produced during the course I took two years ago."

"Well, Gram, why haven't we seen some of your work?" Bridget queried.

"Your grandmother never stays in one spot long enough to do any serious painting, she's always traveling," Barbara commented. "I always wished I had chosen a career like interior design, something that I really could have grown with over the years."

"You know mom," Bridget advised," It's never too late to go back to school."

"That's right", Severn chimes in. "Mom is going to school to be a teacher and she's old."

"Thanks a lot, sport," Bridget says as she ruffles Severn's hair.

"He's right, Mom; your study skills might be a little rusty, but you'd be at the top of your class--you're a bright lady."

"Now that I'm in one spot for awhile I think I'll buy some paint and get started again with some projects," Mary interjects. "I think the kids are right, Barb; why don't you go and take a design course at the Community College to see if you like it? All that is at stake is the cost of the course."

"Hey Mom, remember that pottery class we took at the community school last year?" Severn asks. "I'd like to do that again. Remember the big deal the teacher made about the bowl I threw on the pottery wheel?"

"Yeah, Sev, you really showed some talent. I think you must get it from your grandmother and great grandmother. The pottery teacher had all the right stuff. In fact, his commitment to his students really influenced my decision to teach. I really think I can make a difference in people's lives," Bridget said enthusiastically.

"Bridget, you've always had a positive, can-do attitude. For me I think it's a good dream, just a little too late. I was never the student you were. I struggled just to get out of high school. All I had the skills for was secretarial school. My teachers all said that college just wasn't the place for me," Barbara sighed.

"Terese, since you've climbed up on the stepstool, will you help Mommy wash the dishes in the sink?" Bridget said smiling as she glanced behind her. Terese grinned and nodded "Yes." She stepped off the stool and pushed it over to the sink so she could reach.

1. According to Erikson's stages of psychosocial development what outcome did Bridget encourage by handling the step stool incident in the manner in which she did with Terese? Explain.

2. Using the information from the dialogue, which of Erikson's stages is Severn most likely illustrating?

3. Identify the stage of development that embodies Bridget's view of continuing education for herself.

4. What stage of psychosocial development has Barbara most likely not resolved? What evidence do you have for this?

5. What stage of development has Mary successfully resolved?

An article in a prominent newspaper contained an article entitled "What's a Secretary to Do When the Boss Asks Her to Lie?" The article described some secretaries as being extremely loyal to their bosses, and committing acts, such as shredding important documents that may have destroyed evidence. In one case the secretary explained in court that in her commitment to her boss, her policy was, ". . . not to ask questions and just follow orders."

6. Based on Kohlberg's stages of moral development, in what stage does the secretary's policy fall?

7. The newspaper article further describes a secretary in California who, with the promise of protection from being fired, blew the whistle and corroborated meat-contamination cover-ups, allowing investigators to gather crucial evidence. Based on Kohlberg's work, which stage of moral reasoning does this represent?

8. Another example of what secretaries do when bosses asks them to lie, according to the article, is a woman in the midwest whose boss was falsifying home addresses on payroll records so friends could pay lower taxes in a neighboring state. She confronted him, but was ignored. She decided not to contact the police for fear of losing her job. What stage of moral reasoning, according to Kohlberg, does she best illustrate?

9. What if the same midwestern secretary, described in Item 8, decided–after she confronted her boss's wrong-doing–not to contact the police for fear she might lose her job because she is a single mom charged with raising two small school-aged children. What if instead, she looked for another job and eventually left the company? What stage of Kohlberg's moral development would this illustrate?

10. The relationship and the confidences shared between a minister, priest, or rabbi and a member of his or her congregation is privileged and would prevent that religious leader from revealing to another the nature of any confidence, no matter how dire the incident being described, if the member sharing it did not wish it to be revealed. Often a boss and secretary operate under the same set of ethics. Which stage of moral development is operating here?

FEEDBACK FOR CLASSROOM EXERCISES

1. Bridget encouraged a positive resolution of Autonomy vs. Shame and Doubt. While Terese's age suggests the Initiative vs.Guilt (and this would have been the case if Terese had intended to wash the dishes when she climbed the step stool), in this instance she was climbing the step stool to simply climb. Bridget provided structure and support by suggesting that her climb have a purpose--washing the dishes.

2. Severn's interest and enthusiasm in taking the pottery class, and his enjoyment and the recognition he received from the teacher and his mother suggest that he is successfully resolving the Industry vs. Inferiority stage.

3. Bridget's commitment, as indicated by her comment, "I really think I can make a difference in people's lives," suggests that she is successfully resolving the Generativity vs. Stagnation crisis.

4. Barbara appears to have failed to successfully resolve the Industry vs. Inferiority crisis. In Barbara's eyes her teachers and her academic accomplishments suggested a path other than college or some other career besides secretarial school. It seems from the dialogue that her interests seem to lie in the direction of art/design area, one that was not encouraged or recognized as a strength by significant others.

5. Though being the grandmother of a 40-year-old might suggest Integrity vs Despair, Mary remains in the mainstream of life, and has continued interest in living productively with her travel and painting. This suggests Generativity vs. Stagnation.

6. The secretary is demonstrating Stage 3: Interpersonal Harmony, ethics. Loyalty to someone else illustrates this stage. Since the focus is on loyalty as opposed to fear of repercussion, or some personal favor, we see no evidence of Stage 1 or Stage 2 thinking.

7. This case illustrates Stage 2: Market Exchange. The key is the promise of protection in exchange for providing corroborating evidence.

8. Her reasoning is at Stage 1: Punishment and Obedience. The consequence of being fired if her boss's deed is discovered or reported caused the secretary to keep silent and continue to work for him as she always has.

9. In this case, the secretary's behavior indicates Stage 3: Interpersonal Harmony. Her decision not to contact the police was out of concern for the welfare of her children if she were fired from her job.

10. This reasoning suggests Stage 5: Social Contract. Agreements about keeping confidences is made among the people involved, the sanctity of which is kept until mutually agreed upon changes are made.

CHAPTER 4: GROUP AND INDIVIDUAL DIFFERENCES

CHAPTER OVERVIEW

Learner differences are the focus of this chapter. The chapter begins by outlining different conceptions of intelligence. This discussion is followed by an examination of socioeconomic status, culture–including ethnicity, voluntary and involuntary minorities and culturally responsive teaching–and gender differences. In the last section of the chapter, students placed at risk, the development of resiliency, and effective schools and teachers for students placed at risk are discussed in detail.

CHAPTER OBJECTIVES

- Describe differences in the way intelligence is viewed, and explain how ability grouping can influence learning.
- Define socioeconomic status and explain how it can affect school performance.
- Describe cultural, ethnic, and language diversity and explain how they can influence learning.
- Explain gender role identity and describe steps for eliminating gender bias in classrooms.
- Describe characteristics of schools and qualities of teachers that promote student resilience.

POWERPOINT SLIDES

PP 4.1 Sources of Learner Individuality
PP 4.2 Gardner's Theory of Multiple Intelligences
PP 4.3 Instructional Applications of Gardner's Multiple Intelligences
PP 4.4 Sternberg's Triarchic Model of Intelligence
PP 4.5 Applying Analytic, Creative, and Practical Thinking in Different Content Areas
PP 4.6 Ability Grouping, Behavior, and Achievement
PP 4.7 Types of Ability Grouping in Elementary Schools
PP 4.8 Criticisms of Ability Grouping
PP 4.9 Suggestions for Reducing the Negative Effects of Grouping
PP 4.10 Sources of Learner Individuality
PP 4.11 The Influence of SES on Learning
PP 4.12 U.S. Census Ethnicity Comparisons
PP 4.13 Making Students Feel Welcome in School
PP 4.14 Types of Bilingual Programs
PP 4.15 Teaching Culturally and Linguistically Diverse Students: Instructional Principles
PP 4.16 Gender Differences in the Classroom
PP 4.17 Responding to Gender Differences: Instructional Principles
PP 4.18 Provisions of Title IX
PP 4.19 Characteristics of Students Placed at Risk
PP 4.20 Schools That Promote Resilience
PP 4.21 Teaching Students Placed at Risk: Instructional Principles
PP 4.22 Praxis Practice: Feedback for Short-Answer Questions
PP 4.23 Feedback for Online Case Questions
PP 4.24 Classroom Exercises

VIDEO

DVD 1, Episode 5: "Culturally Responsive Teaching"
In this episode a teacher discusses the adaptations she makes for cultural differences in her students.

CHAPTER OUTLINE

I. Intelligence
   A. Intelligence: One trait or many?
      1. Gardner's theory of multiple intelligences
         a. Applications of Gardner's theory
         b. Criticisms of Gardner's theory
      2. Sternberg's triarchic theory of intelligence
         a. Improving intelligence
   B. Intelligence: Nature versus nurture
   C. Ability grouping
      1. Ability grouping: Research results
      2. Ability grouping: Implications for teachers
   D. Learning styles
      1. Learning preferences: Research results
      2. Learning styles: Implications for teachers
II. Socioeconomic status
   A. Influence of SES on learning
      1. Basic needs and experience
      2. Parental involvement
      3. Attitudes and values
   B. SES: Some cautions and implications for teachers
III. Culture
   A. Ethnicity
   B. Culture and schooling
      1. The cultural basis of attitudes and values
      2. Cultural differences in adult-child interactions
      3. Classroom organization and culture
      4. Culture and schooling: Some cautions
   C. Language Diversity
      1. English dialects: Research findings
      2. Dialects in the classroom: Implications for teachers
      3. English Language Learners
      4. Types of ELL programs
         a. Maintenance ELL programs
         b. Transitional ELL programs
         c. ELL pullout programs
         d. Sheltered English
      5. Evaluating ELL programs
   D. Teaching culturally and linguistically diverse students: Instructional Principles
IV. Gender
   A. Differences in the classroom behavior of boys and girls
   B. Gender stereotypes and perceptions
   C. Responding to gender differences: Instructional Principles
V. Students placed at risk
   A. Resilience
      1. Schools that promote resilience
      2. Teachers who promote resilience
   B. Teaching students placed at risk: Instructional Principles

PRESENTATION OUTLINE

The suggested activities can be completed in small groups and discussed as a whole group, or they can be conducted as whole-class activities. To be consistent with our understanding of knowledge construction, we recommend that you promote as much discussion–both in small groups and with the whole class–as possible.

I. Intelligence
  A. Intelligence: One trait or many?
    1. Gardner's theory of multiple intelligences
      a. Applications of Gardner's theory
      b. Criticisms of Gardner's theory
    2. Sternberg's triarchic theory of intelligence
      a. Improving intelligence
  B. Intelligence: Nature versus nurture
  C. Ability grouping
    1. Ability grouping: Research results
    2. Ability grouping: Implications for teachers
  D. Learning styles
    1. Learning preferences: Research results
    2. Learning styles: Implications for teachers

Teaching Suggestions:

■ ***The following suggestions introduce students to the concept of intelligence and help them understand different views of intelligence including Gardner's and Sternberg's theories :***

1. **Display PP 4.1 "*Sources of Learner Individuality*" and remind students that you have begun your study of learner differences with the study of intelligence.**

2. **Have students take out a sheet of paper and number it from 1 to 10. This activity is most effective if you give them no directions other than to number their paper. They will wonder what is going on, and they usually react to the nature of the questions as you ask them.**

3. **Ask the following questions orally and have them respond in writing to them. (Asking the questions orally is consistent with the way the WISC-III is administered, but the students' responses are also oral, rather than in writing as you're doing here.) (If you have access to the WISC-III, an even better activity would be to select some actual items from it and administer them to the students.)**
    1. **In what continent is Colombia? (South America)**
    2. **What is the capital of Syria? (Damascus)**
    3. **How far is it from Seattle to Atlanta? (2618 miles; Accept 2300-3000)**
    4. **What is the most abundant gas in our atmosphere? (Nitrogen)**
    5. **Who was Albert Einstein? (Creator of theory of relativity)**
    6. **If four pieces of candy cost 10 cents, what will be the cost of 28 pieces? (70 cents)**
    7. **Ed bought a sweater from his friend for $18. He paid 3/4 of what the sweater cost new. What did the sweater cost new? ($24)**
    8. **A pair of walking shorts for $27 was on sale for 1/3 less. When no one bought the shorts, the store owner reduced the sale price by 1/2. How much did the shorts cost after the second reduction? ($9)**
    9. **How are a river and a plateau alike? ("Topographical features" would be a 2-point response; "things we find in nature" would be a 1-point response, and "made of water and rocks" would be a 0-point response)**
    10. **How are freedom and justice alike? ("Social ideals" would be a 2-point response, "civil rights" would be a 1-point response, and "both mean peace" would be a 0-point response.)**

4. **After the students have responded, ask them what they just did. Someone will know that they responded to items similar to those on intelligence tests. Also, ask them what the 2-point answers have in common that make them different from the 1-point answers, and the 0-point answers. Someone will note that the 2-point answers are the most abstract and the 0-point answers are the most concrete.**

5. **Have students discuss what the differences in the 2-point, 1-point, and 0-point answers as well as the items themselves indicate about experts' conceptions of intelligence. Ask them why they think experts believe that an item, such as "What is the capital of Syria?" is an indicator of intelligence. You might also ask them how they feel about the experts' conceptions of intelligence.**

6. **Emphasize that intelligence tests measure experience to a considerable extent. This suggests that we want to provide as much meaningful experience for our learners as possible.**

7. **Display PP 4.2 "*Gardner's Theory of Multiple Intelligences.*" Point out that one of the most important contributions of Gardner's work is that he helps us expand our view of what it means to be intelligent. (This is an emotionally satisfying conception for people who haven't excelled in linguistic or logical-mathematical intelligence, which are the two most strongly emphasized in traditional school curricula.)**

8. **To examine classroom implications of Gardner's work display PP 4.3 "*Instructional Applications of Gardner's Multiple Intelligences.*" Have students identify other topics and describe how they would try to capitalize on the different intelligences in learning activities.**
You might point out that people often misinterpret Gardner's conceptions of intelligence, interpreting them as *preferences* instead. For example, interpersonal intelligence means that an individual has insight into the way other people think and operate. They have a good sense of people's inclinations and needs and what it takes to work effectively with them. It does not necessarily mean that they are socially oriented or prefer being with people to being alone.

9. **Display PP 4.4 "*Sternberg's Triarchic Model of Intelligence.*" Point out that Sternberg's emphasis on the creative and practical aspects of intellect is what sets his theory apart from other views of intelligence. He sees functioning effectively in the real world as intelligent behavior, and because of this emphasis, he believes that individuals considered intelligent in one setting or culture may be viewed as unintelligent in another.**

10. **To illustrate Sternberg's recent views, display PP 4.5 "*Applying Analytic, Creative, and Practical Thinking in Different Content Areas.*" Have the students offer some additional applications in their own specialty areas.**

11. **Have the students compare early conceptions of intelligence, such as Spearman's notion of "g" to today's conceptions. You might also have them compare the implications of Sternberg's and Gardner's theories for their work with their own students.**

12. **Have students describe their position on the nature/nurture debate. Ask them to provide evidence for their positions. Ask them where they believe Gardner and Sternberg would fall. The following correlations might prove interesting to them.**

I. Q. Correlations*

Foster parent-child	**.20**
Parent-child	**.50**
Siblings reared together	**.49**
Fraternal twins	**.53**
Identical twins reared apart	**.75**
Identical twins reared together	**.87**

***Erlenmeyer-Kimling and Jarvik, 1963**

■ ***To help students understand some of the controversies surrounding ability grouping as well as controversies related to the concept of learning styles:***

1. **Display PP 4.6 "*Ability Grouping, Behavior, and Achievement.*" Have the students respond to the four items. Discuss the explanations.**

2. **Display PP 4.7 "*Types of Ability Grouping in Elementary Schools,*" and PP 4.8 "*Criticisms of Ability Grouping.*" Ask students why they think placements are sometimes incorrectly made and why the placements tend to become permanent. Have them relate the process of placing students to intelligence testing and what intelligence tests measure. In the discussion, point out that schools are busy, complex places, and school officials and teachers, like people in general want to simplify their work. Maintaining a placement is simpler than moving students from one ability group to another.**

3. **Ask the students to use Erikson's theory to explain the lowered self-esteem and motivation of students in elementary schools placed in low ability groups. Have them also explain for junior high and high school students placed in low-ability tracks.**

4. **Display PP 4.9 "*Suggestions for Reducing the Negative Effects of Grouping.*" Discuss the suggestions.**

   You might also want to point out that students in high- and low-ability classes, in addition to the amount of time they tend to be off-task, differ in when they're off task. High-ability students tend to complete assignments, such as seatwork, and then go off task, whereas low-ability tend to go off task during the time they're involved in the assignment. As a result, they often fail to complete the assignment in class, it's left to be completed at home, it may not be completed, or may be completed incorrectly, and achievement declines.

5. **Point out that "learning style" means different things to different people, and much of what people refer to as learning style is really learning preference.**

6. **Also note that little research supports the contention that a relationship exists between learning preferences and academic achievement.**

II. Socioeconomic status (SES)
   A. Influence of SES on learning
      1. Basic needs and experiences
      2. Parental involvement
      3. Attitudes and values
   B. SES: Some cautions and implications for teachers

Teaching Suggestions:

■ ***The suggestions in this section are intended to help your students understand the impact of SES on achievement.***

1. **Introduce students to this section of the chapter by again displaying PP 4.10 "*Sources of Learner Individuality,*" and identifying socioeconomic status as the source of individuality that you are focusing on in this section.**

2. **Display PP 4.11 "*The Influence of SES on Learning,*" which summarizes the research on the differences between students from high and low SES backgrounds.**

3. **Strongly emphasize that the information in PP 4.11 is in the form of generalizations, and many exceptions exist. Also emphasize that the results can lead to stereotyping students from low SES backgrounds and inappropriately lowering their expectations as a result. Ask them what**

they would do to accommodate students who come to their classes without some of the school related experiences that other students might have.

III. Culture
  A. Ethnicity
  B. Culture and schooling
    1. The cultural basis of attitudes and values
    2. Cultural differences in adult-child interactions
    3. Classroom organization and culture
    4. Culture and schooling: Some cautions
  C. Language Diversity
    1. English dialects: Research findings
    2. Dialects in the classroom: Implications for teachers
    3. English Language Learners
    4. Types of ELL programs
      a. Maintenance ELL programs
      b. Transitional ELL programs
      c. ELL pullout programs
      d. Sheltered English
    5. Evaluating ELL programs
  D. Teaching culturally and linguistically diverse students: Instructional Principles

Teaching Suggestions:

■ ***The suggestions in this section are designed to increase your students' awareness of the impact that cultural differences can have on learning.***

1. **If you teach in a college or university where Caucasian students are in the majority, begin this section by asking those students to predict how they might feel if they were in a school situation where they were a minority.**

2. **Ask the ethnic minorities in your class, if they were in schools that were largely populated by white students, how they felt during their K–12 experiences. Ask the minority students if they ever felt unwelcome, and if so, why. Discuss their responses.**

3. **Ask minority students who went to schools largely populated by minorities, such as African American students who went to schools largely populated by African Americans, how they felt during their K–12 experiences. Discuss any similarities or differences.**

4. **Refer the students back to your study of Chapter 3 and the issues of ethnic pride and self-esteem.**

5. **Display PP 4.12 "*U.S. Census Ethnicity Comparisons*" to see how the ethnic makeup of our country is changing.**

6. **Display PP 4.13 "*Making Students Feel Welcome in School*," which includes some ideas for making members of cultural minorities feel welcome in teachers' classrooms.**

Here would be a good point to show or discuss **Episode 5 on DVD 1**: "Culturally Responsive Teaching."

■ ***To help your students understand the different types of bilingual programs:***

1. **Display PP 4.14 "*Types of Bilingual Programs.*"**

2. **Have the students explain the research results on bilingual programs using Piaget's and Vygotsky's work as a basis for their explanation. Discuss their explanations.**

3. **With respect to dialects, you might want to remind the students that since the dialect is functional for the child outside the classroom, using it as a base for the gradual evolution of Standard English is a sensible approach. (Interestingly, this is the same approach recommended for parents wanting to develop young children's language; adults use events to elicit language and then build on them by modeling correct language [Snow, Perlmann, & Nathan, 1987]).**

   Most important, students who use different dialects need to feel accepted and valued. Knowing that nonstandard dialects are not inferior forms of language and that students who speak them are as capable as other students can help teachers maintain appropriate expectations.

4. **Display PP 4.15 "*Teaching Culturally and Linguistically Diverse Students: Instructional Principles.*" Refer the students to the case study with Gary Nolan (on page 114 of your text). Have the students identify where Gary applied each of the principles.**

IV. Gender
   A. Differences in the behavior of boys and girls
   B. Gender stereotypes and perceptions
      1. Perceptions of male and female domains
      2. Single-gender classrooms and schools
   C. Responding to gender differences: Instructional principles

Teaching Suggestions:

■ ***The following suggestions are intended to increase your students' awareness of differences in the ways boys and girls are treated in schools.***

1. **Pose the question, "How do girls' behaviors compare to boys' behaviors in classrooms?" After students have offered their perceptions, display PP 4.16 "*Gender Differences in the Classroom*" and discuss the patterns and their implications.**

2. **Display PP 4.17 "*Responding to Gender Differences: Instructional Principles.*" Have the students identify where (in the case study on page 119 of the text) Marti Barnes attempted to apply the principles in her work with her students.**

3. **Display PP 4.18 "*Provisions of Title IX.*" Point out that this federal law dramatically increased girls' and women's participation in sports.**

V. Students placed at risk
   A. Resilience
      1. Schools that promote resilience
      2. Teachers who promote resilience
   B. Teaching students placed at risk: Instructional principles

Teaching Suggestions:

■ ***The following suggestions are designed to help your students understand the characteristics of students placed at risk and the implications these characteristics have for learning and teaching.***

1. **Begin the discussion by asking the students to predict characteristics of students placed at risk.**

2. **Display PP 4.19 "*Characteristics of Students Placed at Risk*" and compare the information to the students' predictions. Discuss the similarities and differences.**

3. **Emphasize that these characteristics are generalizations, and because a student comes from a low SES, inner-city background and is male, for example, doesn't mean that he or she will automatically experience the educational problems displayed in PP 4.19.**

4. **Display PP 4.20 "*Schools That Promote Resilience.*" Point out that these characteristics are important for all schools, not just those with large populations of students placed at risk.**

5. **Display PP 4.21"*Teaching Students Placed at Risk: Instructional Principles.*" Ask the students to identify where in the case study on page 123 that Diane Smith applied each of the principles. After displaying PP 4.21, ask students how instruction for students placed at risk compares to effective instruction in general. They will note that they are essentially the same.**

ENRICHMENT MATERIALS

TEACHER PREP WEBSITE

The *Teacher Prep* website an online resource for students and instructors. Both you and students can access the *Teacher Prep* website by going to http://www.prenhall.com/teacherprep. Enter your user name and password and click on "Log In." The *Teacher Prep* website includes video episodes, student and teacher artifacts, teacher and research resources, and information about licensing and beginning a teaching career. The *Teacher Prep* website is described in detail in the Media Guide.

The following articles are recommended by the *Exploring Further* section of this chapter titled "Culturally Responsive Teaching" on page 115 of the chapter.

Once into the *Teacher Prep* website access the articles by completing the following steps:

1. Click on "Research Resources" on the left panel of the screen, scroll down the middle of the page and again click on "Research Resources."
2. Go to "Classroom Processes" and click on "Diverse Populations."
3. Click on the following articles:
   Bridging Cultures with Classroom Strategies, by C. Rothstein-Fisch, P. M. Greenfield, and E. Trumbull (1999), Ref. No. 2242,
   Exploring World Cultures in Math Class, by C. Zaslavsky (2002), Ref. No. 1684, and
   Closing the Achievement Gap, by K. Haycock (2001), Ref. No. 1789.

These articles describe different ways that teachers can adapt instruction to meet the needs of diverse learners.

The following articles are recommended by the *Exploring Further* section of this chapter titled "Eliminating Gender Bias" on page 120 of the chapter.

Once into the *Teacher Prep* website access the articles by completing the following steps:

1. Click on "Research Resources" on the left panel of the screen, scroll down the middle of the page, and again click on "Research Resources."
2. Go to "Classroom Processes" and click on "Diverse Populations."
3. Click on the following articles:
   Gender Difference on Assessments, by A. S. Latham (1997), Ref. No. 260
   Gender Equity in Cyberspace, by J. Weinman and P. Haag (1999), Ref. No. 549, and
   Raising Better Boys, by G. Canada (1999), Ref. No. 2255.

These articles describe the different ways that teachers can deal with gender issues for both girls and boys in their classrooms.

The following articles are recommended by the *Exploring Further* section of this chapter titled "Effective Instruction for Students Placed At-Risk" on page 125 of the chapter.

Once into the *Teacher Prep* website access the articles by completing the following steps:

1. Click on "Research Resources" on the left panel of the screen, scroll down the middle of the page and again click on "Research Resources."
2. Go to "Classroom Processes" and click on "Diverse Populations."
3. Click on the following articles:
   Building on Urban Learners' Experiences, by B. Williams and M. Woods (1997), Ref. No. 210, and
   Strategies that Close the Gap, by L. I. Bell (2002), Ref. No. 1688.

These articles describe different strategies teachers can use in working with students placed at-risk.

DISCUSSION STARTERS

You may choose to have your students discuss one or more of the following questions to further enrich their understanding of your learning activities.

1. To what extent should schools attempt to make students more homogeneous, i.e., encourage minority students to adopt the behaviors and values of the majority or white culture? What benefits are there to the student? To society? What drawbacks are there to the student? To society? What does educational psychology tell us about the possibility or desirability of this approach?

2. Parents at an elementary school back-to-school night wanted to know why their child wasn't ability grouped in every content area. They felt their child was being held back by the lack of ability grouping. How would you answer their question?

3. A parent comes to see you, says that she has had her daughter tested and that her intelligence is quite high. Still, the daughter only does slightly above average in school. How would you explain these results to the parent?

4. Based on the information in the text on the effects of SES on learning, describe an ideal family learning environment and explain how it promotes intellectual development.

5. There has been an abrupt change of fortune for two families with children. One, an upper class family has suddenly lost most of its wealth. The other, a lower SES family, has recently become unexpectedly wealthy. How might these economic changes influence the educational experiences of the children in these families?

6. Research on the composition of the public school population shows that while 29% of the students are minority, only 3 of the teachers are (National Center for Statistics, 1993). What problems does this cause for culturally responsive teaching? What long and short term solutions to this problem can you suggest?

7. Why is the teaching force primarily female? How does this influence teaching and learning in our schools?

BACKGROUND READINGS

Bleeker, M. M., & Jacobs, J. E. (2004). Achievement in math and science: Do mothers' beliefs matter 12 years later? *Journal of Educational Psychology, 96*(1), 97–109.
This article considers the influence of mothers' beliefs on their daughters' attitudes and expectations for academic success.

Brown, R., & Evans, W. (2002). Extracurricular activity and ethnicity: Creating greater school connection among diverse student populations. *Urban Education, 37*(1), 41–58.
This article examines the impact of minority students' involvement in extracurricular activities on their identification with their schools and its impact on achievement.

Dilworth, M., & Brown, C. (2001). Consider the difference: Teaching and learning in culturally rich schools. In V. Richardson (Ed.), *Handbook of research on learning* (4th ed., pp. 643–667). Washington, DC: American Educational Research Association.
This chapter offers suggestions for capitalizing in learner diversity for enhancing educational experiences for all students.

Doll, B., Zucker, S., & Brehm, K. (2004). *Resilient classrooms: Creating healthy environments for learning*. New York: Guilford Press.
This book offers strategies for promoting resilience in students.

Eisenberg, N, Martin, C., & Rabes, R. (1996). Gender development and gender effects. In D. Berliner, & R. Calfee (Eds.), *Handbook of educational psychology* (pp. 358–397). New York: Macmillan.
This chapter provides a comprehensive review of the influences of gender on learning.

Gardner, H. (1999). *Intelligence reframed: Multiple intelligences for the 21st century*. New York: Basic Books.
This book provides an overview of Gardner's theory.

Grant, C. A., & Gomez, M. L. (2001). *Campus and classroom: Making schooling multicultural* (2nd ed.). Upper Saddle River, NJ: Merrill/Prentice Hall.
This book is a guide for integrating multicultural concepts into the classroom.

Gray, T., & Fleischman, S. (2005). Successful strategies for English language learners. *Educational Leadership, 62*(4), 84–85.
This article offers strategies for helping ELL students succeed in regular classrooms.

Neisser, U. (Ed.) (1998). *The rising curve: Long-term gains in IQ and related measures*. Washington, DC: American Psychological Association.
This book examines the research on the nature versus nurture question.

Ogbu, J. U. (2003). *Black American students in an affluent suburb: A study of academic disengagement*. Mahwah, NJ: Erlbaum.
This controversial book by a prominent author examines the question of Black American students' underachievement compared to their peers who are not members of cultural minorities.

Pressley, M., Raphael, L., & Gallagher, J. G. (2004). Prodience-St. Mel School: How a school that works for African American students works. *Journal of Educational Psychology, 96(2), 216–235.*
This article identifies characteristics of schools that are effective for promoting achievement in students who are members of cultural minorities.

Sand, B. V. (April, 2001). *Toward a definition of creativity; Construct validation the cognitive components of creativity*. Paper presented at the annual meeting of the American Educational Research Association, Seattle.
This paper offers a definition of creativity and a mechanism for identifying creativity in students.

Sternberg, R. J. (2002). Raising the achievement of all students: Teaching for successful intelligence. *Educational Psychology Review, 14*, 383–393.
This article, based on his theory of intelligence offers suggestions for improving learners' intelligence.

FEEDBACK

Developing as a Professional: Praxis Practice: Feedback for Short-Answer Questions

The feedback that appears here is for the short-answer questions that follow the case study on pages 127 and 128 of the text. The feedback is also available to students on the companion website.

1. What strategies did Teri use to eliminate gender bias in her classroom? What else might she have done?
   The most prominent strategy Teri used to eliminate gender bias was to call on all students–both male and female–equally. Other strategies she might have employed include: strategically assigning girls to key roles in small groups, openly talking about the problem in class, and bringing female role models into her class.

2. One of the principles of effective teaching for students placed at risk recommends the use of high-quality examples that supplement students' background knowledge. How well did Teri apply this principle?
   The overheads that Teri used to illustrate mercantilism minimized the role of previous background knowledge by containing all of the essential characteristics.

3. Success and challenge are essential for effective instruction for students placed at risk. Evaluate Teri's attempts to provide these components.
   Teri provided challenge by asking her students to find commonalities between the two examples of mercantilism. She encouraged success by structuring her questioning strategies so that students were able to construct the concept from the examples.

4. What strategies did Teri use to actively involve her students?
   She actively involved her students in two ways. First she had them work in groups, and then she used interactive questioning to involve them in the lesson.

Feedback for Online Case Book Questions

The feedback below is for the *Online Case Book* for Chapter 4 (referenced on page 125 of the chapter). Both you and the students can access the case study by going to www.prenhall.com/eggen, selecting Chapter 4, and clicking on *Online Case Book.*

You may choose to assign the online case as homework or you may want to discuss the case in class. Answers to these questions *do not* appear on the companion website, so students *do not* have access to the feedback.

Multiple-Choice Items:

1. Using the principles of instruction for responding to gender differences as a basis, which of the following statements is the best assessment of Trish's *Math Competition* game?

   a. It is effective, because it is likely to increase a high level of student interest.
   b. It is ineffective because it is likely to emphasize gender differences that can detract from learning.
   c. It is effective, because it adds variety to learning activities, and varying learning activities can increase learning.
   d. It is ineffective because Trish only gave the students 10 minutes for their seatwork before beginning the game.
   b. One of the principles of instruction for responding to gender differences says, "Eliminate gender bias in instructional activities. Regardless of whether the girls or the boys win, gender bias is likely to occur.

2. Base on the principles of instruction for teaching students placed at risk, which of the following is the best assessment of Trish's explanation of the three problems?

   a. The explanations were effective because she carefully explained each and demonstrated the steps as she explained.
   b. The explanations were ineffective because she only explained three problems.
   c. The explanations were effective because she had the students practice solving their own problems after she explained them.
   d. The ineffective because she didn't use a teaching strategy that actively involved the students.
   d. One of the principles of instruction for teaching students placed at risk says, "Use teaching strategies that actively involve all students and promote high levels of success." No evidence of student involvement nor levels of success exist in the lesson. The principles don't address how "carefully" a teacher explains (choice a), the number of problems that should be presented (choice b), or student practice (choice c).

3. During the lesson Trish commented, "These problems may be hard for some of you, but try anyway." Which of the following statements is the best assessment of this comment?

   a. The statement is effective because it is important to give students placed at risk a realistic appraisal of their abilities.
   b. The statement is ineffective because
   c. The statement is effective because Trish made the statement pleasantly.
   d. The statement is ineffective because establishing positive expectations are important for students placed at risk.
   d. A statement such as, "These problems may be hard for some of you, but try anyway," communicates low expectations. And, one of the principles of instruction for teaching students placed at risk states, "Combine high expectations with frequent feedback about learning progress."

Short-Answer Items:

1. Using your understanding of effective instruction for students placed at risk, assess Trish's instruction. Provide evidence from the case study to support your assessment.

Her instruction was basically ineffective for her students placed at-risk. Except for the three problems that she worked at the board, there were few high-quality examples that illustrated the logic behind carrying. In addition, she failed to actively involve students in learning about carrying. This not only made them passive learners but also failed to provide her with valuable information about students' learning progress.

As an alternative she could have had students work several problems both at the board and at their desks and observe them as they worked. Then, the students should be asked to explain how they solved the problems, and why they solved the problems as they did. This would have provided her with insights into the students' understanding.

2. Positive expectations are important for teaching all students and particularly students placed at risk. How effectively did Trish establish positive expectations for her students?

Trish addressed expectations in at least two places in her lesson. First, she said, "I know it's hard to get started in the morning but we have to get going." While it was subtle, the comment could imply that her students might be unenthusiastic or poorly motivated. The second, and more important example occurred when she said, "These may be hard for some of you, but try anyway." Comments such as this suggest to the students that she believes they have low ability. A more positive way to introduce the activity might be to say, "These problems might be challenging, but I know that we can do them if we work hard enough."

CLASSROOM EXERCISES

The classroom exercises that follow appear *only here* in the instructor's manual. Students do not have access to *either the questions or the answers*.

The purpose of keeping the exercises only in the instructor's manual is to allow you to use them as class discussion items, or for homework, if you should choose to do so.

Feedback for the exercises follows immediately.

Gavin, a seventh grader, has more trouble in school than many of his peers, particularly with word problems in math and other areas that aren't tangible. In spite of high motivation, he still struggles, and new situations and problems "throw him" more than they do his classmates. In order to succeed, he needs a lot of practice, and his approach is somewhat more "mechanical" than that of his peers. He comments, "I need to be able to 'see it' to understand it. Some of these ideas are just too abstract for me. Who cares what caused Columbus to want to go to the Far East. I can get it though, if I get enough practice." When he gets frustrated, he retreats to his room where he plays his guitar; he has even done some of his own arrangements. Gavin is very skilled at working with people, and some of his peers turn to him as an arbitrator when clashes occur in club and other organizational meetings.

1. Using traditional conceptions of intelligence, assess Gavin's intelligence compared to his peers. Explain.

2. Consider Gavin's intelligence based on Gardner's Theory of Multiple Intelligences. Assess Gavin's intelligence on this basis. Explain.

3. Consider Gavin's intelligence according to Sternberg's Triarchic Theory of Intelligence. Based on the case study and Sternberg's work, assess Gavin's intelligence. Explain your thoughts.

Carrie is a fifth grader at Gorrie Elementary school—a school near an affluent neighborhood in a suburb of a major city. Carrie, who lives with her divorced mother—a high school dropout with a steady job as a minimum wage housekeeper--seems to have limited background experiences. In a discussion of the "Old West," for example, she asked what a saddle horn was, when Mrs. Williams talked about the saddles cowboys used. Also, she had never heard of a wild turkey, thinking only of the turkeys people eat on Thanksgiving. However, Carrie "picks up" new ideas in class more quickly than most of her classmates, and she periodically asks questions atypical of fifth graders, such as, "Wouldn't our country be better off if some of the money the Congress spends fighting with each other went to educating poor people instead?"

4. Based on the information in the case study, how will Carrie's score on a traditional intelligence test compare to the scores of her typical peers? Explain.

5. Based on researchers' conceptions of intelligence, would Carrie be considered more, less, or similar in intelligence to that of her typical peers? Explain.

6. How does Carrie's socioeconomic status compare to that of her typical peers? Explain.

7. If Carrie fits typical patterns for students with her background and socioeconomic status, is the likelihood of her dropping out of school at some point before graduation greater, less, or similar to the likelihood of her typical peers dropping out? Explain.

8. If Mrs. Williams questioning patterns are similar to those identified by research, is Carrie more, less, or similarly likely to be called on, compared to typical boys in her class. Is she likely to be asked high- or low-level questions? Explain.

9. Of the following groups--Cambodian refugee, Chinese Americans, Native Americans, or Filipino Americans--which is most likely to experience cultural inversion? Explain.

FEEDBACK FOR CLASSROOM EXERCISES

1. He is probably less intelligent than his typical peers. Traditional conceptions of intelligence include the ability to learn, the ability to solve problems, and the ability to think in the abstract. Gavin appears to be a bit behind his classmates in all three areas.

2. Gavin would be described as less intelligent in areas such as logical-mathematical intelligence, more intelligent in others, such as musical and interpersonal. We don't have information about Gavin's behavior or about other intelligences he might possess such as spatial or bodily kinesthetic.

3. Sternberg views the ability to effectively deal with new or novel situations as an indicator of intelligent behavior. Gavin has difficulty with these situations, so according to Sternberg's view, he would be considered less intelligent than his typical peers.

4. Carrie is likely to score lower on traditional intelligence tests, since they measure experience, and Carrie's experience is limited compared to her affluent peers.

5. Traditional conceptions of intelligence include the ability to learn, the ability to solve problems, and the ability to think in the abstract. Carrie picks up ideas rapidly and tends to think more in the abstract than do her peers. According to traditional conceptions of intelligence, Carrie would be considered more intelligent than her typical peers.

6. Her mother is a high school dropout with a low status, low paying job, so Carrie's socioeconomic status would be lower than that of her peers.

7. Students from low SES backgrounds are about twice as likely to drop out as students from the general population, so Carrie would be more likely to drop out than would her typical peer.

8. Teachers typically call on boys more often than girls, so it is likely that Carrie will be called on less than the boys in her class. Also, teachers tend to ask boys more high-level questions than they ask girls.

9. Cultural inversion is the tendency of members of some cultural minorities, because of a long history of separatism and low status, to reject certain attitudes and values of the mainstream culture. Of the choices given, Native Americans are most likely to experience cultural inversion.

CHAPTER 5: LEARNERS WITH EXCEPTIONALITIES

CHAPTER OVERVIEW

This chapter continues the focus on learner differences, looking at students who may need special help to reach their full potential. A theme for this chapter is the classroom teacher's role in identifying and working with students with exceptionalities. The chapter begins by describing The Individuals with Disabilities Education Act together with its amendments. It continues by examining students with learning problems, learners who are gifted and talented, and concludes with a section examining effective practices for working with students with exceptionalities in the regular classroom.

CHAPTER OBJECTIVES

- Describe the provisions of, and amendments to, the Individuals with Disabilities Education Act (IDEA)
- Describe the most common learning problems that classroom teachers are likely to encounter.
- Identify characteristics of learners who are gifted and talented, and describe methods for identifying and teaching these students.
- Explain the roles of classroom teachers and teaching strategies that are effective for working with students having exceptionalities.

POWERPOINT SLIDES

PP 5.1 The Individuals with Disabilities Education Act
PP 5.2 Educational Service Options for Implementing the LRE
PP 5.3 The Population of Students with Disabilities
PP 5.4 Characteristics of Students with Learning Disabilities
PP 5.5 Attention Deficit/Hyperactivity Disorder (AD/HD)
PP 5.6 Characteristics of Students with Behavior Disorders
PP 5.7 Working with Students Having Behavior Disorders
PP 5.8 Kinds of Speech Disorders
PP 5.9 Symptoms of Potential Visual Problems
PP 5.10 Indicators of Hearing Impairment
PP 5.11 Working with Students Who Have Hearing Disabilities
PP 5.12 Characteristics of the Gifted and Talented
PP 5.13 Options in Enrichment and Acceleration Programs
PP 5.14 The Teacher's Role in Inclusive Classrooms
PP 5.15 Principles of Instruction for Teaching Students with Exceptionalities
PP 5.16 Instructional Adaptations for Students with Exceptionalities
PP 5.17 Working with Students with Exceptionalities: An Application
PP 5.18 Praxis Practice: Feedback for Short-Answer Questions
PP 5.19 Feedback for Online Case Questions
PP 5.20 Classroom Exercises

VIDEOS

DVD 1, Episode 6: "Reviewing an IEP"
This episode illustrates the processes involved in preparing an IEP for a student needing extra support.

DVD 1, Episode 7: "Using Peer Tutoring With Students Having Exceptionalities"
This episode illustrates a peer-tutoring program used with students having exceptionalities.

CHAPTER OUTLINE

I. Changes in the way teachers help students with exceptionalities
  A. Individuals with Disabilities Education Act (IDEA)
    1. A free and appropriate public education
    2. Least restrictive environment: The evolution towards inclusion
      a. Collaborative consultation: Help for the classroom teacher
      b. Putting inclusion into perspective
    3. Protection against discrimination in testing
    4. Due process and parents' rights
    5. Individualized education program
  B. Amendments to the Individuals with Disabilities Education Act
II. Students with learning problems
  A. The labeling controversy
  B. Mental retardation
    1. Levels of mental retardation
    2. Programs for students with mental retardation
  C. Learning disabilities
    1. Characteristics of students with learning disabilities
    2. Identifying and working with students who have learning disabilities
      a. The use of classroom-based information for identification
      b. Adaptive instruction
  D. Attention deficit/hyperactivity disorder
  E. Behavior disorders
    1. Kinds of behavior disorders
    2. Teaching students with behavior disorders
      a. Behavior management strategies
      b. Teacher sensitivity
  F. Communication disorders
    1. Helping students with communication disorders
  G. Visual disabilities
    1. Working with students who have visual disabilities
  H. Hearing disabilities
    1. Working with students who have hearing disabilities
  I. Assessment and Learning: Assessment trends in special education
    1. Curriculum-based assessment
    2. Adaptive behavior
III. Students who are gifted and talented
  A. Creativity
  B. Identifying students who are gifted and talented
  C. Teaching students who are gifted and talented: Instructional principles
IV. The teacher's role in inclusive classrooms
  A. Identifying students with exceptionalities
  B. Teaching students with exceptionalities: Instructional principles
    1. Provide additional instructional support
    2. Adapt seatwork and homework
    3. Supplement reading materials
    4. Teach learning strategies
  C. Social integration and growth
    1. Developing classmates' understanding and acceptance
    2. Helping students learn acceptable behaviors
    3. Strategies for promoting interaction and cooperation

PRESENTATION OUTLINE

The suggested activities can be completed in small groups and discussed as a whole group, or they can be conducted as whole-class activities. To be consistent with our understanding of knowledge construction, we recommend that you promote as much discussion—both in small groups and with the whole class—as possible.

I. Changes in the way teachers help students with exceptionalities
    A. Individuals with Disabilities Education Act (IDEA)
        1. A free and appropriate public education
        2. Least restrictive environment: The evolution towards inclusion
            a. Collaborative consultation: Help for the classroom teacher
            b. Putting inclusion into perspective
        3. Protection against discrimination in testing
        4. Due process and parents' rights
        5. Individualized education program
    B. Amendments to the Individuals with Disabilities Education Act

Teaching Suggestions:

■ ***The suggestions in this section are designed to help your students understand the law and their roles as teachers in working with students having exceptionalities.***

1. **Ask them what Public Law 94-142 (PL 94-142), the Individuals with Disabilities Education Act (IDEA), means to them. This will give you some insight into their backgrounds and perceptions. You might then want to highlight some information about it, such as:**
    - **it was passed in 1975; updated in 1997.**
    - **it is commonly associated with the term "mainstreaming and inclusion."**
    - **it ensures a free and appropriate public education for all students with exceptionalities.**
    - **it means that regular classroom teachers are highly likely to have students with exceptionalities in their classrooms.**

    PP 5.1 "*The Individuals with Disabilities Education Act*" summarizes this information.

2. **Ask the students to what other topics that they've already studied PL 94-142 relates. They should identify it as an anti-discrimination law, which makes it a moral issue, so it relates to Chapter 3. Having exceptionalities also represents learner differences, so the topic also relates to the study of Chapter 4.**

3. **To help the students summarize the information in this section, display PP 5.2 "*Educational Service Options for Implementing the LRE.*"**

4. **Remind the students that a sample IEP is shown in Figure 5.2 on page 137 of their text.**

5. **To help students understand the options for implementing the LRE, and how they relate to mainstreaming and inclusion you might consider using the following examples:**

    The first student has a learning disability, and in the judgment of the student's individualized implementation plan team, this student is able to cope with the regular classroom environment when given some extra support from the regular classroom teacher. As a result, the student is at or near the top of the options for implementing the LRE.

    The second student is mainstreamed for most of the day, and is pulled out for part of the day to receive specialized help with reading. The second student would be at the third or fourth position down of the options for implementing the LRE; the exact location would be determined by the IEP team.

The least restrictive environment for the first student is full mainstreaming; the least restrictive environment for the second student is partial mainstreaming.

If an inclusion model were implemented, a special resource teacher would be in the regular classroom to work with the second student, and the regular classroom teacher and the specialist would collaborate in working with the student. The student would not be pulled out of the regular classroom.

Here would be a good point to show or discuss **Episode 6 on DVD 1**: "Reviewing and IEP."

II. Students with learning problems
  A. The labeling controversy
  B. Mental retardation
    1. Levels of mental retardation
    2. Programs for students with mental retardation
  C. Learning disabilities
    1. Characteristics of students with learning disabilities
    2. Identifying and working with students who have learning disabilities
      1. The use of classroom-based information for identification
      2. Adaptive instruction
  D. Attention deficit/hyperactivity disorder
  E. Behavior disorders
    1. Kinds of behavior disorders
    2. Teaching students with behavior disorders
      a. Behavior management systems
      b. Teacher sensitivity

Teaching Suggestions:

■ ***The purpose in the following suggestion is to introduce students to the exceptional student population and their relative frequencies.***

1. **Display PP 5.3 "*The Population of Students with Disabilities.*" They will see that students with learning problems–mental retardation, learning disabilities, and behavior disorders–make up the majority of the population (actually 66%).**

2. **PP 5.4 "*Characteristics of Students with Learning Disabilities*" summarizes the characteristics of students with learning disabilities.**

3. **PP 5.5 "*Attention Deficit/Hyperactivity Disorder (AD/HD)*" summarizes the legal issues and characteristics of AD/HD.**

   In clarifying the relationship between AD/HD and learning disabilities you might emphasize that AD/HD is not a type of learning disability nor is it a subset of learning disabilities. It does not qualify for special funding and support under IDEA as its own category. It is, however, commonly associated with learning disabilities, and this is the reason it is presented in this section of the chapter. If a learner who has AD/HD is also classified as learning disabled, the learner then qualifies for special education support. Since the laws and policies governing special education are often somewhat murky, these descriptions may quickly change.

4. **PP 5.6 "*Characteristics of Students with Behavior Disorders*" summarizes the general characteristics of behavior disorders and both externalizing and internalizing behavior disorders.**

5. **PP 5.7 "*Working with Students Having Behavior Disorders*" summarizes behavior management strategies for working with students having behavior disorders.**

6. **To summarize and relate the information in this section, have the students identify the similarities and differences between mental retardation, learning disabilities, and behavioral disorders (emotional disabilities or emotional handicaps).**

7. **To help the students apply the content of this section to a classroom situation, have them examine the case study at the end of the chapter (pp. 158-159 of the chapter) , and have them determine how Mike Sheppard, the teacher in the case study, worked with his students having learning disabilities and behavior disorders. Have them identify the specific strategies Mike used, and have them also assess the extent to which Mike applied the strategies for working with students having learning disabilities and the strategies for working with students having behavior disorders.**

F. Communication disorders
   1. Helping students with communication disorders
G. Visual disabilities
   1. Working with students who have visual disabilities
H. Hearing disabilities
   1. Working with students who have hearing disabilities
I. Assessment and learning: Assessment trends in special education
   1. Curriculum-based assessment
   2. Adaptive behavior

Teaching Suggestions:

■ ***The purpose in the following suggestions is to increase your students' awareness of communication, visual, and hearing problems in learners.***

1. **In the lower elementary grades identifying communication, visual, or hearing problems is important. A communication disorder in a first grader, for example, may be undetected, whereas an undetected communication disorder in an 8th grader is unlikely.**

2. **Emphasize that a primary role of teachers in the middle elementary grades and beyond in working with students having communication disorders is to ensure that they feel like they belong and that they are welcome in the classroom.**

3. **PP 5.8 "*Kinds of Speech Disorders*" describes and illustrates common speech disorders.**

4. **PP 5.9 "*Symptoms of Potential Visual Problems*," summarizes some of the signs and symptoms of possible visual problems.**

5. **Point out that even though most children are visually screened, a young child with a visual impairment may remain undetected, so sensitivity to the symptoms is important.**

6. **Emphasize that lowered self-concept and the possibility of learned helplessness are possibilities for visually impaired learners.**

7. **PP 5.10 "*Indicators of Hearing Impairment*," summarizes some of the symptoms of hearing problems.**
8. **PP 5.11 "*Working with Students Who Have Hearing Disabilities*" offers suggestions for regular classroom teachers in working with hearing impaired students who are mainstreamed into their classrooms.**

III. Students who are gifted and talented
  A. Creativity
  B. Identifying students who are gifted and talented
  C. Teaching students who are gifted and talented: Instructional principles

Teaching Suggestions:

■ ***The suggestions in this section are intended to help your students understand the characteristics of gifted and talented students, together with options for maximizing their learning.***

1. **Display PP 5.12 "*Characteristics of the Gifted and Talented,*" which summarizes the characteristics of gifted and talented students.**

   Myths associated with giftedness. As you discuss the information on PP 5.12, emphasize some of the myths associated with giftedness such as: people who are gifted being poorly adjusted, having emotional problems, or other difficulties with life. While some people who are gifted and talented certainly do have problems, the percentage in the gifted population is lower than the percentage in the population as a whole.

   Also point out that learners who are gifted and talented tend to somewhat naturally do the things that we encourage in all learners, such as searching for relationships, identifying applications, solving problems, and thinking in the abstract. In fact, students who are gifted and talented will sometime identify relationships in ideas that technically don't exist.

2. **To introduce the students to the concept of creativity, have students identify as many uses as possible for a brick, a discarded car tire, or some other object of your choice. If you do the activity in groups, you might want to have the groups compete to see which group can come up with the most uses. (If you want to focus the groups somewhat, you might also require that the uses be practical.) Discuss the groups' results with the whole class.**

3. **After the students have reported, you might examine the list in terms of flexibility, originality, and fluency.**

4. **Have students think back to the conceptions of intelligence discussed in Chapter 4, such as traditional IQ tests (e.g., the WISC-III), Gardner's Multiple Intelligences, and Sternberg's view of intelligence. Have the students consider how effective or difficult identifying students who are gifted and talented would be based on these conceptions.**

5. **PP 5.13 "*Options in Enrichment and Acceleration Programs,*" outlines some options for working with students who are gifted and talented.**

   Point out that while some students are gifted and talented, they still have the same needs and concerns that are typical of students in general. Also note that some irony exists in programs and courses for the gifted. Teachers tend to assume that because the students are gifted that they don't need instructional support, and students in these programs are often given long, detailed projects without adequate instruction. These criticisms are somewhat controversial, of course.

IV. The teacher's role in inclusive classrooms
  A. Identifying students with exceptionalities
  B. Teaching students with exceptionalities: Instructional principles
    1. Provide additional instructional support
    4. Adapt seatwork and homework
    5. Supplement reading materials
    6. Teach learning strategies

C. Social integration and growth
 1. Developing classmates' understanding and acceptance
 2. Helping students learn acceptable behaviors
 3. Strategies for promoting interaction and cooperation

Teaching Suggestions:

■ ***The suggestions in this section are designed to help your students understand their roles in working with students in their classrooms who have exceptionalities.***

1. **Display PP 5.14 "*The Teacher's Role in Inclusive Classrooms*" which summarizes teachers' roles and responsibilities.**

2. **PP 5.15"*Principles of Instruction for Teaching Students with Exceptionalities*" provides a framework for regular classroom teachers who have students with exceptionalities in their classrooms.**

3. **PP 5.16 "*Instructional Adaptations for Students with Exceptionalities*" offers some suggestions for helping students with exceptionalities in the regular classroom.**

Here would be a good point to show or discuss **Episode 7 on DVD 1**: "Using Peer Tutoring With Students Having Exceptionalities."

4. **Display PP 5.17 "*Working with Students with Exceptionalities: An Application,*" and have the students respond to the questions. Discuss their response with the whole class. They should have identified the following in their responses:**

 Question 1: Based on the evidence in the case study Joan implemented prereferral strategies by calling Lon's parents and checking on the school procedures. No evidence exists, however, to indicate that she tried alternative strategies with Lon, that she documented any strategies, or that she checked Lon's records.

 Question 2: The school officials violated the provisions of IDEA by giving him the test in English. A second possible violation depends on interpretation and judgment. The placement appears to have depended largely on the WISC-III, and if this is the case it is a violation, since IDEA calls for more than one measure. On the other hand, Joan's observations of Lon's performance and behavior are other measures, and if they were considered in the placement, it could be argued that the placement decision was not a violation.

 Question 3: Lon appears to have a learning disability. This is based both on his classroom performance and his uneven performance on the WISC-III.

 Question 4: Since a disproportionate number of cultural minorities exist in the special education population, school officials should ask themselves if the performance is in fact an exceptionality, or is it a developmental lag, a language-based problem, or a lack of school-related experience.

ENRICHMENT MATERIALS

TEACHER PREP WEBSITE

The *Teacher Prep* website an online resource for students and instructors. Both you and students can access the *Teacher Prep* website by going to http://www.prenhall.com/teacherprep. Enter your user name and password and click on "Log In." The *Teacher Prep* website includes video episodes, student and teacher artifacts, teacher and research resources, and information about licensing and beginning a teaching career. The *Teacher Prep* website is described in detail in the Media Guide.

The following articles are recommended by the *Exploring Further* section titled "Inclusion" on page 136 of the chapter.

Once into the *Teacher Prep* website access the articles by completing the following steps:
1. Click on "Research Resources" on the left panel of the screen, scroll down the middle of the page and again click on "Research Resources."
2. Go to "Classroom Processes" and click on "Diverse Populations."
3. Click on the following articles:
   Small victories in inclusive classrooms, by M. Mahony (1997), Ref. No. 384,
   "Our school doesn't offer inclusion" and other legal blunders, by P. Kluth, R. Villa, and J. Thousand (2001), Ref. No. 1679, and
   Contemporary Issues: The legal basis of inclusion, by M. Yell (1998), Ref. No. 2265

These articles describe different ways that inclusion is changing classrooms in the United States.

The following articles are recommended by the *Exploring Further* section titled "Instructional Strategies" on page 148 of the chapter.

Once into the *Teacher Prep* website access the articles by completing the following steps:
1. Click on "Research Resources" on the left panel of the screen, scroll down the middle of the page and again click on "Research Resources."
2. Go to "Classroom Processes" and click on "Diverse Populations."
3. Click on the following articles:
   What's in a name? The labels and language of special education, by W. Heward (2003), Ref. No. 2190,
   Neverstreaming: Preventing learning disabilities, by R. Slavin (1996), Ref. No. 2275, and
   Understanding disabilities, by R. Hartwell (2001), Ref. No. 1721.

These articles describe the process of categorization within special education as well as different ways to help students with learning problems.

The following articles are recommended by the *Exploring Further* section titled "Teaching Students Who are Gifted and Talented" on page 152 of the chapter.

Once into the *Teacher Prep* website access the articles by completing the following steps:
1. Click on "Research Resources" on the left panel of the screen, scroll down the middle of the page, and again click on "Research Resources."
2. Then, go to "Classroom Processes" and click on "Diverse Populations."
3. Click on the following articles:
   For gifted students, full inclusion is a partial solution, by J. Delisle (1999), Ref. No. 2272, and
   Using Multiple Intelligence Theory to identify gifted children, by C. Reid and B. Romanoff (1997), Ref. No. 810

These articles describe different ways to identify and teach students who are gifted and talented.

DISCUSSION STARTERS

You may choose to have your students discuss one or more of the following questions to further enrich their understanding of your learning activities.

1. Given the past trends in these areas of special education what do you predict for the future? In particular, what would you predict about the future of inclusion?

2. Will the future role of classroom teachers expand or contract in terms of dealing with students with exceptionalities? Why do you think so?

3. Research shows that a disproportionate number of minorities are placed in special education classes. How might we explain this finding? What can be done to address this problem?

4. Should all teachers be required to take a course in teaching students with exceptionalities? If so, what should it contain? If not, why is such a course unnecessary?

5. How are effective strategies and programs for children with exceptionalities similar to those for at-risk students? How are they different?

6. How well do the following practices in the general area of special education meet the special needs of students who are gifted and talented?
   - mainstreaming
   - IEP
   - mainstream assistance teams
   - collaborative consultation

BACKGROUND READINGS

Clark, B. (2002). *Growing up gifted* (6th ed.). Upper Saddle River, NJ: Merrill/Prentice Hall.
An excellent overview of issues and practices in gifted education.

Hallahan, D., & Kauffman, J. (2003). *Exceptional children* (9th ed.). Upper Saddle River, NJ: Prentice-Hall. This is an excellent introduction to the field of special education. It clearly describes the different kinds of mental and physical handicaps and what the classroom teacher can do to accommodate the special needs of these students in the regular classroom.

Hardman, M., Drew, C. & Egan, W. (2005). *Human exceptionality* (8th ed.). Needham Heights, MA: Allyn & Bacon.
This book does an excellent job of exploring the social issues involved with exceptionalities.

Heward, W. (2006). *Exceptional children: An introduction to special education* (8th ed.). Upper Saddle River, NJ: Merrill/Prentice Hall.
The author provides an overview of the field that is both comprehensive and practical. This book is especially useful for the classroom teacher.

Karten, T. (2005). *Inclusion strategies that work: Research-based methods for the classroom*. Thousand Oaks, CA: Corwin Press.
This text offers strategies for classroom teachers in their efforts to meet the needs of all the students in their classrooms.

Keogh, B., & MacMillan, D. (1996). Exceptionality. In D. Berliner, & R. Calfee (Eds.), *Handbook of educational psychology* (pp. 311–330). New York: Macmillan.
This chapter focuses on three groups of students with exceptionalities: mildly mentally retarded, learning disabled, and gifted and talented.

Piirto, J. (1999). *Talented children and adults: Their development and education* (2nd ed.). Upper Saddle River, NJ: Merrill/Prentice Hall.
An interesting look at developmental aspects of giftedness.

Turnbull, A., Turnbull, R., Shank, M., Smith, S., &. Leal, D. (2004). *Exceptional lives: Special education in today's schools* (4th ed.). Upper Saddle River, NJ: Merrill/Prentice Hall.
This introductory special education text has an update of the 1997 IDEA principles, takes a humanistic, philosophical approach in its description of inclusion and collaboration. It is an innovative and definitive text that describes all categories of disabilities including AD/HD as covered by Section 504.

In addition to the above references, you may also wish to contact the National Information Center for Children and Youth with Disabilities (NICHCY) for video information and other resource materials:

NICHCY
P.O. Box 1492
Washington, DC 20013-1492
http://www.nichcy.org

FEEDBACK

Developing as a Professional: Praxis Practice: Feedback for Short-Answer Questions

The feedback that appears here is for the short-answer questions that follow the case study on pages 158 and 159 of the text. The feedback is also available to students on the companion website.

1. Describe specifically what Mike did to create a supportive academic climate for his students.
   Mike helped create a supportive climate in several ways. Some seem minor, but they were all significant. For example, he smiled at his students, willingly repeated part of the problem for Gwenn, and offered encouragement by telling them in a positive tone that he was going to call on them first in the lesson. He also provided support for other students, such as whispering, "That's terrific," to Todd and giving him a light "thump" on the back and encouraging Herchel when he said, "I . . . I . . . don't know." While each of these behaviors—alone—is relatively minor, when combined they result in a climate of support and positive expectations.

2. How did Mike attempt to ensure success in his teaching?
   First, Mike was consistently positive with the students, and he stated positive expectations throughout the lesson. Second, he taught the lesson in small steps and prompted students, such as Herchel, whenever they were unable to answer.

3. What did Mike do to alter instruction for his students with learning disabilities? How effective were these modifications?
   First, he had the three students with learning disabilities come to class a few minutes early, so he could carefully read his warm-up problem to them and be sure they understood what was asked for in the problem before the rest of the students began. Then he worked with them in a small group while the rest of the students were doing seatwork to give them the extra scaffolding they needed to help get them to the point where they could work on their own.

4. What did Mike do to meet the needs of his students with behavior disorders? How effective were these interventions?
   He helped Todd develop a system in which Todd would chart his own behavior, with the goal being the development of self management. He also provided Todd with the emotional support and reinforcement needed to help make the system work.

   We don't have evidence in the case study about support for Horace. This can be a problem, since Horace is shy and withdrawn, and he can become "lost in the shuffle." A relatively simply way to provide support would be to include him in the question and answer activity and prompt him if necessary to ensure that he is able to answer successfully before turning to another student. In this way, he can involve Horace, and hopefully, in time, make significant progress with him.

Feedback for Online Case Book Questions

The feedback below is for the *Online Case Book* for Chapter 5 (referenced on page 156 of the chapter). Both you and the students can access the case study by going to www.prenhall.com/eggen, selecting Chapter 5, and clicking on *Online Case Book.*

You may choose to assign the online case as homework or you may want to discuss the case in class. Answers to these questions *do not* appear on the companion website, so students *do not* have access to the feedback.

Multiple-Choice Items:

1. Based on Kelly's description of Craig, "He can't seem to sit still long enough to learn anything. And he doesn't just interfere with his own learning; he bothers everyone around him and seems totally unaware of his behavior," it is most likely that he has what type of exceptionality?
   a. Mental retardation
   b. Learning disability
   c. Behavior disorder
   d. Communication disorder
   c. His impulsive behavior suggests he has a behavior disorder.

2. Based upon Kelly's description of Amanda, "She tries so hard and is really sweet, but she just can't seem to keep up with the others. She has difficulty with abstract ideas like multiplication and can't seem to pick up anything unless we go over it again and again," it is most likely that she has what type of exceptionality?
   a. Mental retardation
   b. Learning disability
   c. Behavior disorder
   d. Communication disorder
   a. Amanda's behavior profile suggests she may be mildly mentally retarded.

3. Based upon Kelly's description of Jared, "He's bright! I've checked his file! But he can't seem to learn when it involves anything written. I put word problems on the board, and he just spaces out," it is most likely that he has what type of exceptionality?
   a. Mental retardation
   b. Learning disability
   c. Behavior disorder
   d. Communication disorder
   b. Jared's behavior suggests that he has a learning disability. He seems bright, but has trouble with reading, both characteristic of a learning disability.

Short Answer Items:

4. What is curriculum-based assessment, and how was it illustrated in the case?
   Curriculum-based assessment attempts to measure learners' performance in specific areas of the curriculum. Because of its specificity, it is especially helpful in constructing I. E. P.'s. Maria suggested curriculum-based assessment when she said, "The first thing you need to do is gather some work samples that document the kinds of problems these kids are having in class. Then try to be as specific as possible about the specific problems they are having in specific areas. This will help us figure out exactly what these students need."

5. Identify how the following concepts were illustrated in the case study:

a. Inclusion
b. Protection against discrimination in testing
c. Due process and parents' rights.

a. Inclusion is a comprehensive approach to educating students with exceptionalities that advocates a total, systematic, and coordinated web of services. Maria suggested this when she said, "The ideal solution would be to get you some help so these students can succeed in your classroom."

b. Protection against discrimination in testing attempts to protect students and their parents from bias in testing resulting from language or other factors. Maria advocated this when she said, "We'll need to make sure that English as a second language isn't the cause for some of these learning problems. That will be important if we decide to do some additional testing."

c. Due process and parents rights is a provision that attempts to make sure that safeguards are followed to ensure that parents are integrally involved in decisions about their child's educational future. Maria suggested this when she said, "We'll also want to involve the parents. You'll need to check the students' files and see if the parents have been alerted to problems in the past."

CLASSROOM EXERCISES

The classroom exercises that follow appear *only here* in the instructor's manual. Students do not have access to *either the questions or the answers*.

The purpose of keeping the exercises only in the instructor's manual is to allow you to use them as class discussion items, or for homework, if you should choose to do so.

Feedback for the exercises follows immediately.

Teress, age 3, loves to observe her friends as they play at a mothers' "morning out" program she attends three times a week. Her teachers describe her as very well behaved little girl who is somewhat shy, but usually all smiles. Teress is happy to draw and color and seldom talks unless she says "please" and "tank-you". One-day Teress's mother, Anita, overhears one of her daughter's classmates tell her mother that she thinks Teress doesn't like her because she doesn't answer her questions.

At home she is quite imaginative as she sets up tea parties and school for her stuffed animals. Teress is also quite adept at using the family computer and has several preschool programs that she uses at will. Outside, she enjoys kicking the soccer ball with Roberto, her brother, or playing a game of two-square. Her chalk drawings on the driveway rival the stick figures that her brother makes.

When Teress talks however, she asks her mother and her brother to help her communicate her needs. Teress's father looks to Anita and Roberto to help him understand Teress's answers to his questions about her day. Anita and Roberto frequently have to help neighbors; friends and grandparents decipher Teress's answers to their questions.

Anita takes Teress and Roberto to have physicals each year which include hearing and vision tests. Both children come away with a clean bill of health each time. Neither child has ever experienced ear infections. One day Anita expressed her concern to her sister-in-law, Louisa, about having to continually decipher Teress's responses to her husband's questions, who Anita thought by now should be as adept at understanding Teress as she and Roberto are.

Louisa, a pediatric nurse, told Anita about a screening program that was available through the public school system free of charge and suggested taking Teress there for evaluation.

A preliminary screening and a more comprehensive screening administered separately within a three month period revealed that Teress didn't need therapy. Anita, however, pressed the point that Teress's father continues to have difficulty understanding his daughter and Teress continues to be shy among teachers, school mates, friends and relatives. In some cases the shyness overcomes her completely and Teress will ignore someone's question or ask her mother or brother to respond for her. Anita further explained that Teress would be attending private school (affiliated with their religion) and that the kindergarten class was 25 strong and that this large number of children might promote Teress becoming lost in the numbers due to her hesitancy to talk other than in a comfortable setting.

The elementary school's speech therapist agreed to include Teress in her program two days a week for a three-month period at which time Teress's progress would be reviewed. Anita was asked to attend a meeting three days later with the speech therapist, her supervisor and the school district's director. During the meeting a simple plan was drawn up for Teress's therapy. With some discussion and agreement on all points three documents were signed by Anita.

1. Based on the anecdotal evidence present in the paragraphs above describe the (pattern) type of disability illustrated in Teress's behavior.

2. List the behavioral symptoms that may indicate a disorder, and make a case for or against Teress being referred to a school specialist.

3. If Teress were a cultural minority, what impact might this factor have on the identification of any disorder Teress might have? Explain.

4. Based on the available evidence, does Teress have a specific learning disability? Explain.

5. Based on the available evidence, is Teress mentally retarded? Explain.

6. Suppose you are a classroom teacher responsible for someone like Teress. Identify some actions you can take to ensure a safe learning environment.

7. Using your knowledge of the IEP and the information provided describe the legal components and ascertain if all the components were present in the episode.

8. Is LRE (least restrictive environment) being met by having Teress attend speech class at a public elementary school before her mom takes her to her preschool?

In a class of 28 students is Hector Sanchez, a Brazilian-American boy, whose parents make a combined income of $61,000 per year; Sonja Jackson, an African American student, whose mother is an administrative assistant and whose father is an electronics technician; Franklin Jordan, an African American student whose parents are divorced and whose mother is a janitor, and Christopher Montcinous, a Mexican-American boy whose parents make a combined income of $45,000 as language specialists.

9. If the students fit patterns identified by research, which of the four is least likely to be diagnosed as behaviorally disordered? Explain.

10. Which student is most likely to be diagnosed as behaviorally disordered? Explain.

FEEDBACK FOR CLASSROOM EXERCISES

1. Teress's symptoms suggest an expressive communication disorder. Expressive (articulation) disorders involve forming and sequencing sounds. While there is no evidence that Teress is stuttering, she is mispronouncing sounds as in the case of "tank-you." Receptive disorders involve using language to express ideas, and there is no direct evidence of this type of problem.

2. Teress indicates the following symptoms: 1) Seldom speaking even during play, 2) using few words or very short sentences, and 3) over-relying on gestures to communicate. There is anecdotal evidence that Teress seldom speaks to people other than her brother and mother. While there is no evidence about the use of gestures, Teress's strong dependence on the interpretive skills of her brother and mother and her one or two word answers, coupled with the evidence that her father doesn't understand some of her language, would suggest that testing is in order. A school specialist should be contacted.

3. Language disorders are more difficult to detect in non-native English speakers, because they are initially learning English, and their problems may indicate difficulty with the language instead of truly being a disorder.

4. No evidence of a specific learning disability exists. Specific learning disabilities are most commonly problems with learning to read, write, or do math when students are involved in formal schooling. We have no evidence of this in Teress's case.

5. No evidence of mental retardation exists. In fact, Teress's imagination as well as her work with the computer indicates above average intelligence.

6. Some of your actions would include: 1) Identifying the disorder and referring Teress to a specialist, 2) modeling acceptance of Teress for her classmates, 3) following through to be sure that actions are taken, and 4) providing opportunities for small-group interaction.

7. The components include the following: 1) Assessment of a student's current level of performance, 2) long and short term objectives, 3) description of services or strategies, 4) schedule for implementing the plan, 5) criteria to be used in evaluating the plan's success. Although a re-evaluation date was made, there is no evidence that the specifics of how Teress's progress would be evaluated was discussed. Long term

objectives seem to hinge on the evaluation at the end of the three-month therapy. All other components were present.

8. The LRE is being met. Teress receives therapy in a small group, but she attends regular preschool.

9. Sonja is least likely to be diagnosed as behaviorally disordered. Girls are less likely than boys to be diagnosed as behaviorally disordered. Since all the students are minorities, no indicators can be identified on that basis.

10. Franklin is most likely to be diagnosed as behaviorally disordered. Franklin comes from a low socioeconomic background and is a cultural minority. Research indicates minority students from low SES backgrounds tend to be labeled behaviorally disordered more often than other students.

CHAPTER 6: BEHAVIORISM AND SOCIAL COGNITIVE THEORY

CHAPTER OVERVIEW

This chapter begins with an introduction to behaviorism and continues with a discussion of classical and operant conditioning and their applications. The chapter then turns to social cognitive theory, and the differences between behaviorism and social cognitive theory are outlined. The discussion of social cognitive theory continues by examining different types of modeling and vicarious learning, the effects of modeling on learner behavior, and the processes involved in modeling. The chapter concludes by examining behaviorism and social cognitive theory in the context of working with learners having diverse backgrounds.

CHAPTER OBJECTIVES

- Identify examples of operant conditioning concepts in classroom activities.
- Use social cognitive theory concepts, such as the nonoccurrence of expected consequences, reciprocal causation, and vicarious learning, to explain examples of people's behaviors.
- Identify examples of social cognitive theory concepts, such as types of modeling, modeling outcomes, effectiveness of models, and self regulation in people's behaviors.
- Identify examples of behaviorist and social cognitive theory concepts in teachers' work with students having diverse backgrounds.

POWERPOINT SLIDES

PP 6.1 An Introduction to Classical Conditioning
PP 6.2 Classical Conditioning Examples
PP 6.3 Learning to Like School
PP 6.4 A Comparison of Classical and Operant Conditioning
PP 6.5 Consequences of Behavior
PP 6.6 Operant Conditioning in the Classroom
PP 6.7 Shaping Learner Behavior
PP 6.8 Schedules of Reinforcement
PP 6.9 Reinforcement Schedules and Examples
PP 6.10 Reinforcement Schedules in the Classroom
PP 6.11 Punishment, Satiation, and Extinction
PP 6.12 Applied Behavior Analysis
PP 6.13 Vicarious Learning on the Interstate
PP 6.14 Differences Between Behaviorism and Social Cognitive Theory
PP 6.15 Different Forms of Modeling
PP 6.16 Effects of Modeling on Behavior
PP 6.17 Modeling Outcomes in the Classroom
PP 6.18 Processes Involved in Learning From Models
PP 6.19 Effectiveness of Models
PP 6.20 Under-muscled and Embarrassed
PP 6.21 Principles of Instruction for Applying Social Cognitive Theory in Classrooms
PP 6.22 Praxis Practice: Feedback for Short-Answer Questions
PP 6.23 Feedback for Online Casebook Questions
PP 6.24 Classroom Exercises

VIDEOS

DVD 1, Episode 8: "Using Reinforcement in Classrooms"
This episode illustrates a number of examples of a second grade teacher using reinforcement with her students.

DVD 1, Episode 9: "Demonstrating Problem Solving in High School Chemistry"
This video illustrates a high school teacher directly modeling a technique for solving problems with beginning chemistry students.

CHAPTER OUTLINE

I. Behaviorist views of learning
  A. What is behaviorism?
  B. Classical conditioning
    1. Classical conditioning in the classroom
    2. Generalization and discrimination
    3. Extinction
  C. Operant conditioning
    1. Reinforcement
      a. Positive reinforcement
      b. Negative reinforcement
      c. Shaping
      d. Reinforcement schedules
      e. Extinction
      f. Satiation
    2. Punishment
      a. Using punishment effectively
      b. Ineffective forms of punishment
    3. The influence of antecedents on behavior
      a. Environmental conditions
      b. Prompts and cues
      c. Generalization and discrimination
  D. Behaviorism in the classroom: Applied behavior analysis
    1. Steps in applied behavior analysis
      a. Identify target behaviors
      b. Establish a baseline
      c. Choose reinforcers and punishers
      d. Measure changes in behavior
      e. Reduce frequency of reinforcers
    2. Functional analysis
  E. Putting behaviorism into perspective
II. Social cognitive theory
  A. Comparing behaviorism and social cognitive theory
    1. Definition of learning
    2. The role of expectations
    3. Reciprocal causation
  B. Modeling
    1. Cognitive modeling
  C. Vicarious learning
  D. Nonoccurrence of expected consequences
  E. Functions of modeling
    1. Learning new behaviors
    2. Facilitating existing behaviors
    3. Changing inhibitions
    4. Arousing emotions
  F. Processes involved in learning from models
  G. Effectiveness of models
  H. Self-regulation
    1. Setting goals
    2. Monitoring progress
    3. Self assessment
    4. Self reinforcement
    5. Cognitive behavior modification
  I. Social cognitive theory in the classroom: Instructional principles
  J. Putting social cognitive theory into perspective
III. Addressing diversity: Behaviorism and social cognitive theory
  A. Classical conditioning: Learning to like school
  B. Motivating hesitant learners
  C. Capitalizing on minority role models

PRESENTATION OUTLINE

The suggested activities can be completed in small groups and discussed as a whole group, or they can be conducted as whole-class activities. To be consistent with our understanding of knowledge construction, we recommend that you promote as much discussion–both in small groups and with the whole class–as possible.

I. Behaviorist views of learning
   A. What is behaviorism?
   B. Classical conditioning
      1. Classical conditioning in the classroom
      2. Generalization and discrimination
      3. Extinction

Teaching Suggestions:

■ ***The following suggestions are designed to help students understand classical conditioning and use classical conditioning concepts to explain events in and out of classrooms.***

1. **Display PP 6.1 "*An Introduction to Classical Conditioning*?" Ask the students what Rod "learned." Lead them to conclude that he learned to feel excited when he heard Latin Music.**

2. **Ask them how he learned to feel excited when he heard Latin music, and lead them to conclude that he associated the music with his encounter with Kim.**

3. **Display PP 6.2 "*Classical Conditioning Examples*" and have the students identify the common features in the examples. Have them relate the examples to the example with Rod learning to feel excited at the sound of Latin music.**

4. **Display PP 6.3 "*Learning to Like School*" and have the students identify the conditioned and unconditioned stimuli, and the unconditioned and conditioned responses in each case.**

   The following are the answers.

	Problem 1	**Problem 2**
UCS	**Jennifer's father**	**Mrs. Rodriguez's reassuring manner**
UCR	**Security (with her father)**	**Feeling better**
CS	**Mrs. Abbott**	**Mrs. Rodriguez's classroom**
CR	**Comfortable**	**Relaxed**

5. **Ask the students to compare the examples, so they will see that in one case there is an association between Mrs. Abbott and Jennifer's father ("She puts her arm around Jennifer and chats with her dad as the three of them stand together near the door."), whereas in the second example there is no association between Mrs. Rodriguez and Natasha's mother. There is an association, however, between Mrs. Rodriguez's manner and her classroom ("Each day, Ms. Rodriguez greets Natasha with the same smile and reassuring manner. Now Natasha jumps out of the car and feels quite relaxed as she enters Mrs. Rodriguez's classroom.").**

6. **Again display PP 6.1 "*An Introduction to Classical Conditioning*" and have the students explain why Rod reacts to Reggae the same way he does to Latin music, and why doesn't he react the same way to Rock and Jazz. Typically generalization and discrimination are quite easy for students to understand, and they will identify them quickly in the examples.**

7. **Ask the students what would happen if Rod continued to listen to Latin music, but he never had another encounter with Kim, or if Pavlov's lab assistants kept coming in the room but stopped bringing meat, or Tim kept taking tests but didn't fail. In each case the conditioned response gradually disappears.**

8. **To summarize classical conditioning, have the students explain the following examples using classical conditioning**
- **test anxiety**
- **a medical patient breaking into a sweat when he sees a needle.**
- **a kindergartner developing a pain in the stomach when she and her parents drive into the school parking lot.**
- **a junior high student becoming nervous before gym after a class in which his gym shorts split and other students laughed.**

C. Operant conditioning
  1. Reinforcement
     a. Positive reinforcement
     b. Negative reinforcement
     c. Shaping
     d. Reinforcement schedules
     e. Extinction
     f. Satiation
  2. Punishment
     a. Using punishment effectively
     b. Ineffective forms of punishment
  3. The influence of antecedents on behavior
     a. Environmental conditions
     b. Prompts and cues
     c. Generalization and discrimination

Teaching Suggestions:

■ ***The following suggestions are intended to help the students understand operant conditioning and the difference between reinforcers and punishers.***

1. **To introduce this section display PP 6.4 "*A Comparison of Classical and Operant Conditioning*" to help the students make the transition to operant conditioning. Then display PP 6.5 "*Consequences of Behavior*," discuss the consequences and PP 6.5 "*Operant Conditioning in the Classroom*," and have students explain the teachers' and the students' behaviors in each case.**

In both cases the teachers were punished. For example, Ann Johnson decreased the length of her assignment (from 30 to 20 to 15 problems), and Jim Gann decreased the difficulty of his tests.

The students were negatively reinforced for their complaining. Both Ann's and Jim's students complained sooner and sooner.

2. **The *Exploring Further* suggestion on page 170 of the chapter suggests that the students go to the *Exploring Further* module of Chapter 6 for a more detailed discussion of negative reinforcement.**

3. **Ask the students for additional examples of reinforcers and punishers. Some examples include:**

Positive reinforcers:	**Praise, high test scores, good grades**
Negative reinforcers:	**Allowing them to avoid a homework assignment because of their conscientious work**
Presentation punishers:	**Reprimands, such as being told "Shh."**
Removal punishers:	**Loss of privileges, timeout, detention.**

Here would be a good point to show or discuss **Episode 8 on DVD 1**: "Using Reinforcement in Classrooms" as additional examples of positive reinforcers and presentation punishers.

4. **To illustrate shaping display PP 6.7 "*Shaping Learner Behavior.*" Ask the students for additional examples of shaping.**

5. **The different types of reinforcement schedules are outlined in PP 6.8 "*Schedules of Reinforcement*" and they're illustrated in PP 6.9 "*Reinforcement Schedules and Examples.*" To increase their understanding of the different schedules, have them identify the reinforcement schedules illustrated on PP 6.10 "*Reinforcement Schedules in the Classroom.*" In item 1 on PP 6.10 tell them to focus on the students doing seatwork. Discuss their conclusions. They should conclude the following:**
   1. **For the students doing seatwork, a variable-interval schedule is being used. It is based on time and is unpredictable.**
   2. **This is a variable-ratio schedule. It is based on a student's response and is unpredictable.**
   3. **Mr. Lombardo's homework system is a fixed-interval schedule, whereas Mrs. Aschliman's is a variable interval schedule. Their quizzes are both fixed interval.**
   4. **Mr. Lombardo's policy with finishing homework illustrates a fixed-ratio schedule. The students can predict when they will be rewarded with free time, and it is based on their behaviors--not on time.**

6. **Display PP 6.11 "*Punishment, Satiation, and Extinction*" which illustrates the difference in the three concepts. Students often have difficulty in distinguishing among the three. Point out that a difference between removal punishment and extinction depend on the situation. For instance, you might ask students what would make the situation with the student who isn't being called on an example of removal punishment. (If the teacher had been calling on her, and then stops, it would be punishment--being called on is removed. If the student wasn't being called on in the first place, it is extinction--there is nothing removed.)**

7. **To help the students understand the influence of antecedents on behavior ask them to identify examples of environmental conditions that serve as cues. Point out that prompting questions are one of the most common forms of cues that teachers use in classrooms. Ask students for some additional examples.**

8. **Have students explain the difference between generalization and discrimination in a classical conditioning situation and generalization and discrimination in an operant conditioning situation.**

9. **Present the following examples and ask the students to explain whether generalization or discrimination is being illustrated.**
   - **Junior high students go from classroom to classroom to meet with different teachers. In some classes they're well behaved; in others they're rowdy.**
   - **Kevin's English teacher taught outlining skills in his class. Kevin now uses the study strategy in biology and social studies.**
   - **Students are wild and loud on the playground but quiet down when they enter the classroom.**

- **Joe's seventh grade language arts teacher is working on his handwriting. Other teachers have noticed an improvement, too.**

D. Behaviorism in the Classroom: Applied behavior analysis
  1. Steps in applied behavior analysis
     a. Identify target behaviors
     b. Establish a baseline
     c. Choose reinforcers and punishers
     d. Measure changes in behavior
     e. Reduce frequency of reinforcers
  2. Functional analysis

E. Putting behaviorism into perspective

Teaching Suggestions:

■ ***The suggestions in this section are designed to help students understand applied behavior analysis.***

1. **Display PP 12 "*Applied Behavioral Analysis*," which outlines the steps in performing applied behavioral analyses.**

2. **Have the students turn to the case study at the end of Chapter 5 (pp 15–159), and identify 2here in the case study Mike Sheppard completed each of the steps involved in an applied behavioral analysis.**

3. **Have them identify the step for which we have the least evidence.**

4. **The students should find the following:**
   - **He identified talking out, swearing, hitting and touching, out of seat and being friendly as his target behaviors.**
   - **He established a baseline during the week of 2/9 to 2/13.**
   - **He chose praise as his primary reinforcer.**
   - **He measured changes in the target behaviors during the weeks of 2/16 to 2/20 and 2/23–2/27.**
   - **We have the least evidence for gradually reducing the reinforcers as the behavior improves.**

5. **To help students put behaviorism into perspective, point out that since behaviorism focuses on observable learning is organized into isolated, specific, and decontextualized pieces that allow instructors to determine if learners display the desired behaviors. If they do, they're reinforced. If not, they're given feedback until they do display the desired behaviors. Gradually, these isolated pieces accumulate, with higher order processes being the final outcome of the cumulative process.**

6. **Also point out that the criticisms of behaviorism as a basis for guiding instruction continue to increase. For example, the gap between having students complete decontextualized exercises, such as, "Please come with Karen and (I, me) to the mall," and being effective writers is indeed large.**

7. **On the other hand, behaviorism continues to be a very powerful influence as a basis for managing learners and the learning environment. Whether or not this should be the case is open to debate, and you may want to have your students discuss this issue.**

II. Social cognitive theory
   A. Comparing behaviorism and social cognitive theory
      1. Definition of learning
      2. The role of expectations
      3. Reciprocal causation
   B. Modeling
      1. Cognitive modeling
   C. Vicarious learning
   D. Nonoccurrence of expected consequences

Teaching Suggestions:

■ *The following suggestions are intended to help the students understand modeling, vicarious learning and the nonoccurrence of expected consequences.*

1. **To introduce social cognitive theory display PP 1.13 "*Vicarious Learning on the Interstate.*" Have the students try to explain why we slow down when we see the other car pulled over. Lead them to conclude that behaviorism is unable to explain our behavior, which leads us to social cognitive theory.**

   Point out that this is the reason we study different theories. Behaviorism is able to explain the production of emotional and physiological responses based on associations, and it is also able to explain changes in overt behaviors as a result of consequences applied directly to the behaviors, but it cannot explain changes in behavior as the result of observing others. It can't explain why we slow down because nothing directly happened to us.

   Also point out that we slowed down because we *expect* to be pulled over if we continue to exceed the speed limit, which helps the students understand the role of expectations in social cognitive theory.

   You can also note that we were *vicariously punished.* Our behavior decreased as a result of observing the consequences for someone else's behavior.

   Finally ask the students what would happen if we were traveling in the flow of traffic where everyone is exceeding the speed limit. They will say that we will continue to speed. This will allow you to introduce *the nonoccurrence of expected consequences.* We expect to be pulled over if we speed, but when we speed, but are not pulled over, the nonoccurrence of the expected punisher acts as a reinforcer, which increases the likelihood that we will continue to speed. Ask the students for additional examples of the nonoccurrence of expected consequences. Many exist, such as students turning in homework but not having it graded, which results in them taking the homework less seriously, or a school faculty being asked for input into a policy but not having the input ever used, making it less likely that they will offer input in the future.

2. **Display PP 6.14 "*Differences Between Behaviorism and Social Cognitive Theory*" and point out the differences. Also emphasize the importance of feedback based on social cognitive theory. (Since reinforcers only work when learners are aware of the behaviors that are being reinforced, feedback helps them become aware, by specifying the behaviors they've displayed that are being reinforced, e.g., learners getting feedback on a writing assignment are then better equipped to display the desired behaviors on the next assignment.)**

3. **Display PP 6.15 "*Different Forms of Modeling,*" which describes and illustrates the different forms of modeling. Ask the students which form has the most impact on behavior. Discuss the influence of television on behavior, and the enormous number of celebrity endorsements that exist. These are forms of symbolic modeling.**

E. Functions of modeling
  1. Learning new behaviors
  2. Facilitating existing behaviors
  3. Changing inhibitions
  4. Arousing emotions
F. Processes involved in learning from models
G. Effectiveness of models

Teaching Suggestions:

■ ***The suggestions in this section are intended to help students understand the different effects of modeling, the processes involved in learning from models, and what makes some models more effective than others.***

1. **Display PP 6.16 "*Effects of Modeling on Behavior*," which describes and illustrates the effects.**

2. **Display PP 6.17 "*Modeling Outcomes in the Classroom*" and have students respond to the questions. Have them share their responses.**

3. **Display PP 6.18 "*Processes Involved in Learning from Models*." Have students identify one or more topics and describe how the processes would be involved with the topic of their choice.**

4. **To illustrate the factors that influence a model's effectiveness, display PP 6.19 "*Effectiveness of Models*," which outlines and illustrates factors influencing a model's effectiveness.**

5. **PP 6.20 "*Under-Muscled and Embarrassed*" which is taken from a newspaper clipping is a real-world example of the importance of perceived similarity in modeling effectiveness. The models are not effective because the people going to the gym don't perceive themselves as similar enough to the models. On the other hand, overweight, out-of-shape models would also be ineffective, because the people would not perceive the models as competent.**

> Here would be a good point to show or discuss **Episode 9 on DVD 1**: "Demonstrating Problem Solving in High School Chemistry" as an example of *direct modeling* with *learning new behaviors* as the modeling outcome.

H. Self-regulation
  1. Setting goals
  2. Monitoring progress
  3. Self assessment
  4. Self reinforcement
  5. Cognitive behavior modification
I. Social cognitive theory in the classroom: Instructional principles
J. Putting social cognitive theory into perspective

Teaching Suggestions:

■ ***To illustrate the characteristics of self-regulation and the application of social cognitive theory in classrooms:***

1. **Pose the question, "Why is self-regulation an important part of social cognitive theory?" The students' responses will give you some insight into both their perception of social cognitive theory compared to behaviorism and what self-regulation means to them.**

2. **Point out that many reinforcers are delayed significantly, such as studying to get a good grade in a course. Without self-regulation, they wouldn't maintain the behavior until they received the reinforcer.**

3. **Also point out that behaviorism has a difficult time explaining why people will maintain a behavior when reinforcers are significantly delayed. (As a discussion topic, you might ask them to explain the difference between delayed reinforcement, as social cognitive theorists describe it, and intermittent reinforcement, as behaviorists describe it.)**

4. **To help them understand self regulation have them identify goals related to the class, such as setting a goal of writing a response to each of the margin questions, responding to all the applications in the student study guide, or writing a summary statement for each of the sections of the chapters. They will then see how goals, self-observation, self-assessment, and self-reinforcement promote learning.**

5. **To help students understand how social cognitive theory can be applied in classrooms Display PP 6.21 "*Principles of Instruction for Applying Social Cognitive Theory in Classrooms.*" Have the students identify where Sally Campese (in the case study beginning on page 188) applied each of these principles in her teaching.**

III. Addressing diversity: Behaviorism and social cognitive theory
   A. Classical conditioning: Learning to like school
   B. Motivating hesitant learners
   C. Capitalizing on minority role models

Teaching Suggestions:

■ ***To apply their understanding of behaviorism to issues of learner diversity:***

1. **Have students use classical conditioning to explain why Carlos felt welcome in school, whereas Roberto felt unwelcome.**

2. **Bring in some newspaper clippings of syndicated columnists who are members of cultural minorities. Point out that they can be effective symbolic models for minority youth.**

ENRICHMENT MATERIALS

TEACHER PREP WEBSITE

The *Teacher Prep* website an online resource for students and instructors. Both you and students can access the *Teacher Prep* website by going to http://www.prenhall.com/teacherprep. Enter your user name and password and click on "Log In." The *Teacher Prep* website includes video episodes, student and teacher artifacts, teacher and research resources, and information about licensing and beginning a teaching career. The *Teacher Prep* website is described in detail in the Media Guide.

The following article is recommended by the *Exploring Further* section titled "Practicing What We Preach" on page 181 of the chapter.

Once into the *Teacher Prep* website access the article by completing the following steps:

1. Click on "Research Resources" on the left panel of the screen, scroll down the middle of the page, and again click on "Research Resources."
2. Go to "Classroom Processes" and click on "Classroom Management."
3. Click on the following article:
   Attaining Credibility with Students: Teacher Attitude and Modeling Behaviors, by R. Kellough (1999), Ref. No. 454.

This brief excerpt offers examples of important behaviors that teachers should model in order to create a productive learning environment.

ADDITIONAL EXPLORING FURTHER SUGGESTIONS

Page 170 of the chapter suggests that students go to the *Exploring Further* module of Chapter 6, for a more detailed discussion of negative reinforcement.

Page 175 of the chapter suggests that students go to the *Exploring Further* module of Chapter 6, for a discussion of mastery learning and programmed instruction, both considered to be instructional applications of behaviorism.

Page 180 of the chapter suggests that students go to the *Exploring Further* module of Chapter 6 to read the journal article that describes Bandura's original research. A brief summary of his research is also included.

DISCUSSION STARTERS

You may choose to have your students discuss one or more of the following questions to further enrich their understanding of your learning activities.

1. Should corporal punishment be used in the schools today? If so, under what circumstances? If not, why not?

2. Should students or their parents be informed if teachers are trying to change or shape students' behavior through behavioral principles?

3. What does research on social cognitive theory suggest about the ethical and moral behavior of teachers?

4. On what point or points would Piaget and Skinner agree about the nature of learning? On what points would they disagree?

5. How would Skinner explain the development of moral behavior? How would his explanation differ from Kohlberg's?

6. Do all learners respond to basically the same reinforcers? Do all cultures? What implications do your answers have for teaching?

7. A great deal of controversy exists about the potentially harmful influences of television and movies on young people. Do you believe that the criticisms of the television and film industry are valid? What would social cognitive theorists say about these criticisms?

8. Cultural minorities and women sometimes complain about the lack of opportunity for them in upper management levels in the business world. How important is it that minorities and women be in these positions? How would social cognitive theorists explain the need for minorities and women in these positions?

BACKGROUND READINGS

Alberto, P., & Troutman, A. (2006). *Applied behavior analysis for teachers* (7th ed.). Upper Saddle River, NJ: Merrill/Prentice Hall.
The authors do a good job of explaining how behaviorist principles can increase learning in the classroom.

Baldwin, J., & Baldwin, J. (2001). *Behavior principles in everyday life* (4th ed.). Upper Saddle River, NJ: Prentice Hall.
This book provides a number of concrete examples of classical and operant conditioning in the everyday world.

Bandura, A. (1997). *Self-efficacy: The exercise of control.* New York: Freeman.
This book does a good job of describing the role of self-efficacy in self regulation.

Gentile, J. (1996). Setbacks in the "Advancement of learning?" *Educational Researcher, 25*, 37–39.
In this article, Gentile provides an additional perspective on classical conditioning.

Kohn, A. (1996). By all available means: Cameron and Pierce's defense of extrinsic motivators. *Review of Educational Research, 66*, 1–4.
In this article Kohn argues against the use of behaviorally based motivational systems.

Kratochwill, T., & Bijou, S. (1987). The impact of behaviorism on educational psychology. In J. Glover & R. Ronning (Eds.), *Historical foundations of educational psychology* (pp. 131–158). New York: Plenum.
This excellent historical overview of behaviorism, includes the contributions of the most important figures in the field presented in an historical context.

Mazur, J. E. (2006). *Learning and behavior* (6th ed.). Upper Saddle River, NJ: Prentice Hall.
This book provides a comprehensive look at different theories of learning, including behaviorism and social cognitive theory.

Schunk, D. E. (2004). *Learning theories: An educational perspective* (4th ed.). Upper Saddle River, NJ: Merrill/Prentice Hall.
Behaviorism and social cognitive theory are covered in detail in this text.

Skinner, B. F. (1968). *The technology of teaching.* New York: Appleton-Century-Crofts.
This is a classic in the field written by one of the giants. It is quite readable, and Skinner is persuasive in describing learning and teaching from a behaviorist perspective.

Zirpoli, T. J. (2005). *Behavior management: Applications for teachers* (4'h ed.). Upper Saddle River, NJ: Merrill/Prentice Hall.
This book is a good resource for teachers.

FEEDBACK

Developing as a Professional: Praxis Practice: Feedback for Short-Answer Questions

The feedback that appears here is for the short-answer questions that follow the case study on pages 194 and 195 of the text. The feedback is also available to students on the companion website.

1. Describe where classical conditioning occurred in the case study. Identify the classical conditioning concepts in your description.

Helen's nervousness, as indicated in her comment to Jenny, in reaction to having to go to the chalkboard is a conditioned response. Having to go to the board became associated with "blanking out." Blanking out was the unconditioned stimulus, and through the association, going to the board is the conditioned stimulus. Blanking out resulted in Helen feeling like an idiot as the unconditioned stimulus.

Warren could help Helen's nervousness become extinct by ensuring that she was successful as she worked at the board. This might require some extra scaffolding and emotional support as she worked through the problems.

2. Warren allowed himself to be punished in two different places in the case study. Explain where they occurred, and describe their likely impact on learning.

The first example of punishment occurred when Warren reduced his first homework assignment from 6 to 5 word problems. The students' complaints were presentation punishers. They presented him with their complaints, and he reduced the length of the assignment.

The second example occurred when students complained again and he reduced the assignment from 5 to 4 problems. While longer homework assignments don't necessarily result in more learning, students need to practice the problem-solving skills Warren was trying to teach. Reducing the homework assignments too much is likely to decrease learning.

3. Warren inadvertently negatively reinforced the students at two points in the lesson. Identify and explain each of the two points.

Warren negatively reinforced students by reducing the length of the homework assignments when they complained. Their behavior increased as indicated by the fact that they complained about the homework assignment sooner on Friday than they did on Thursday. Taking away some of the homework assignment was the negative reinforcer.

Warren also negatively reinforced Pamela for not answering his question by removing the question and turning it to Callie. This is likely to result in Pamela saying she doesn't know more quickly the next time she is called on and is uncertain about the answer. A more effective move would be to prompt Pamela and then positively reinforce her for her efforts. We want to reinforce students for answering instead of for not answering.

4. Warren's modeling had both effective and ineffective features. Identify and explain one effective and one ineffective feature.

Warren's modeling was effective in two ways. First, he demonstrated the solution to a problem, and second, he capitalized on cognitive modeling as he articulated his thinking during the demonstration in saying, "Now,... the first thing I think about when I see a problem like this one is, 'What does the jacket cost now?' I have to figure out the price, and to do that I will take 25% of the $84. . . ."

Warren's modeling was ineffective when he said, "I realize that percentages and decimals aren't your favorite topic, and I'm not wild about them either, but we have no choice, so we might as well buckle down and learn them." Since people tend to imitate behaviors they observe in others, modeling distaste for a topic increases the likelihood that students will decide that the topic is boring.

5. Warren capitalized on the effects of perceived similarity and vicarious learning in the case study. Explain where and how this occurred.

When Cris caught his error and corrected himself, Warren commented, "Good, . . . that's what we're trying to do. We are all going to make mistakes, but if we catch ourselves, we're making progress. Keep it up." His comment reinforced Cris and simultaneously vicariously reinforced the other students. He also used Cris as a model, and, since everyone in the class is similar in that they are all students, Cris was likely to be an effective model because of perceived similarity. (Warren's praise suggested that Cris was also competent, which would further increase his effectiveness as a model.)

Feedback for Online Case Book Questions

The feedback below is for the *Online Case Book* for Chapter 6 (referenced on page 177 of the chapter). Both you and the students can access the case study by going to www.prenhall.com/eggen, selecting Chapter 6, and clicking on *Online Case Book*.

You may choose to assign the online case as homework or you may want to discuss the case in class. Answers to these questions *do not* appear on the companion website, so students *do not* have access to the feedback.

Multiple-Choice Items

1. Which of the following concepts is best illustrated by Pamela's response to Jeff?
   a. Positive reinforcement
   b. Negative reinforcement
   c. Presentation punishment
   d. Satiation
   a. Pamela gave Jeff a compliment in saying, "Good, Jeff," which increased the likelihood of him attempted to answer in the future.

2. Which of the following concepts is best illustrated by Pamela's response to Lonnie?
   a. Positive reinforcement
   b. Negative reinforcement
   c. Presentation punishment
   d. Satiation
   c. In saying, "Not quite, Lonnie," the likelihood of Lonnie giving a similar response in the future was decreased. Since Pamela presented Lonnie with the comment, it is an example of presentation punishment.

3. When Pamela returned the tests on Monday she commented, "Here are your papers. You did fine on the sentences, but your paragraphs need a lot of work. Why did you have so much trouble with them, when we had so much practice?"

The students responded with comments, such as, "It was hard, Mrs. Lane," "Not enough time," and "I hate to write."

Which of the following best explains why the students had difficulty with this portion of the test?
   a. The students said they didn't like writing, and when students dislike an activity they're less likely to do well on it.
   b. The students weren't given enough time to complete a quality paragraph.
   c. The students perceived the assignment as difficult, and students generally do less well on difficult assignments.
   d. They didn't practice writing, and practice is necessary in order to learn to write.
   d. The most likely reason the students had difficulty with the writing portion of the test is that they didn't practice writing. Your study of Chapter 2 suggested that learners' development depends

on their experiences. Without experiences, development doesn't occur. The students' experiences were limited to the specific sentences in which they selected the correct pronoun case. As Pamela pointed out, they did well on this portion of the test. This makes sense, since they had experiences with this type of task. To be able to apply the rules for pronoun cases in their writing, the students must be given experiences with writing.

Short-Answer Items

4. Explain why Pamela's instruction was based primarily on behaviorism. Cite specific evidence from the case study to support your explanation.

Pamela's lesson was based primarily on behaviorism because it focused on observable responses followed by reinforcers or corrective feedback. For example, Pamela had displayed the following exercises.

Did you get the gift from Kerri and (I, me)?
Will Robert and (she, her) work at the football game?
Mr. Chang treats (whoever, whomever) he hires very well.
Areiel looked for someone (who, whom) could give her directions to the concert.

Pamela: Okay, look at the first one. Which is correct? . . . Jeff?
Jeff: Me.
Pamela: Good, Jeff. How about the second one? . . . Lonnie?
Lonnie: Her.
Pamela: Not quite, Lonnie. Listen to this. . . .

Jeff was reinforced for his correct response, and Lonnie received corrective feedback for his incorrect response. (The corrective feedback was a form of punishment. The likelihood of him making a similar response in the future was decreased by Pamela's feedback. Remember, a punisher merely decreases a behavior; it isn't necessarily hurtful or destructive.)

5. Assess the effectiveness of the feedback Lonnie received from Pamela when she said, "Not quite, Lonnie. Listen to this. Suppose I turn the sentence around a little and say, 'Robert and her will work at the football game.' See, that doesn't sound right, does it? Robert and she is a compound subject, and when we have a subject, we use the nominative case."

While giving feedback is appropriate and important, the feedback must be meaningful. It is unlikely that Lonnie's understanding was significantly increased as a result of Pamela's explanation, because she didn't explain why 'her' didn't sound right. Presumably, it sounded correct to Lonnie, or he wouldn't have chosen it as the answer.

Pamela could increase the meaningfulness of the feedback by providing several examples of sentences involving the nominative case and several others involving the objective case and discussing each in the process. (Doing so would be a shift to a more cognitive approach to instruction, which you will study in Chapters 7, 8, and 9.)

Near the end of the lesson Pamela again provided feedback that wasn't meaningful, as illustrated in the following dialogue.

Pamela: Are there any questions?
Enrique: Number 4.
Pamela: Okay, let's look at 4. It says, 'I didn't know to (who, whom) to give the letter.' There, the answer is whom.

Again, a series of examples illustrating using the nominative and objective cases correctly would help clear up the misconception.

CLASSROOM EXERCISES

The classroom exercises that follow appear *only here* in the instructor's manual. Students do not have access to *either the questions or the answers.*

The purpose of keeping the exercises only in the instructor's manual is to allow you to use them as class discussion items, or for homework, if you should choose to do so.

Feedback for the exercises follows immediately.

1. Teachers are discouraged from giving students writing assignments as a form of punishment for misbehavior. Using classical conditioning as a basis, explain why using writing assignments as punishment is unwise practice. Be specific in your explanation.

2. For many people a song, a picture, or even an odor sometimes conjures up feelings or moods that they can't otherwise capture. You've probably had this experience yourself. a) What concept from classical conditioning is illustrated by the song, picture, or odor, and b) what concept from classical conditioning is illustrated by the mood or feeling? Explain in both cases.

3. Suppose you repeatedly hear a song that elicits a warm feeling, but you don't have another positive experience similar to the original one that caused the warm feeling. a) What will eventually happen to the feeling, and b) what concept from classical conditioning does this illustrate? Explain.

4. A teacher says, "Okay, everyone. You've done such a good job of turning in your homework this week that you don't have to do your assignment for the weekend. We'll do it Monday instead." a) What concept from behaviorism is the teacher attempting to apply in this case, b) What is the teacher's goal in making this statement, and c) what is the situation the students must be in, in order for the teacher's strategy to work? Explain.

5. A teacher says, "If everyone is sitting quietly in his or her seat when the bell rings, we'll go to lunch. If not, we'll miss some of our lunch period." Suppose that the students are then sitting quietly when the bell rings, and they go to lunch as scheduled. What concept from behaviorism is the teacher applying in this case? Explain.

6. In Chapter 1 we asked, "Have you ever done one job to get it out of the way and saved a more enjoyable one for later?" Assuming the answer is yes, what idea from behaviorism is being illustrated? Explain.

7. Suppose that, in an effort to increase car pooling, a city allowed cars with three or more people to pass through toll booths without paying. Using the information in this section, explain the city's efforts.

8. What reinforcement schedule is best illustrated by people playing slot machines? Explain.

9. You're working with your students in a question and answer session and you ask:

"How does the direction of the ocean current off the coast of Chile affect the rainfall in the Chilean Desert?"

Tanya responds, "The current comes from the south, so the water is cold. The air over the water is more dense than the air over the land, so the air that goes over the land is warmed up, and it doesn't rain."

You want to praise Tanya for her answer. Write down what you would say.

Suppose instead that Tanya responded, "I . . . I'm not sure. The current goes from the south, . . . I think, . . . so . . . the water should be . . . cold. So, . . . the air above is . . . less . . . let's see . . . no, . . . more dense, so the air . . . over the land . . . gets cold, . . . no, warm . . . and, it rains, no . . . doesn't rain."

Again, you want to praise Tanya for her answer. Write down what you would say this time.

10. A person studies hard for a test, takes the test, and receives a high score several days later. Before receiving the score, however, the person continues to study other material related to the course. Behaviorists maintain that the high score is a reinforcer that directly causes the studying behavior. How do social cognitive theorists view the high score? Why do they believe the behaviorist account is inadequate?

11. Suppose a teacher has a classroom rule requiring students to raise their hands before speaking, and further suppose that a student speaks without permission and isn't reprimanded. a) Using social cognitive theory as a basis, what is the likely effect on the rest of the class of not reprimanding the student, and b) what modeling effect does this best illustrate? Explain this effect using the concept of expectations as a basis for your explanation.

12. Look again at the case study that introduces the chapter. Susan and Karen, Tim's classmates, were both successful, but Tim chose to imitate Susan's rather than Karen's behavior. Explain why this might have been the case?

FEEDBACK FOR CLASSROOM EXERCISES

1. Being punished is an event that can cause an instinctive negative emotion, so being punished is an unconditioned stimulus, and the emotion is the unconditioned response. The writing assignment can become associated with being punished, so it is a conditioned stimulus causing a negative emotion, as a conditioned response, that is similar to the one that results from being punished. As a result, students can learn to dislike writing assignments. We don't want to teach students to dislike writing.

2. The song, picture, or odor are conditioned stimuli that have become associated with some unconditioned stimulus that produced the original mood or feeling. The mood or feeling is a conditioned response that is similar to the original mood or feeling produced by the unconditioned stimulus.

3. The feeling will eventually disappear. The concept is extinction. If a conditioned stimulus occurs repeatedly in the absence of the unconditioned stimulus, the conditioned response will eventually disappear (become extinct).

4. The teacher is attempting to use negative reinforcement by allowing the students to avoid doing homework. Her goal is to increase the students' "doing homework" behaviors. The students must be in a situation of normally doing homework, or there would be nothing for them to avoid.

5. The teacher is applying negative reinforcement. The teacher is focusing on a desired outcome (sitting quietly) versus an undesired outcome (stopping talking). Also, the students are in control of the outcome. If they're quiet, they get to go to lunch. Negative reinforcement is being illustrated because the students can avoid missing some of their lunch period. Under typical conditions, they would get to go to lunch. The teacher is threatening the students with punishment, but she isn't actually punishing them.

6. The idea is the Premack Principle, which says that a more desirable activity can serve as a positive reinforcer for a less desirable activity.

7. The city is attempting to apply negative reinforcement by allowing people to avoid the tolls.

8. Slot machines illustrate variable-ratio schedules. The reinforcers depend on behaviors, not time, and they're unpredictable.

9. In the first case, specific praise in the first case wasn't necessary because the student gave a clear, confident answer. If Tanya's answer were tentative, however, specific praise would emphasize important information and help eliminate uncertainty.

An example in the second case could be: "Very good, Tanya. You recognized that the air would be warmed as it moved over the land. This was because the air above the water was cold, caused by the cold water itself flowing from the south. Good analysis."

10. Social cognitive theorists view the high score as causing expectations. According to social cognitive theorists, students study because they "expect" to be reinforced for doing so. They believe the behaviorist account is inadequate because in many cases too much elapses between the behavior and receiving the reinforcer.

11. If students break a rule they expect to be punished. If the punisher isn't given, its nonoccurrence can serve as a reinforcer, and the undesirable behavior is likely to increase. Decreasing inhibitions is the modeling effect that is illustrated.

12. When learners are fearful about a situation, as Tim was, they are more likely to imitate a coping model, or one who struggles to achieve competence, than a mastery model, or one whose competence is an accomplished fact (Schunk, 1991). This is where competence and similarity interact. Tim perceived both Karen and Susan to be competent, but he perceived himself to be more similar to Susan, because she too had to struggle, so he imitated her.

CHAPTER 7: COGNITIVE VIEWS OF LEARNING

CHAPTER OVERVIEW

This chapter is the first of three that expands the discussion of internal cognitive processes, such as attention, perception, rehearsal, encoding, and retrieval. The chapter begins with a description of information processing, one of the most thoroughly studied cognitive learning theories. Our information processing systems consist of information stores–sensory memory, working memory and long-term memory, cognitive processes–attention, perception, rehearsal, encoding, and retrieval–that move information from one store to another, and metacognition, which regulates processing.

CHAPTER OBJECTIVES

- Describe the principles on which cognitive learning theories are based, and identify illustrations of the principles.
- Use the characteristics of the memory stores in our information processing system to explain events in and outside the classroom. .
- Describe the cognitive processes in our information processing system, and identify examples of the processes in classroom events.
- Define metacognition, and identify examples of metacognition in classroom events.
- Describe the principles for applying information processing theory in classrooms, and identify examples of the principles in learning activities.

POWERPOINT SLIDES

PP 7.1 Tall in the Saddle
PP 7.2 Principles of Cognitive Learning Theory
PP 7.3 An Information Processing Model.
PP 7.4 Research Results and Working Memory
PP 7.5 The Limitations of Working Memory
PP 7.6 Schema Representing Randy's Understanding
PP 7.7 Schema Representing Juan's Understanding
PP 7.8 Characteristics of the Memory Stores
PP 7.9 Strategies for Attracting Attention
PP 7.10 Making Information Meaningful
PP 7.11 Elaborating on Past Experiences
PP 7.12 Types and Examples of Mnemonic Devices.
PP 7.13 Active and Passive Study Strategies,
PP 7.14 Review Exercise (The Role of Prior Knowledge).
PP 7.15 Children and Metacognition
PP 7.16 Principles of Instruction for Applying Information Processing in Classrooms.
PP 7.17 Background Knowledge and Encoding
PP 7.18 Praxis Practice: Feedback for Short-Answer Questions
PP 7.19 Feedback for Online Case Questions
PP 7.20 Classroom Exercises

VIDEOS

DVD 1, Episode 10: "Applying Information Processing: Attracting Students' Attention"
This episode illustrates two teachers attempting to begin their lesson with a demonstration that will attract students' attention.

DVD 1, Episode 11: "Applying Information Processing: Organizing Information"
This episode includes four teachers using different ways of organizing information for students.

DVD 1, Episode 11: "The Scarlet Letter in a High School English Class"
This episode illustrates a teacher's attempts to help her students understand the characters in the novel *The Scarlet Letter*. (This is the chapter's closing case study.)

CHAPTER OUTLINE

I. Cognitive Perspectives on Learning
   A. Principles of cognitive learning theory
      1. Learners are mentally active
      2. Learning and development depend on learners' experiences
      3. Learners construct knowledge
      4. Knowledge that is constructed depends on learners' prior knowledge
      5. Learning is enhanced in a social environment
      6. Learning requires practice and feedback
   B. A definition of learning
II. Memory Stores in our Information Processing System
   A. Sensory Memory
   B. Working Memory
      1. Limitations of working memory
      2. Reducing cognitive load: Overcoming the limitations of working memory
         a. Chunking
         b. Automaticity
         c. Dual processing
   C. Long-Term Memory
      1. Representing declarative knowledge in memory: Schemas
         a. Meaningfulness: Reducing cognitive load on working memory
         b. Meaningfulness and cognitive load: Implications for learning and teaching
         c. Schemas as scripts
      2. Representing procedural knowledge in memory: Conditions and actions
         a. Developing procedural knowledge
         b. Developing procedural knowledge: Implications for learning and teaching
III. Cognitive processes in our information processing system
   A. Attention: The beginning of information processing
      1. Attracting and maintaining attention
   B. Perception: Finding meaning in stimuli
   C. Rehearsal: Retaining information through repetition
   D. Meaningful encoding: Making connections in long-term memory
      1. Organization: Representing relationships in content
      2. Imagery: Applying Dual-Coding Theory
      3. Elaboration: Extending understanding
      4. Activity: Capitalizing on a learning principle
   E. Forgetting
      1. Forgetting as interference
      2. Forgetting as retrieval failure
IV. Metacognition: Knowledge and control of cognitive processes
   A. The development of metacognition
V. Information processing in the classroom: Instructional principles
   A. The impact of diversity on information processing
      1. Diversity and perception
      2. Diversity, encoding, and retrieval
      3. Instructional adaptations for background diversity
   B. Putting information processing into perspective

PRESENTATION OUTLINE

I. Cognitive Perspectives on Learning
   A. Principles of cognitive learning theory
      1. Learners are mentally active
      2. Learning and development depend on learners' experiences
      3. Learners construct knowledge
      4. Knowledge that is constructed depends on learners' prior knowledge
      5. Learning is enhanced in a social environment
      6. Learning requires practice and feedback
   B. A definition of learning

Teaching Suggestions:

■ *The following activities are suggestions for introducing the chapter and the principles of cognitive learning theory.*

1. **Tell the students that you're going to do two simple activities, and the point in them will be clear after you've completed and discussed them.**

2. **Tell them to say "Pots." After they say it, tell them to repeat it, and after they do, then tell them to say it one more time. Then ask, "What do we do at a green light?" Most of them will say, "Stop." Repeat, "What do we do at a green light?" and they will catch themselves.**

3 **For the second activity, tell the students that you're going to display a phrase on the overhead for just a second, and that you want them to write it down. Then display PP 7.1 "Tall in the Saddle" for about a second. (Most of the students will miss the second "the" in the phrase.)**

4. **Ask the students how either behaviorism or social cognitive theory would explain the fact that they said "Stop" in response to the question about the green light, and that they missed the second "the" in the phrase "Tall in the the saddle."**

Point out that neither behaviorism nor social cognitive theory can explain their responses, which leads us to cognitive learning theory. Also note that they were responding more to their past experiences and expectations than to the stimuli in each case. (For example, saying "Pots," established expectations for them, and they responded to their expectations instead of the actual stimulus.)

5. **Point out also that they missed the second "the" in the phrase because the phrase "Tall in the saddle" makes sense, whereas the phrase "Tall in the the saddle" does not. This can then lead you to the principles of cognitive learning theory. Remind the students that some people believe that making sense of their experiences is the strongest cognitive need that exists in people.**

6. **Display PP 7.2 "*Principles of Cognitive Learning Theory*" and ask the students to offer examples that illustrate each principle.**

II. Memory Stores in our Information Processing System
   A. Sensory Memory
   B. Working Memory
      1. Limitations of working memory
      2. Reducing cognitive load: Overcoming the limitations of working memory
         a. Chunking
         b. Automaticity
         c. Dual processing

C. Long-Term Memory
   1. Representing declarative knowledge in memory: Schemas
      a. Meaningfulness: Reducing cognitive load on working memory
      b. Meaningfulness and cognitive load: Implications for learning and teaching
      c. Schemas as scripts
   2. Representing procedural knowledge in memory: Conditions and actions
      a. Developing procedural knowledge
      b. Developing procedural knowledge: Implications for learning and teaching

Teaching Suggestions:

■ ***The purpose of the suggestions in this section is to help the students understand that models, such as the information processing model, are representations that help them visualize what they can't observe directly.***

1. **Ask the students to give you some examples or definitions of models. Some possibilities are:**
   - **A miniature representation of something, such as a model car or a globe**
   - **Someone who poses for an artist**
   - **Someone who displays merchandise**
   - **Someone who displays behavior that is imitated (as was presented in Chapter 6)**

2. **Now point out that the definition that is useful when we discuss information processing is: "A representation that allows us to visualize what we can't observe directly." Note that even though we can't directly observe the information this model represents, it is valuable nevertheless, because it helps us visualize and think about the information stores and cognitive processes involved in processing information.**

3. **Display PP 7.3 "*An Information Processing Model.*" Have the students make observations of the model such as, "In the model there are fewer lines to the right of 'attention' than there are to the left of attention," or "In the model, working memory is smaller then either sensory memory or long-term memory." Then, ask them what conclusions they can make based on their observations, such as attention serving as a screen, and working memory being limited in capacity.**

4. **To help the students understand the characteristics of sensory memory have them wiggle their fingers back and forth in front of them and ask them what they observe (a "shadow" of their fingers as it's moving). Then have them press their forefingers on their opposite arms and note that the feeling of pressure remains briefly after their fingers are removed. Point out that the "shadow" that "trails" after their fingers as they wiggle them, and the slight feeling of pressure that briefly remains are the memory traces retained in sensory memory.**

   Note also that in reading we must retain the first part of the sentence in sensory memory long enough to extract meaning from the whole sentence. If information was lost immediately, it would be impossible to get any meaning from reading.

   Ask the students to summarize the characteristics of sensory memory (this can be done either as a small-group or whole-group activity). They should identify the following characteristics:
   - **Virtually unlimited capacity**
   - **Retains exact copy of stimuli (information is "unprocessed")**
   - **Holds information very briefly (a second or two)**

5. **Display PP 7.4 "*Research Results and Working Memory,*" and ask the students to try and identify what the examples have in common.**

6. **Then display PP 7.5 "*The Limitations of Working Memory.*" Tell the students that you're going to show them some letters for about 1 second, and that after you've shown them, they should**

write them down. Then show the first row only (for about a second). Have the students write the letters. Then repeat the process with the other four rows. (Be careful to avoid displaying the words at the bottom of PP 7.5.)

7. **After you're finished, display the letters and ask them how many got the letters in each case. Nearly all will get the letters in the five-letter row, and fewer will get all the letters in each succeeding row. Point out that the typical adult capacity is from 5 to 9 bits of information, and that these capacities are lower for younger children.**

8. **Ask students to recall some of the observations and inferences (conclusions) they made about working memory. They should note that:**
   - **It is limited in capacity.**
   - **It is the "conscious" part of our processing system.**
   - **If it becomes overloaded, information from it will be lost.**

   Again display PP 7.4 to emphasize the importance of working memory's limited capacity.

■ ***To help students understand chunking, automaticity, and dual processing and their roles in reducing cognitive load:***

1. **Display the words at the bottom half of PP 7.5. This displays the same letters in the exercise "chunked" into one or two units. They will see that remembering all the letters in the "chunked" information is easy to remember in each case.**

2. **Point out that remembering patterns and relationships is also a form of chunking which frees working memory space. This is the reason that in this class we emphasize relationships rather than isolated pieces of information. When several items of information are related to each other, they essentially become a "chunk." (For example, with continued thought and effort, the information processing model becomes a chunk rather than several pieces of information.)**

3. **Ask the students to identify some things they do "without thinking about it." These are essentially automatic. After you have a list, offer the term "automaticity" if they haven't already used it. Some examples include:**
   - **typing on a computer keyboard.**
   - **recognizing words.**
   - **math facts.**
   - **writing.**

4. **Ask them to identify several ideas that must be automatic for them to do well in this class. The information processing model and its components are examples. Definitions of concepts are other examples. Have them explain why these ideas must be automatic.**

5. **Point out that–in virtually all cases–you supplement your descriptions with visual materials, such as information on the power point.**

6. **Point out that these visual representations, combined with you class discussions, are intended to capitalize on the dual-processing capabilities of working memory.**

7. **Summarize dual processing by having the students explain what dual processing means. Lead them to conclude that dual processing theory suggests that working memory consists of a visual and an auditory store that work independently and additively, i.e., combining visual and verbal representations not only does not overload working memory, but in fact help overcome its limitations.**

■ *To help students understand the implications for instruction of working memory's limitations:*

1. **Have them identify as many implications of working memory's limitations as possible.**

   Some include:
   - **practicing basic skills to automaticity, so that they don't have to use working memory space to recall basic information.**
   - **forming schemas of interrelated information, so the schemas become chunks of information instead of isolated pieces.**
   - **teaching in short steps and providing practice to allow learners time to process information and transfer it to long-term memory.**

2. **You might want to point out that some experts (e.g., Bruer, 1993) believe that a limited working memory is the most significant aspect of our information processing systems. Further, cognitive load theorists (e.g. Sweller, van Merrienboer, & Paas, 1998) point out that while our working memories can hold about 7 bits of information, processing also requires working memory space, so we are probably only able to hold–and process–about 2 bits of information.**

   On the other hand, Sweller, et al., (1998) point out that while the number of bits of information is limited, the size is not. This makes the development of inter-related schemas an even more important goal for learning.

■ *To help students understand the characteristics of long-term memory:*

1. **Display PP 7.6 "*Schema Representing Randy's Understanding*" and PP 7.7 "Schema Representing Juan's Understanding." Have the students describe and compare the information in the transparencies. Remind the students that they are models that help us visualize the way Randy and Juan organized and stored information in their long-term memories. Guide them to the definition that schemas are the way knowledge is organized in memory.**

2. **Point out that while there are 10 concepts in each "schema" Juan's has 12 links, whereas Randy's only has 6. Juan's behaves more nearly like a chunk which reduces the cognitive load on his working memory.**

3. **Have the students describe as much information as they can about the information processing model and what implications this information has for learning and teaching. The information they offer will be in the form of declarative knowledge organized in a schema.**

4. **As you ask them to tell you how they recalled the information, some are likely to say that they "pictured" the model, which you can point out as an example of imagery. They might also say that they saw sensory memory on the left, working memory in the middle and long-term memory on the right. You can then offer this as a form of linear ordering.**

5. **Point out that virtually infinite numbers of schemas exist. You can also point out that one of your goals in this section is for them to develop a complex and integrated schema about information processing and what implications it has for learning and teaching.**

6. **Review declarative knowledge and use it as a link to procedural knowledge by pointing out that the focus of your discussion to this point has been on declarative knowledge. Ask them to describe some procedural knowledge related to your discussion. (When they actually teach based on the implications of information processing, they will demonstrate procedural knowledge.)**

7. **Also ask the students to give you some additional examples of procedural knowledge. Some examples include:**
   - **finding a book in the library.**
   - **changing a tire.**
   - **using a computer.**
   - **solving a word problem in math.**
   - **writing an essay.**

8. **Ask the students why we care about the difference between declarative and procedural knowledge--the "so what" question. They should note that the two types of knowledge are learned differently; declarative knowledge involves items of information being linked to each other, whereas procedural knowledge involves conditions and actions. Ask the students to offer some examples of conditions and actions, such as in the case of finding a book in the library, writing a persuasive versus a descriptive essay, or different types of word problems.**

9. **Summarize this section by asking the students what kind of knowledge has predominated to this point in the course you're teaching (declarative). Ask them how conditions and actions have been illustrated to help them develop procedural knowledge. (The classroom examples and the written and video cases are the best examples, primarily because they provide context for the topics they're studying.)**

10. **Display PP 7.8 "*Characteristics of the Memory Stores*" which summarizes the similarities and differences.**

III. Cognitive processes in our information processing system
   A. Attention: The beginning of information processing
      1. Attracting and maintaining attention
   B. Perception: Finding meaning in stimuli
   C. Rehearsal: Retaining information through repetition
   D. Meaningful encoding: Making connections in long-term memory
      1. Organization: Representing relationships in content
      2. Imagery: Applying Dual-Coding Theory
      3. Elaboration: Extending understanding
      4. Activity: Capitalizing on a learning principle
   E. Forgetting
      1. Forgetting as interference
      2. Forgetting as retrieval failure

Teaching Suggestions:

■ ***The purpose of the activities in this section of the chapter is to help students understand how the cognitive processes move information from sensory memory to working memory, and from working memory to long-term memory.***

1. **Begin this section by asking students to recall what you did to begin your discussion of the chapter. They should remember that you began with the "Say 'pots'," and "Tall in the saddle," examples. Ask them what these examples illustrated. They should note that first the examples were attention getters. Second, they should recall that "Say 'pots'" set up expectations in them that influenced their perceptions, which in turn resulted in them saying "Stop," when you asked, "What do you do at a green light?" Perception was also involved with the other example. They tend to miss the second 'the' in "Tall in the the saddle," because we rarely see it (experience).**

2. **PP 7.9 "*Strategies for Attracting Attention*" provide some additional examples of ways to attract attention. Have the students identify other examples of attention getters that you've used throughout your instruction in the course.**

Then have the students identify other topics, and have them determine how they might begin a lesson on the topic to best attract attention.

Here would be a good point to show or discuss **Episode 10 on DVD 1**: "Applying Information Processing: Attracting Students' Attention."

3. **Ask the students how they will determine if their learners are accurately perceiving the information they present. (Asking students is the simplest and most effective way.)**

   Ask them what kinds of questions are particularly effective. They should identify open-ended questions as being ideal. You can then remind them that open-ended questions are also very effective in working with cultural minorities, so they are appropriate for an additional reason.

4. **Ask the students how they remember a phone number long enough to dial it. The technique they describe will likely illustrate a form of rehearsal, since they will have repeated the number enough times to retain it in working memory until they could dial it.**

5. **Point out that rehearsal is a low-level process, used to retain factual information. Point out that rehearsal and practice are not the same process. Practice can involve high-high level operations, such as problem solving and writing whereas rehearsal is low level, involving memorization.**

■ ***To help students understand the concept of "meaningfulness" and that meaningfulness is increased with organization, imagery, elaboration, and activity:***

1. **Display PP 7.10 "*Making Information Meaningful*" as an organizer for this section. To illustrate the concept of meaningfulness, again display PP 7.6 and PP 7.7 that illustrate the difference between Randy's and Juan's schemas. In them we see the same numbers of ideas, yet more links exist among the ideas in Juan's schema than exist in Randy's. As a result, Juan's understanding is greater. (For example, as you saw above, there are 12 links in Juan's schema, whereas there are only 6 in Randy's. This helps visualize the idea that the information is more meaningful for Juan than it is for Randy.)**

2. **To illustrate organization, display transparencies that you have used to teach topics from earlier chapters, such as a matrix, a hierarchy, and another form of organizer (such as the information processing model from this chapter). Ask the students what they have in common. Guide them to conclude that they all helped organize the content you were teaching. Then, take one or two specific examples and have the students describe how the organizer makes the information more meaningful. (Emphasize that each organizer illustrates associations or connections in the content.)**

3. **As you discuss the organizers in each case, point out how they all incorporate imagery, and remind the students that dual-coding theory suggests that information that can be visualized is stored more efficiently in long-term memory than is information that can only be described verbally. This helps us understand why a concept like *tree* is easier to remember than a concept like *honesty*.**

Here would be a good point to show or discuss **Episode 11 on DVD 1**: "Applying Information Processing: Organizing Information."

■ ***To illustrate the process of elaboration:***

1. **Display PP 7.11 "*Elaborating on Past Experiences.*" As the students to explain the two examples and then display the feedback.**

2. **Point out that producing examples is probably the most effective form of elaboration that exists. Also note that this is the reason you've emphasized the use of examples so strongly in your teaching.**

3. **Point out that using analogies and mnemonic devices are two strategies that capitalize on elaboration. Display PP 7.12 "*Types and Examples of Mnemonic Devices.*"**

■ ***To illustrate the importance of activity:***

1. **Display PP 7.13 "*Active and Passive Study Strategies,*" and have the students decide which of the three students are likely to learn the most.**

2. **Ask the students what other kinds of learning experiences promote activity.**

■ ***To illustrate the importance of prior knowledge in meaningful encoding:***

1. **Display PP 7.14 "*Review Exercise (The Role of Prior Knowledge).*" It offers an example of the role of prior knowledge in making information meaningful. Have the students respond to the exercise and then discuss the results.**

■ ***To help students understand that interference is one explanation for why we forget information:***

1. **Ask students to offer two related ideas that are confusing for them. Ask them to try and explain why they're confusing. Point out that theorists would explain that one interferes with the other.**

2. **Identify some concepts, such as *assimilation* and *accommodation* in Chapter 2 or *positive* and *negative reinforcement* in Chapter 6, which can potentially involve interference.**

■ ***To help students understand that some theorists suggest that "forgetting" is really the inability to retrieve information:***

1. **Use the discussion of interference to emphasize that effective encoding is the key to retrieval. Ask the students what would help them clarify the confusing ideas.**

2. **Ask one of the students to state the months of the year. He or she will quickly say "January, February, . . . December."**

3. **Now ask the student to name the months of the year alphabetically. He or she will struggle and laborously say, "April, August, . . . " Point out that this illustrates the fact that we've encoded the months of the year in a chronological context. When we have to state the months alphabetically, we have to reprocess the information.**

IV. Metacognition: Knowledge and control of cognitive processes
   A. The development of metacognition

Teaching Suggestions:

■ ***To help students understand metacognition and how it influences learning:***

1. **Ask the students what they might do if they were up late the night before class and know they might have trouble staying awake in class. Some examples might be:**
   . Drink some coffee before (or during) class.
   . Move to the front of the room.

. Take more notes.
. Fidget/move around in their seats.

2. Point out that these examples illustrate that they're aware of, and are exercising control over, their attention.

3. Also point out that their tendency to take notes and/or highlight parts of the book, work the exercises in the Student Study Guide, take the practice quizzes, and respond to the margin notes in the book illustrate metacognition, because by doing these activities they demonstrate knowledge of and control over their understanding of the content they're studying.

4. Also note that exercising metacognition and using study strategies is part of being self-regulated.

5. Again display PP 7.3 "*An Information Processing Model*" to illustrate metacognition in our information processing systems.

■ ***To illustrate developmental differences in metacognition:***

1. Display PP 7.15 "*Children and Metacognition*" and have the students offer a brief explanation for the child's behavior in the cartoon. (The students will likely say that the child is egocentric, and from a Piagetian perspective egocentrism is demonstrated. From an information processing perspective, the cartoon illustrates lack of metacognition; the child is unaware that he isn't able to communicate clearly.)

2. Remind the students that meta-attention and metamemory are types of metacognition, and then ask what type is illustrated by the cartoon and see if they're able to identify "metacommunication," as a type of metacognition.

3. Also, have the students predict what the two children will do in the example at the bottom of PP 7.15. (The kindergartner will likely do nothing, whereas the 6th grader will say something, such as, "I can't hear," or do something such as try to move closer to the front of the room.)

4. Summarize this section by asking how a first grader and a fifth grader might differ in their approach to learning how to spell a list of words.

V. Information processing in the classroom: Instructional principles
  A. The impact of diversity on information processing
    1. Diversity and perception
    2. Diversity, encoding, and retrieval
    3. Instructional adaptations for background diversity
  B. Putting information processing into perspective

Teaching Suggestions:

■ ***The suggestions in this section are intended to help students identify instructional applications of information processing and to see how learner diversity influences the way they perceive information.***

1. Display PP 7.16 "*Principles of Instruction for Applying Information Processing in Classrooms.*" Have the students identify where Lisa Johnson (in the case study beginning on page 223 of the chapter) applied each of the principles in her teaching.

Here would be a good point to show or discuss **Episode 12 on DVD 1**: "Applying Information Processing: The *Scarlet Letter* in High School English," and assess the extent to which the teacher applied information processing theory in her instruction.

■ ***To illustrate how diversity in backgrounds influences encoding and retrieval:***

1. **Display PP 7.17 "*Background Knowledge and Encoding.*" Have the students decide what each passage is about and offer their interpretations.**

   After they've offered their interpretations point out that the first is about Christopher Columbus and his voyage to the New World, and the second is about washing clothes.

2. **Ask students why neither passage was very meaningful for some of them. They will probably point out that they weren't told what the passages were about. In the discussion, note that being told what the passages are about activates background knowledge of Columbus and their experience with washing clothes. Point out that in these examples background knowledge was there, just needing to be activated. Often, background knowledge is absent and needs to be provided.**

■ ***To help the students understand how instruction can be adapted to accommodate differences in their learners' backgrounds:***

1. **Tell them to think of themselves as teachers with classes having students with widely varying backgrounds. Ask them what kinds of relatively simple and practical things they might do to accommodate those differences in backgrounds.**

   Based on information processing theory and their reading, they should identify the following:
   - **Ask students what they know about the topic you're planning to teach.**
   - **Provide background for the students in the form of examples and other representations.**
   - **Check students' perceptions of your examples by using open-ended questions.**
   - **Have students in your classes share experiences to increase each others' backgrounds.**

2. **You might also point out that you're doing a perception check whenever you ask students to interpret some information, or when you simply ask them what a display or example represents.**

■ ***To help the students understand some of the strengths and weaknesses of information processing:***

1. **Ask them to identify some factors that influence the amount they study. Some of their responses can include:**
   - **how well they like the material.**
   - **how well they like the teacher.**
   - **how they feel.**
   - **what they expect to learn and what they expect from the teacher.**
   - **what they believe about the content, the teacher, and the course.**

2. **Point out that information processing doesn't take learners' emotions, beliefs, needs, and expectations into account, and its failure to do so is commonly cited as weaknesses and limitations in the information processing view of learning.**

3. **Point out that, on the other hand, most researchers and theorists accept the basic architecture of information processing–a sensory memory, working memory, and long-term memory, together with cognitive processes that move information from one store to another. Note that areas of study, such as cognitive-load theory and dual-processing theory focus on the limitations of working memory and what can be done to help overcome them.**

ENRICHMENT MATERIALS

TEACHER PREP WEBSITE

The *Teacher Prep* website an online resource for students and instructors. Both you and students can access the *Teacher Prep* website by going to http://www.prenhall.com/teacherprep. Enter your user name and password and click on "Log In." The *Teacher Prep* website includes video episodes, student and teacher artifacts, teacher and research resources, and information about licensing and beginning a teaching career. The *Teacher Prep* website is described in detail in the Media Guide.

The following articles are recommended by the *Exploring Further* section titled "Metacognition and Emotional Development" on page 221 of the chapter.

Once into the *Teacher Prep* website access the articles by completing the following steps:
1. Click on "Research Resources" on the left panel of the screen, scroll down the middle of the page and again click on "Research Resources."
2. Go to "Classroom Processes" and click on "Instructional Methods."
3. Click on the following article:
   Socratic Seminars: Engaging Students in Intellectual Discourse, by L. Tredway (1995), Ref. No. 385

This article suggests that teachers use Socratic dialogue to help students become more metacognitive about their emotions and motivations. The approach is unique in that it relates metacognitive abilities to the affective domain.

ADDITIONAL EXPLORING FURTHER SUGGESTIONS

Page 203 of the chapter suggests that students to go the *Exploring Further* module of Chapter 7 for a more detailed discussion of models.

Page 206 of the chapter suggests that students to go the *Exploring Further* module of Chapter 7 for a more detailed discussion of cognitive load theory.

Page 218 of the chapter suggests that students to go the *Exploring Further* module of Chapter 7 for a discussion of levels of processing, an alternative view of meaningful encoding.

DISCUSSION STARTERS

You may choose to have your students discuss one or more of the following questions to further enrich their understanding of your learning activities.

1. What similarities and differences exist between behaviorist, social cognitive, and information processing views of learning? Are either more valuable to teaching at different grade levels? In different subject matter areas? For different topics? Which and why?

2. Is information processing more closely related to Piaget's or to Vygotsky's theory? What specific concepts from each are related? Describe the relationship.

3. Which aspect or aspects of an information processing view of memory and learning have the most important implications for instruction? What are these implications?

4. Using information from this chapter explain how long-term memory might differ for the following groups of people:
    a. A three-year-old vs. senior citizen
    b. A first year biology student and a doctoral student in the same area
    c. A first year and experienced teacher
    4. A student who has memorized information for a fill-in-the-blanks test and one who studies for an essay exam

5. How useful are mnemonic devices in the classroom? Should teachers place more emphasis on these strategies? Are they more useful at some levels and in certain content areas than others? Which and why?

6. Which theory of forgetting--interference or retrieval failure--seems most useful to teachers? Why? What are the implications of each for instruction?

7. Does diversity primarily influence the information stores or the processes in the information-processing model? Explain, using information from the chapter.

BACKGROUND READINGS

Bransford, J., Brown, A., & Cocking, R. (Eds.). (2000). *How people learn: Brain, mind, experience, and school.* Washington, DC: National Academy Press.
This comprehensive book cognitive learning in detail and the implications these views of learning have for planning, instruction, and assessment.

Bruning, R., Schraw, G., Norby, M., & Ronning, R. (2004). *Cognitive psychology and instruction* (4th ed.). Upper Saddle River, NJ: Prentice Hall.
This book provides in-depth coverage of information processing and constructivism. Separate chapters discuss memory, encoding, and retrieval, as well as cognitive frameworks for reading, writing, math, and science.

Byrnes, J. P. (2001). *Minds, brains, and learning: Understanding the psychological and educational relevance of neuroscientific research.* New York: Guilford Press.
This book describes neuroscientific research and relates it to cognitive theories of learning.

Greeno, J., Collins, A., & Resnick, L. (1996). Cognition and learning. In D. Berliner & R. Calfee (Eds.), *Handbook of Educational Psychology* (pp. 15–46). New York: Macmillan.
This chapter examines learning, motivation and transfer from behaviorist, cognitive, and situative/sociohistoric views. It includes discussions of assessment and creating classroom environments that facilitate learning.

Mayer, R. (2002). *The promise of educational psychology, Volume II: Teaching for meaningful learning.* Upper Saddle River, NJ: Prentice Hall.
This book by a well-known author discusses a variety of topics related to cognitive learning.

Schunk, D. (2004). *Learning theories: An educational perspective* (4th ed.). Upper Saddle River, NJ: Merrill/Prentice Hall.
This text provides a detailed description of information processing, among other views of learning.

Veenman, M. V., & Spaans, M. A. (2005). Relation between intellectual and metacognitive skills: Age and task differences. *Learning and Individual Differences*, 15, 159–176.
This article provides some insights into the relationships between learner ability, development, and metacognition.

FEEDBACK

Developing as a Professional: Praxis Practice: Feedback for Short-Answer Questions

The feedback that appears here is for the short-answer questions that follow the case study on pages 228 and 229 of the text. The feedback is also available to students on the companion website.

1. Assess the extent to which Sue applied the principles of cognitive learning theory in her lesson. Include both strengths and weaknesses in your assessment.

Six principles of cognitive learning theory were outlined in the chapter. The following identifies the principle and offers an assessment of Sue's implementation of each.

1. Learners are active. Sue put the students in active roles with her questioning and by having them write in their journals.

2. Learning and development depend on learners' experiences. The students acquired experience through their reading of the novel together with the class discussion of it. The understanding of the themes of the novel was developed through these experiences.

3. Learners construct knowledge. The fact that the students offered different interpretations of Hester's reaction to Dimmesdale's speech is evidence that they construct their own understanding. For instance, Nicole viewed Hester as angry, whereas Sarah saw her as devoted. Because one of Sue's goals was for students to understand Dimmesdale's character, she might have been more focused in her questioning, helping students to form a more complete picture of his character. This might have been accomplished by referring the students to specific passages in the novel that would give the students insights into his character.

4. Knowledge that is constructed depends on learners' prior knowledge. Sue helped her students build on their prior knowledge by encouraging them to think about their discussion of Hester's character from previous lessons.

5. Learning is enhanced in a social environment. This is the principle Sue perhaps implemented most effectively. She had students work in groups, and she conducted much of the whole-group portion of the lesson through her questioning. Social interaction was prominent throughout the lesson.

6. Learning requires practice and feedback. Sue's students were given the opportunity to practice their developing understanding both in writing in their journals and also as they practiced articulating their understanding. This is the principle that Sue applied least effectively. The students offered their perceptions of Dimmesdale's character and Hester's reaction to his speech, but they received little feedback about the validity of their perceptions or how their analysis related to her goals for having them read the novel. The lesson was largely a sharing of perceptions.

2. Assess the extent to which Sue applied information processing theory in her lesson. Include both strengths and weaknesses in your assessment.

Applying information processing theory requires that teachers consciously attempt to attract and maintain students' attention, check their perceptions, and promote meaningful encoding without imposing a cognitive load that exceeds their working memory capacities. Sue's lesson was an effective application of information processing theory. She helped attract and maintain students' attention by challenging them to find evidence in the book that Dimmesdale was the illicit lover and by using the passage from the book describing Dimmesdale's speech. She also used class discussion as a mechanism to maintain attention. In each instance she used student responses to check their perceptions. Sue avoided imposing too heavy a cognitive load by asking one question at a time and giving them time to consider their answers. She promoted meaningful encoding by encouraging the students to use imagery to gain more insights into Dimmesdale's character. When they wrote in their journals and discussed Hester's reaction to Dimmesdale's speech they were in active roles. Through the discussion they elaborated on each other's understanding. Imagery, activity, and elaboration are all processes that make information meaningful.

3. Which cognitive process from information processing theory was most prominent in Sue's lesson? Explain.

Encoding was cognitive process most prominent in her lesson. As we saw in item 2, Sue promoted encoding by encouraging tstudents to use imagery to gain more insights into Dimmesdale's character, by putting them in active roles with their journal writing and class discussion, and promoting elaboration in the class discussion.

While encoding was most significant, perception was prominent as well. For instance, when the students offered different views of Hester's reaction to Dimmesdale's speech, they were presenting their perceptions.

4. Identify at least one instance in Sue's lesson in which she focused on declarative knowledge. Identify another in which she focused on procedural knowledge. Was the primary focus of Sue's lesson the acquisition of declarative knowledge or procedural knowledge?

Declarative knowledge is knowledge of facts, definitions, procedures, and rules; procedural knowledge involves knowing how to perform tasks. Sue focused on declarative knowledge when she reviewed the novel's plot at the beginning of the lesson. The primary focus of the lesson was on declarative knowledge—helping the students develop an understanding of the characters in the novel. When the students wrote in their journals, they were demonstrating procedural knowledge.

Feedback for Online Case Book Questions

The feedback below is for the *Online Case Book* for Chapter 7 (referenced on page 224 of the chapter). Both you and the students can access the case study by going to www.prenhall.com/eggen, selecting Chapter 7, and clicking on *Online Case Book.*

You may choose to assign the online case as homework or you may want to discuss the case in class. Answers to these questions *do not* appear on the companion website, so students *do not* have access to the feedback.

Multiple-Choice Items

1. Look again at the third paragraph of the case study which describes what Steve did on the first day of his unit. *As an application of information processing*, which of the following is the best assessment of Steve's instruction on this day?

a. It was effective because he presented the students with information, and information processing begins with stimuli entering sensory memory.

b. It was ineffective because presenting information as he did was likely to impose a heavy cognitive load on the students, which decreased the likelihood of them being able to encode the information.

c. It was effective because he showed the students a transparency on which the inner and outer lanets were represented.

d. It was ineffective, because all of the information was at a fact level.

b. Presenting information without interacting with students is likely to impose a heavy load on working memory. If the load is too heavy some information is likely to be lost before it can be encoded into long-term memory. Information processing does begin with stimuli entering sensory memory, but that doesn't address whether or not Steve's presentation was effective (choice a), and presenting the information on a transparency doesn't solve the problem of the earlier cognitive load. If he had displayed the transparency and referred to it as he was presenting the information, it would have been more effective (choice c). Teachers sometimes have learning objectives that involved fact level learning. To suggest that a lesson is ineffective because it involves fact learning is not valid (choice d).

2. At the end of his first day's lesson, Steve displayed a transparency that illustrated the inner and outer planets. As an application of dual processing theory, which of the following is the best assessment of Steve's teaching strategy?

a. It was an effective application of dual processing theory because he presented the information both verbally and visually.
b. As an application of dual processing theory, it would have been more effective if Steve had first presented the transparency and then presented the information verbally, so the students would have had something concrete to observe.
c. As an application of dual processing theory it would have been more effective if he had shown one transparency with the inner planets and a separate transparency with the outer planets.
d. As an application of dual processing theory, it would have been more effective if he had displayed the transparency at the same time as he presented the information, referring to the transparency during the presentation.
*d. Dual processing theory suggests that word and visual representations should be presented **simultaneously.** As the quote on page 207 of the chapter states, "The integration of words and pictures is made easier by lessons that present the verbal and visual information together rather than separated."*

3. The second day Steve began class by saying, "All right everyone, what have we learned about the solar system so far?" Which of the following best describes the purpose of a review such as this?

a. It helps students retrieve information from long-term memory which can then be used for further processing.
b. It provides the students with opportunities to rehearse important information
c. It promotes metacognition by making students aware of what they've already studied.
d. It acts as a script which will guide the students' future actions.
a. The primary function of reviews is to help students retrieve information from long-term memory.

Short-Answer Items

4. Based on evidence taken from the case study, how meaningful was the lesson for students. (Hint: Keep the definition of *meaningfulness* in mind as you respond to this question.)

As you saw in the chapter, meaningfulness describes the number of connections that students make in the different aspects of the topic. Based on the evidence in the case study, the topic wasn't as meaningful for the students as would be desired. First, most of what Steve did was at the knowledge-recall level. For example, he wrote the names of the planets in their order from the sun, and he presented other factual information about the planets. While this information is important, a meaningful lesson goes beyond these facts to identify characteristics of the planets, and why those characteristics exist, such as why Mercury is so hot on one side and so cold on the other, and why planets, such as Saturn have a low density. Steve didn't present any of this type of information in his lesson. Steve's homework assignment also focused on knowledge-level information.

We saw additional evidence that the lesson wasn't meaningful in the exchange between Benjie and Janet:

Benjie: What did he say about orbits? . . . I didn't get it.
Janet: I'm not sure. He said the planets came off the sun, I think.
Benjie: How?
Janet: I don't know. Just came off I guess.

A greater focus on relationships among the parts of the solar system would have made the lesson more meaningful.

5. How effectively did Steve accommodate the limitations of working memory in his lesson? Provide evidence from the case study to support your assessment.

The limitations of working memory can be accommodated through chunking, practicing procedural knowledge to automaticity, and dual processing. Steve presented some of his information in both visual and verbal form, which helps take advantage of dual processing, but, because much of his lesson focused on specific facts, opportunities to make connections and chunk information were limited. He also presented much of the information in a lecture format, and lecturing commonly overloads working memory. The students also had little opportunity to practice with the content which could lead to automaticity.

CLASSROOM EXERCISES

The classroom exercises that follow appear *only here* in the instructor's manual. Students do not have access to *either the questions or the answers.*

The purpose of keeping the exercises only in the instructor's manual is to allow you to use them as class discussion items, or for homework, if you should choose to do so.

Feedback for the exercises follows immediately.

1. Look at the following telephone numbers:
   731-9586
   249-7132
   852-1657
   965-3841

What do they have in common?
Why do you suppose this commonality exists?

2. Lecture has always been and still remains the most common teaching method in junior highs, high schools, and universities. Using the characteristics of working memory as the basis, explain why lecture is so popular. (Respond to this item from the perspective of the teacher. In other words, how does the use of lecture relate to teachers' working memories?)

3. Teachers are encouraged to used sophisticated forms of instruction, such as guided discovery in their teaching. (A discussion and example of guided discovery begins on page 293 of your text.). Again, using the characteristics of working memory as the basis, explain what the teachers must do in order to successfully use a strategy such as guided discovery.

4. When teachers become expert at using a strategy, such as guided discovery, are they primarily demonstrating declarative knowledge or procedural knowledge? Explain.

5. You have an electric garage door opener, and one morning as you're in a bit of a rush to get to school or work, you realize that you can't remember if you've put the garage door down or not, so you drive back several blocks to check, and you see that you have indeed put the garage door down. What concept from information processing best explains why you originally couldn't remember if you put the garage door down?

6. Research indicates that experts in a field, as widely ranging as teaching, physics, or even chess, think differently than novices in those same fields. Some of the differences include the following:
- Experts are more metacognitive in their approaches to problems.
- Experts have more of their knowledge stored in interconnected schemas, whereas novices have more of their knowledge stored in isolated bits.
- More of experts' knowledge is automatic than is the knowledge of novices.

Which of the following concepts–sensory memory, attention, perception, working memory, or rehearsal–is most closely related to these expert-novice differences? Explain the relationship between the concept and these differences in the thinking of experts and novices.

7. Missy Somers, a business consultant and mother, was asked to attend a meeting of an auxiliary which raises money for an organization that helps abused children. Before Missy agreed to attend she asked her friend to send her information about the charity and the auxiliary's financial budget. After poring over the information her friend sent her, which Missy found impressive, she agreed to attend the next meeting with

the knowledge that some of her energies would be devoted to participating in one of the group's fundraisers.

While attending the meeting the following month, Missy met other first-time members who were unaware of the auxiliary's track record and were simply there at the invitation of friends to meet other women. During the meeting, the charity's director shared some statistics on the number abused children taken in by the agency on a monthly basis. She continued her talk by including details of the direct impact of the money raised by the auxiliary on the children's lives. Murmurs among the prospective members after the meeting revealed that some of them were unaware of the group's three fund raising efforts and the requirement to work on at least one. Others talked of their shock on the number of children abused each year. Missy was not surprised by either of these concerns, but she did detect a sort of factionalization of the group in terms of interest in belonging.

Using the information from the chapter, explain why Missy's reaction differs with other first-time members.

8. Would Missy's schema for the organization apt to be more or less detailed than another business consultant whose mother had died from a long-term battle with breast cancer and who attended a similar membership drive for the American Cancer Society?

9. You are working on these exercises. What concept from "making information meaningful" in the chapter is best illustrated by your work on these exercises?

FEEDBACK FOR CLASSROOM EXERCISES

1. Each of the numbers is composed of seven digits. Working memory is capable of holding approximately seven bits of information.

2. Lecture is the simplest form of instruction, so it is less likely to overload teachers' working memories than are more sophisticated forms of instruction. The instructor only has to think about organizing and presenting the content, and the students are typically not disruptive. In addition to organizing and presenting the content, more sophisticated forms of instruction, such as guided discovery, require the teacher to ask questions, monitor students' answers and ask questions based on those answers, and look for inattention or disruptive behavior. These requirements can overload teachers' working memories.

3. Skills, such as questioning, must be automatic, so working memory space is available to monitor the students and the flow of the lesson.

4. They are demonstrating procedural knowledge. They are identifying conditions and taking actions based on the appropriateness of the conditions.

5. The concept is automaticity. You put the garage door down "without thinking about it."

6. These differences most closely relate to working memory. Interconnected schemas become large chunks of information that actually take up less working memory space than do isolated pieces, and automaticity also frees working memory space. Since experts are more effective at saving working memory space, they have working memory available for metacognition.

7. Because of her background knowledge, Missy's perception of the meeting's details was different from the perceptions of the other women.

8. Missy's schema would be more detailed about the abused children's charity than the other consultant. Her schema was based on her study. The other consultant's experiences weren't relevant to the organization.

9. These exercises are intended to put you in an active role in applying the information in the chapter to new situations.

CHAPTER 8: CONSTRUCTING KNOWLEDGE

CHAPTER OVERVIEW

This chapter includes a discussion of constructivism, including different interpretations of constructivism, characteristics common to most views of constructivism, and the suggestions for classroom practice that can be derived from constructivism. The chapter continues with an examination of the products of knowledge construction, including concepts, schemas, and conceptual change, and the role of assessment in constructivist classrooms. It concludes with a discussion of instructional applications of constructivist views of learning.

CHAPTER OBJECTIVES

- Describe the primary difference between cognitive and social constructivism, and identify examples of each in descriptions of learning activities.
- Identify characteristics and applications of constructivism in events in and outside of classrooms.
- Analyze applications of concept learning including teaching for conceptual change.
- Identify suggestions for classroom practice in descriptions of learning activities.
- Analyze applications of constructivist learning theory in classroom activities.

POWERPOINT SLIDES

PP 8.1 Some Conclusions from Kids
PP 8.2 Constructing Understanding About Movie Ratings
PP 8.3 Characteristics of Constructivism
PP 8.4 Principles of Cognitive Learning Theory
PP 8.5 Concepts from Educational Psychology
PP 8.6 Theories of Concept Learning
PP 8.7 First Learner's Network for the Concept Novel
PP 8.8 Second Learner's Network for the Concept Novel
PP. 8.9 Constructing Understanding of Balance Beams
PP 8.10 Suzanne's Thinking About Balance Beams
PP 8.11 The Persistence of Suzanne's Thinking About Balance Beams
PP 8.12 Assessing Understanding of Balance Beams
PP 8.13 Suggestions for Classroom Practice
PP 8.14 Praxis Practice: Feedback for Short-Answer Questions
PP 8.15 Feedback for Online Case Questions
PP 8.16 Classroom Exercises

VIDEOS

DVD 1, Episode 13: "Constructing Knowledge of Balance Beams."
This episode illustrates the thinking of fourth graders as they attempt to construct understanding of the principle that makes a beam balance. (This is the chapter's opening case study and it is integrated throughout the chapter.)

DVD 1, Episode 14: "Constructing Concepts: Using Concrete Examples"
This episode illustrates a middle school English teacher attempting to use concrete examples to teach the concept *concrete poem* and a middle school science teacher attempting to teach the concept *bilateral symmetry*.

CHAPTER OUTLINE

I. What is constructivism?
    A. Cognitive constructivism
    B. Social constructivism
        1. Sociocultural learning theory
        2. The classroom as a community of learners
        3. Cognitive apprenticeship
        4. Situated cognition
II. Characteristics of constructivism
    A. Learners construct knowledge that makes sense to them
    B. New learning depends on current understanding
    C. Social interaction facilitates learning
    D. Meaningful learning occurs within real-world tasks
III. Outcomes of knowledge construction
    A. Concepts
        1. Theories of concept learning
        2. Examples: The key to learning and teaching concepts
        3. Concept mapping: A learning strategy
    B. Schemas
    C. Misconceptions and conceptual change
        1. Misconceptions' resistance to change
        2. Teaching for conceptual change
IV. Implications of constructivism for teaching
    A. The teacher's role in constructivist classrooms
    B. Suggestions for classroom practice
        1. Provide a variety of examples and representations of content
        2. Connect content to the real world
        3. Treat verbal explanations skeptically
        4. Promote high levels of quality interactions
    C. Assessment and learning: The role of assessment in constructivist classrooms
    D. Putting constructivism into perspective
V. Constructivism in classrooms: Instructional principles
    A. Learning contexts: Knowledge construction in urban environments
        1. Need for examples
        2. Real-world connections
        3. Interaction

PRESENTATION OUTLINE

I. What is constructivism?
  A. Cognitive constructivism
  B. Social constructivism
    1. Sociocultural learning theory
    2. The classroom as a community of learners
    3. Cognitive apprenticeship
    4. Situated cognition
II. Characteristics of constructivism
  A. Learners construct knowledge that makes sense to them
  B. New learning depends on current understanding
  C. Social interaction facilitates learning
  D. Meaningful learning occurs within real-world tasks

Teaching Suggestions:

■ *The following suggestions are designed to help students understand the basic process of knowledge construction.*

1. **Begin your discussion by displaying PP 8.1 "*Some Conclusions from Kids.*" Beginning with PP 8.1 allows you to accomplish at least three goals:**
   a. **To remind the students that you're beginning your presentation with an attention getter.**
   b. **To show the students some examples that are attractive and funny.**
   c. **To illustrate the process of knowledge construction.**

2. **Then, display PP 8.2 "*Constructing Understanding About Movie Ratings.*" Point out that, obviously, the students who made these conclusions developed or "constructed" them on their own; they weren't presented by a teacher. (The examples in PP 8.1 come from 6th graders, and Andrew, in PP 8.2, was a seventh grader when he made the statement).**

3. **Display PP 8.3 "*Characteristics of Constructivism*" and ask students which of the characteristics they believe are best illustrated in PP 8.1 and PP 8.2.**

> Here would be a good point to show or discuss **Episode 13 on DVD 1**: "Constructing Knowledge of Balance Beams."

4. **After showing the episode, ask the students how Suzanne (the little dark-haired girl) arrived at the conclusion that the number of tiles was all that was needed to make the beam balance.**

5. **Display PP. 8.4 "*Principles of Cognitive Learning Theory*". (This is the same as PP 7.2, which you first displayed in your discussiòn of Chapter 7.) The students will conclude that she constructed the idea on her own, because it made sense to her.**

III. Outcomes of knowledge construction
  A. Concepts
    1. Theories of concept learning
    2. Examples: The key to learning and teaching concepts
    3. Concept mapping: A learning strategy
  B. Schemas
  C. Misconceptions and conceptual change
    1. Misconceptions' resistance to change
    2. Teaching for conceptual change

Teaching Suggestions:

■ ***The following suggestion is to introduce your students to concepts and concept learning.***

1. **Tell the students that what you're about to do may seem a little silly but to simply pay attention to what you're doing.**

2. **Walk over to the wall and push on it. Ask the students what you're doing. Prompt them to simply say that you're pushing on the wall. Then pull on the chalkboard tray, or a cabinet or some other object. Again prompt them to say that you're pulling. Ask them if they know what a push or a pull is called. Someone is likely to say "force." (If they don't, simply tell them that any push or pull is called a force.)**

3. **Now, have a student come and sit on a chair in front of the room, and pull the student and the chair across the front of the room.**

4. **Ask the class what you're doing and prompt them to say that you're exerting a force (pulling). Ask them what is different about the force you're exerting now and the force you exerted when you pulled on the chalkboard tray (or whatever you pulled on). Prompt them to say that movement was involved.**

5. **Ask them if they know what the combination of force and movement is called. (If they don't know, simply tell them "work".)**

6. **Point out that they constructed the concepts of *force* and *work* based on the examples you displayed (your demonstrations). Again, display PP. 8.4 "*Principles of Cognitive Learning Theory*." Point out that people—in their attempts to understand how the world works—form categories, which are concepts, so constructing concepts is one outcome of knowledge construction.**

Here would be a good point to show or discuss **Episode 14 on DVD 1**: "Constructing Concepts: Using Concrete Examples."

7. **Have the students respond to the questions in the DVD episode, and emphasize the importance of high-quality examples.**

8. **Display PP 8.5 "*Concepts from Educational Psychology*" for additional examples of concepts from educational psychology that they've studied to this point.**

9. **Display PP 8.6 "*Theories of Concept Learning*" and ask the students which theory of concept learning: rule-driven, prototype, or exemplar best explains how they learned the concepts force and work. Point out that the concepts have very well-defined characteristics, so rule-driven theories provide an effective explanation.**

10. **Have the students offer cases of concepts best explained by rule-driven, prototype, and exemplar theories. Have them explain why they chose the cases they did. Lead them to conclude that prototype and exemplar theories best explain concepts that don't have specific and well-defined characteristics.**

11. **Ask them how "easy" it was for them to learn the concepts force and work compared to concepts such as *square* and *socialism*. They will see that *force, work*, and *square* are all much easier to learn than is socialism. Ask them why. They should note that *force, work,* and *square* are easy to learn because they have only a few characteristics, and the characteristics are**

tangible or observable, whereas the concept *socialism* has abstract characteristics and there isn't universal agreement on what the characteristics are. Point out that prototype theories probably better explain how we learn socialism than do rule-driven theories.

12. **Ask the students how the ease of learning concepts relates to the developmental level of the students. They will see that kindergartners, for example, understand concepts, such as square, whereas concepts like socialism are rarely taught before the middle or junior high school years, and even then students' understandings of them are often uncertain.**

■ *To help the students understand concept mapping:*

1. **Display PP 8.7 "*First learner's network for the concept novel*" and PP 8.8 "*Second learner's network for the concept novel.*" Then, have them construct a concept map of content in their subject matter area or at their level.**

■ *To help students understand misconceptions and conceptual change:*

1. **Push again on the wall. Ask the students if you're doing any work. In spite of the activity you've just completed, a number of them are likely to say "yes." Ask them why they responded as they did.**

2. **Point out that this experience illustrates that many learners have misconceptions about the concepts they study. Remind the students about Suzanne's misconception about beam balances and the fact that she retained the misconception from the lesson and into the beginning of the interview in spite of hearing three correct explanations for the balance-beam principle.**

IV. Implications of constructivism for teaching
   A. The teacher's role in knowledge construction
   B. Suggestions for classroom practice
      1. Provide a variety of examples and representations of content
      2. Connect content to the real world
      3. Treat verbal explanations skeptically
      4. Promote high levels of interaction
   C. Assessment and learning: The role of assessment in constructivist classrooms
   D. Putting constructivism in perspective

Teaching Suggestions:

■ *The suggestions in this section are designed to help students understand the implications of constructivist views of learning for teaching.*

1. **Refer the students again to the DVD Episode After the students have seen the video segment, display PP 8.9 "*Constructing Understanding of Balance Beams*," and have the students respond to the questions. Discuss their responses.**

2. **As you discuss their responses, display PP 8.10 "*Suzanne's Thinking About Balance Beams*," and PP 8.11 "*The Persistence of Suzanne's Thinking About Balance Beams.*" They concretely illustrate Suzanne's thinking during the lesson and interview.**

3. **Display PP 8.12 "*Assessing Understanding of Balance Beams.*" It illustrates how understand of the balance beam principle could be systematically assessed. Emphasize that, since learners construct their own knowledge, learners constructions are likely to vary, so assessment is essential.**

4. **Display PP 8.13 "*Suggestions for Classroom Practice.*" Link each of the suggestions back to the DVD episode and the students' thinking.**

5. **Also point out that conceptual change only occurred for Suzanne when her thinking was directly confronted and was found to be invalid (The group tried her solution and the beam didn't balance.)**

■ ***To help students understand the limitations of constructivism:***

1. **Point out that while evidence overwhelmingly indicates that learners do indeed construct knowledge, not all forms of understanding are equally good, and a reality independent of individual understanding exists. If this weren't true, teachers would have little role in education.**

2. **Also point out that the fact that learners construct their own knowledge makes the teacher's job more difficult, not easier. As they saw with the DVD episode with the balance beams, simply explaining often doesn't work very well, which makes guiding learners' understanding more demanding and sophisticated.**

3. **Also note that constructivism, as with all theories, has limitations. Aspects of learning exist that are better explained with behaviorism, social cognitive theory, and information processing. This is the reason a variety of theories are presented.**

V. Constructivism in classrooms: Instructional principles
   A. Learning contexts: Knowledge construction in urban environments
      1. Need for examples
      2. Real-world connections
      3. Interaction

Teaching Suggestions:

■ ***The following activities are designed to help students further understand classroom applications of constructivism and the process of knowledge construction in urban environments.***

1. **Again display PP 8.13 "*Suggestions for Classroom Practice*" and have the students identify each of the suggestions in Judy Nelson's lesson (beginning on page 254 of the chapter).**

2. **Refer again to the DVD episodes, and point out how important high-quality examples, real-world connections, and interaction are for all students and particularly for students in urban environments.**

■ ***To summarize the chapter:***

1. **Point out the applications of constructivism that are being employed in your class. Some examples of applications could be:**
   - **You do a considerable amount of groupwork followed by discussion of the groups' findings. This is an application of social interaction as a factor that facilitates learning.**
   - **As the students discuss the topics, complete the exercises, take quizzes, and receive feedback, they are in the process of constructing understanding.**
   - **You are making an effort to link each topic to topics that you have already studied. This capitalizes on the role of background knowledge in learning.**
   - **You link the topics you study to classrooms through the case studies, video episodes, applications, and examples. Since classroom application is a major theme of the class, these are authentic learning tasks.**

2. **Point out that you are attempting to use your class as a model of instruction based on constructivist views of learning.**

ENRICHMENT MATERIALS

TEACHER PREP WEBSITE

The *Teacher Prep* website an online resource for students and instructors. Both you and students can access the *Teacher Prep* website by going to http://www.prenhall.com/teacherprep. Enter your user name and password and click on "Log In." The *Teacher Prep* website includes video episodes, student and teacher artifacts, teacher and research resources, and information about licensing and beginning a teaching career. The *Teacher Prep* website is described in detail in the Media Guide.

The following articles is recommended by the *Exploring Further* section titled "Assessing Constructivism in Classrooms" on page 237 of the chapter.

Once into the *Teacher Prep* website access the articles by completing the following steps:

1. Click on "Research Resources" on the left panel of the screen, scroll down the middle of the page and again click on "Research Resources."
2. Go to "Classroom Processes" and click on "Instructional Methods."
3. Click on the following article:
   Caution: Constructivism Ahead, by J. H. Holloway (1999) Ref. No. 2280.

This article provides an evenhanded analysis of "constructivist" approaches to instruction, neither wholeheartedly endorsing, nor severely criticizing, these approaches.

The following article are recommended by the *Exploring Further* section titled "Analyzing Authentic Instruction" on page 241 of the chapter.

Once into the *Teacher Prep* website access the articles by completing the following steps:

1. Click on "Research Resources" on the left panel of the screen, scroll down the middle of the page and again click on "Research Resources."
2. Go to "Classroom Processes" and click on "Instructional Methods."
3. Click on the following article:
   Five Standards for Authentic Instruction, by F. M. Newmann and G. G. Wehlage (1993), Ref. No. 2282

This article specifies and details standards the authors believe must be met in order for instruction to be validly described as "authentic."

ADDITIONAL EXPLORING FURTHER SUGGESTIONS

Page 256 of the chapter suggests that students to go the *Exploring Further* module of Chapter 8 for an examination of "Classroom Discussions" as an application of constructivist views of learning.

Page 257 of the chapter suggests that students to go the *Exploring Further* module of Chapter 8 to see the rest of the teacher's examples as she attempted to personalize the content for her urban students.

DISCUSSION STARTERS

You may choose to have your students discuss one or more of the following questions to further enrich their understanding of your learning activities.

1. What are some important similarities and differences between information processing and constructivism?

2. If teachers lecture, do learners still construct their own understanding? Why or why not?

3. If teachers are basing their instruction on constructivist views of learning, will they have their students practice basic skills to automaticity? Why or why not?

4. Some educational psychologists suggest that constructivism is more a principle than a theory. Explain why you either agree or disagree with that assertion.

5. Do teachers have a more important or a less important role when conducting learner-centered instruction than when conducting teacher-centered instruction?

6. Is assessment a more or less important for learner-centered instruction compared to teacher-centered instruction?

7. Teachers often have goals for which real-world applications are not immediately apparent. If they are basing their instruction on constructivist views of learning, should they avoid teaching those topics? Why or why not?

8. To what extent to learners' beliefs influence their constructions of understanding? Explain.

BACKGROUND READINGS

Abed-El-Khalick, F., & Akerson, V. L. (2004). Learning as conceptual change: Factors mediating the development of preservice elementary teachers' views of nature of science. *Science Education, 88,* 785–810.
This article illustrates the process of conceptual change in preservice teachers.

Bransford, J., Brown, A., & Cocking, R. (Eds.). (2000). *How people learn: Brain, mind, experience, and school.* Washington, DC: National Academy Press.
This comprehensive book discusses the implications that constructivist views of learning have for planning, instruction, and assessment.

Bransford, J., Darling-Hammond, L., & LePage, P. (2005). Introduction. In L. Darling-Hammond & J. Bransford (Eds.), *Preparing teachers for a changing world: What teachers should learn and be able to do* (pp. 1–39). San Francisco: Jossey-Bass/Wiley.
This book, by prominent authors, links the process of knowledge construction to teacher preparation.

Bruning, R., Schraw, G., Norby, M., & Ronning, R. (2004). *Cognitive psychology and instruction* (4th ed.). Upper Saddle River, NJ: Prentice Hall.
This book provides in-depth coverage of information processing and constructivism. Separate chapters discuss memory, encoding, and retrieval, as well as cognitive frameworks for reading, writing, math, and science.

Cassady, J. (1999, April). *The effects of examples as elaboration in text on memory and learning.* Paper presented at the annual meeting of the American Educational Research Association, Montreal.
This paper describes the role of examples in the process of knowledge construction.

Donovan, M. S., & Bransford, J. D. (2005). Introduction. In M. S. Donovan, & J. D. Bransford (Eds.), *How students learn: Science in the classroom* (pp. 1–26). Washington, DC: National Academies Press.
This book provides a comprehensive look at the process of knowledge construction in science classrooms.

Ferrari, M., & Elik, N. (2003). Influences on intentional conceptual change. In G. M. Sinatra & P. R. Pintrich (Eds.), *Intentional conceptual change* (pp. 21–54). Mahwah, NJ: Erlbaum.
This chapter discusses the process of conceptual change in detail.

Greeno, J., Collins, A., & Resnick, L. (1996). Cognition and learning. In D. Berliner & R. Calfee (Eds.), *Handbook of Educational Psychology* (pp. 15–46). New York: Macmillan.
This chapter examines learning, motivation and transfer from behaviorist, cognitive, and situative/sociohistoric views. It includes discussions of assessment and creating classroom environments that facilitate learning.

Mayer, R. (2002). *The promise of educational psychology, Volume II: Teaching for meaningful learning.* Upper Saddle River, NJ: Prentice Hall.
This book by a well-known author discusses a variety of topics including applications of constructivist views of learning, such as guided discovery.

Shepard, L. (2001). The role of classroom assessment in teaching and learning. In V. Richardson (Ed.), *Handbook of research on learning* (4th ed., pp. 1066–1101). Washington, DC: American Educational Research Association.
This chapter provides a detailed discussion of the role of assessment in learning.

FEEDBACK

Developing as a Professional: Praxis Practice: Feedback for Short-Answer Questions

The feedback that appears here is for the short-answer questions that follow the case study on pages 259 and 260 of the text. The feedback is also available to students on the companion website.

1. Describe the extent to which the characteristics of constructivism were demonstrated in Scott's lesson.

The characteristics of constructivism were demonstrated in Scott's lesson quite clearly. For example, the characteristic, learners construct understanding that makes sense to them, was illustrated in the students' tendency to try and solve the problem by changing more than one variable at a time. Changing two—or even all three—variables made sense to the students.

The characteristic, new learning depends on current understanding, was also illustrated in the students' tendency the change more than one variable at a time. They knew that they had to manipulate the variables, but didn't have sufficient background experiences to help them understand that the variables had to be changed systematically, varying only one at a time.

The characteristic, social interaction facilitates learning, was demonstrated in at least two ways. First, Scott's questions helped them reconsider their procedures, and talking to each other provided different perspectives on ways to identify and isolate key variables.

The characteristic, meaningful learning occurs within real-world tasks, was perhaps the strongest aspect of Scott's lesson. By actually handling the equipment, students could see how the abstract variables they were considering related to the real world.

2. Scott's students held some misconceptions about controlling variables, failing to keep length constant, for example, as they changed the weight. How effectively did Scott teach for conceptual change in responding to this misconception? Explain.

When students said, "Mr. Sowell, we found out that the shorter it is and the heavier it is, the faster it goes," this indicated that they had changed both variables and revealed a misconception about controlling variables. Scott then asked which of the two variables was responsible for the change in the frequency.

When Wensley and Jonathan said simultaneously, "They both changed," Scott responded, "Think about that. You need to come up with a conclusion about length, about weight, and about angle-how each of them influences the frequency of your pendulum." This question challenged their thinking, but probably not directly enough to result in conceptual change. Scott later demonstrated and explained the need to control variables, but whether or not the explanation would have been effective for promoting conceptual change is uncertain, because we don't know about the results of his subsequent assessments.

3. Assess how effectively Scott implemented the "Suggestions for Classroom Practice" (see Figure 8.6).

We will consider these suggestions one at a time, starting with the strengths of the lesson.

The suggestion: "Promote high levels of interaction", was effectively accomplished through his groupwork, which allowed students to discuss the process in detail, as well as his strategic questions during the lesson.

A second suggestion: "Treat verbal explanations skeptically" was also effectively implemented. Scott didn't lecture about controlling variables; instead, he provided experiences and asked questions, guiding students in their knowledge construction.

The suggestion: "Connect content to the real world", was effectively implemented. The students had a real-world experience with controlling variables, and they also acquired real-world experience with working cooperatively and making decisions.

The suggestion: "Provide learners with a variety of examples and representations of content", was probably the least well demonstrated in the lesson. While Scott presented students with a concrete, hands-on problem, they likely will need a number of additional problems where they will be required to control variables in order to develop a deep understanding of the process.

The suggestion: "Make assessment an integral part of the teaching-learning process" was implemented informally. However, we have no evidence of formal assessment.

4. Assess the effectiveness of Scott's lesson for learners with diverse backgrounds.

Scott's lesson was quite effective for learners with diverse backgrounds. First, the group that was showcased in his lesson consisted of an Asian American, an African American, and two Caucasians, one a recent immigrant from Russia. Scott used groupwork for a part of his lesson, which is effective for students such as these. It provides opportunities for students from different backgrounds to learn to work together, and they learn that they are much more alike than they are different. The task required that they worked together to solve a common problem, and, as was evident in the videotaped episode from which the transcript was taken, the students worked together very cooperatively.

In addition, his task provided concrete experiences for the students, which is also effective for learners with backgrounds that are diverse.

Feedback for Online Case Book Questions

The feedback below is for the *Online Case Book* for Chapter 8 (referenced on page 254 of the chapter). Both you and the students can access the case study by going to www.prenhall.com/eggen, selecting Chapter 8, and clicking on *Online Case Book*.

You may choose to assign the online case as homework or you may want to discuss the case in class. Answers to these questions *do not* appear on the companion website, so students *do not* have access to the feedback.

Multiple-Choice Items

1. Of the following, student comments such as, "I don't get this 'division by zero is undefined.' I just don't understand what they mean by 'undefined'," and "Division is division. You divide, you get an answer. Everybody knows that. So, 'undefined' is . . . I don't get it," suggest that students are struggling with which of the following characteristics of constructivism?
   a. Learners construct knowledge that makes sense to them.
   b. New learning depends on current understanding.
   c. Social interaction facilitates learning.
   d. The most meaningful learning occurs in real world tasks.
   a. The students were attempting to construct knowledge about division by zero, and they were unable to do so.

2. Of the following, which principle for using constructivism as a guide for instruction is best illustrated by the table Sandy created on the chalkboard?
   a. Provide learners with a variety of examples and representations of content.
   b. Connect content to the real world.
   c. Treat verbal explanations skeptically.
   d. Promote high levels of interaction.
   e. Make assessment an integral part of the teaching-learning process.
   a. Sandy's table represented the increase in the product as 12 was divided by ever smaller numbers.

3. Look at the dialogue between Sandy and the students after the table on the chalkboard was completed. Of the following, which instructional principle for using constructivism as a guide for instruction is best illustrated by this dialogue?

a. Provide learners with a variety of examples and representations of content.
b. Connect content to the real world.
c. Treat verbal explanations skeptically.
d. Promote high levels of interaction.
e. Make assessment an integral part of the teaching-learning process.

d. After the table was prepared Sandy promoted the interaction that helped the students construct their understanding of the idea that division by zero must be undefined. She also was aware that verbal explanations are unlikely to work (choice c), but the social interaction was most evident in the case study.

Short-Answer Questions:

4. Which of the principles for using constructivism as a guide for instruction was *least* illustrated in the case study? Explain.

We saw no formal evidence that Sandy assessed the students' understanding of the idea that division by zero is undefined. The only evidence indicating that the students understood this abstract idea was Troy's comment, "That must be what 'undefined' is." (Admittedly, assessing students' understanding of an idea such as "division by zero is undefined" is very difficult.)

5. Provide an assessment of the extent to which Sandy applied the principles for using constructivism as a guide for instruction in her lesson.

The lesson was strongly grounded in constructivist views of learning. For example, Sandy provided a representation of the relationship between dividing by smaller and smaller numbers and the bigger and bigger products. Then, instead of trying to explain why division by zero was undefined, Sandy used social interaction to guide the students into constructing their own understanding by first having them divide 12 by a series of smaller and smaller numbers and looking for patterns in the results. While trying to understand that division by zero is undefined isn't technically a "real-world" task, understanding the idea is fundamental to understanding mathematics. So, each of the characteristics except, "Make assessment an integral part of the teaching-learning process," was illustrated in the lesson.

CLASSROOM EXERCISES

The classroom exercises that follow appear *only here* in the instructor's manual. Students do not have access to *either the questions or the answers.*

The purpose of keeping the exercises only in the instructor's manual is to allow you to use them as class discussion items, or for homework, if you should choose to do so.

Feedback for the exercises follows immediately.

1. Teachers commonly believe that children must memorize basic math facts, such as 7 x 8 = 56, and 9 x 6 = 54. Assume that the teachers' beliefs are valid. Which theory–information processing or constructivism–better explains this assertion? Explain.

2. You are in a class where the teacher lectures virtually all the time. Does this imply that you do not construct understanding of the ideas being presented? Explain why it does or does not.

3. What is meant by the term cognitive architecture? Where in our cognitive architectures is understanding constructed? Explain.

4. Tim, a fourth-grader, concludes that we're closer to the sun in the summer than we are in the winter. When asked to explain why he thinks so, he says, "When I stand close to the fireplace, I feel warm, and when I stand far away, I feel cooler." Which two characteristics of constructivism are illustrated by Tim's reasoning? Explain.

5. Offer one important reason why guided discovery is considered to be more nearly grounded in constructivist views of learning than is lecture. (Judy Nelson's lesson on page 254 of the chapter is an example of guided discovery.)

6. Which of the following least illustrates a learning activity based on constructivist views of learning? Describe what could be done to more nearly apply principles of instruction that guide teachers as they plan and conduct instruction based on constructivist views of learning.

a. Geography students use longitude and latitude to describe how to tell a friend to find a remote camping location in the mountains.

b. Math students look at manufacturing costs and the prices marked on a series of soap products to determine the percentage of profit.

c. Science students explain why a can of pork and beans explodes--if a hole isn't poked in the can--when placed in a campfire.

d. Language arts students rewrite a series of sentences, each of which contains grammatical errors.

Explain your thinking.

Use the following vignette for exercises 7 and 8.

Four teachers want their students to understand the rule saying that non-essential clauses in sentences are set off by commas.

Janet Reeve displays six sentences on the overhead, three of which contain essential clauses and three others that contain non-essential clauses. She points out the clauses, correctly punctuates them, and explains why they are punctuated in this way. She then gives the students several sentences for practice, directing them to correctly punctuate the clauses in the sentences.

Javier Sanchez presents a paragraph which contains three underlined essential clauses and three other underlined non-essential clauses, each punctuated correctly. The class discusses the common features of the underlined and italicized clauses, and, with Javier's guidance they arrive at a rule for punctuating essential and non-essential clauses. Javier then directs the students to write a paragraph containing at least three examples of essential clauses and three other examples of non-essential clauses, all punctuated correctly.

Steve Smith presents several sentences which contain essential clauses and other sentences that contain non-essential clauses. He directs the students to look for clauses in the sentences that have commas around them, and he guides them to conclude that the clauses set off by commas are not essential, whereas those that don't have commas around them are essential. He then gives the students some additional sentences to punctuate correctly.

Susan Welna presents a passage in which several examples of essential and non-essential clauses are embedded. She asks the students to describe the passages, and after they have made several observations, she punctuates the sentences properly, explaining the rule in the process.

7. Which teacher in the vignette most nearly based his or her learning activity on the principles of instruction that guide teachers as they plan and conduct instruction based on constructivist views of learning? Explain.

8. Which teacher in the vignette least nearly based his or her learning activity on the principles of instruction that guide teachers as they plan and conduct instruction based on constructivist views of learning? Explain.

FEEDBACK FOR CLASSROOM EXERCISES

1. Information processing better explains this assertion. The memorized facts are automatic, so they don't use working memory space. Constructivism doesn't address this issue.

2. It does not imply that you are not constructing understanding. However, constructing understanding on the basis of a lecture is more difficult than constructing understanding based on effective representations of content and social interaction.

3. Cognitive architecture refers to our information processing system–sensory memory, working memory, long-term memory, and the cognitive processes that move information from one memory store to another. The process of constructing understanding occurs in working memory, and it depends on our attention, perception, and existing background knowledge.

4. The characteristics "Learners construct understanding that makes sense to them" and "New learning depends on current understanding" are both illustrated in Tim's thinking. To him, it made sense that we're closer to the sun in summer, since he got warmer when he got closer to the fireplace. And, his experience with fireplaces was the background knowledge he used to construct his conclusion.

5. The primary reason guided discovery is views as more nearly grounded in constructivist views of learning is the emphasis on social interaction. The importance of social interaction is a characteristic of constructivism, and "Promote high levels of interaction" is one of the instructional principles that guide teachers in their attempts to base instruction on constructivism. In addition, as students describe their thinking during guided discovery lessons, teachers can informally assess their current levels of understanding, and assessment is an essential part of instruction based on constructivism.

6. Choice d least illustrates a learning activity based on constructivist views of learning. It is the least "real world" of the tasks. It could be more nearly based on constructivism if the grammatical errors were first embedded in the real-world context of a written passage instead of isolated sentences. Then, students could discuss the parts of the passage that were punctuated correctly and other parts that were not, so social interaction would be incorporated, and finally students should again write passages rather than isolated sentences.

7. Javier Sanchez most nearly based his learning activity on the principles of instruction that guide teachers as they plan and conduct instruction based on constructivist views of learning. First, Javier presented the rules in the context of a paragraph, which is more nearly connected to the real world than presenting the rules in isolated sentences. Second, he capitalized on social interaction by having the class discuss the common features of the underlined and italicized clauses, and, he further capitalized on social interaction by guiding the students to the rule for punctuating essential and non-essential clauses. Finally, he further connected his content to the real world by having the students write a paragraph containing at least three examples of essential clauses and three other examples of non-essential clauses, all punctuated correctly.

8. Janet Reeve least nearly based her learning activity on the principles of instruction that guide teachers as they plan and conduct instruction based on constructivist views of learning. First, Janet illustrated the rule in the form of sentences which is less connected to the real world than embedding the rule in the context of a passage would have been. Then, she did not capitalize on social interaction when she pointed out the clauses, correctly punctuated them, and explained why they were punctuated in this way. Finally, she again failed to connect her content to the real world by giving the students sentences for practice.

CHAPTER 9: COMPLEX COGNITIVE PROCESSES

CHAPTER OVERVIEW

Our analysis of cognitive learning continues in this chapter with a focus on complex cognitive processes. The chapter includes a discussion of problem solving, including a discussion of a well-defined and ill-defined problems, a general problem solving strategy, expert-novice differences in problem solving ability, and what teachers can do to help students become better problem solvers.

The second section of the chapter examines the strategic learner with emphasis on basic and complex study strategies, and the third examines critical thinking. The chapter closes with a discussion of transfer, including general and specific transfer, and factors that influence transfer of learning.

CHAPTER OBJECTIVES

- Identify examples of ill-defined and well-defined problems and describe the role of deliberate practice in solving them.
- Explain differences between effective and ineffective strategies in studying behaviors.
- Define critical thinking and identify its characteristics in classroom activities.
- Identify factors that influence transfer in examples of classroom activities.

POWERPOINT SLIDES

PP 9.1 Cases That Are and Are Not Problems
PP 9.2 A General Problem-Solving Model
PP 9.3 The Druggists' Problem
PP 9.4 Expert-Novice Differences in Problem-Solving Ability
PP 9.5 Principles of Instruction for Promoting Problem-Solving Ability
PP 9.6 Characteristics of Effective Strategy Users
PP 9.7 Utilizing SQ3R with This Text
PP 9.8 Principles of Instruction for Developing Strategic Learning
PP 9.9 Elements of Critical Thinking
PP 9.10 Principles of Instruction for Promoting Critical Thinking
PP 9.11 Factors Affecting the Transfer of Learning
PP 9.12 Praxis Practice: Feedback for Short-Answer Questions
PP 9.13 Feedback for Online Case Questions
PP 9.14 Classroom Exercises

VIDEOS

DVD 1, Episode 15: "Using a Problem-Solving Model: Finding Areas in Elementary Math."
This episode illustrates the thinking of fifth graders as they deal with the problem of how much carpeting they need to cover an irregularly shaped portion of their classroom. In the episode we see problem-solving processes illustrated concretely. (It is the opening case study of the chapter.)

DVD 2, Episode 16: "Guiding Students' Problem Solving: Graphing in Second Grade."
This video lesson illustrates a teacher attempting to use real-world experiences to help her second graders understand bar graphs. The lesson includes several applications at learning centers around the classroom.. (It is the closing case study of the chapter.)

CHAPTER OUTLINE

I. Problem solving
   A. Well-defined and ill-defined problems
   B. A problem solving model
      1. Identifying the problem
      2. Representing the problem
      3. Selecting a strategy
         a. Algorithms
         b. Heuristics
      4. Implementing the strategy
      5. Evaluating the results
   C. Expert-novice differences in problem-solving ability
      1. Developing expertise: The role of deliberate practice
   D. Helping learners become better problem solvers: Instructional principles
      1. Present problems in real-world contexts and take students' prior knowledge into account
      2. Capitalize on social interaction
      3. Provide scaffolding for novice problem solvers
         a. Analyzing worked examples
      4. Teach general problem-solving strategies
   F. Problem-based learning
II. The strategic learner
   A. Metacognition: The foundation of strategic learning
      1. Prior knowledge
      2. A repertoire of strategies
   B. Study strategies
      1. Note taking
      2. Using text signals
      3. Summarizing
      4. Elaborative questioning
      5. SQ3R
   C. Developing strategic learning in students: Instructional principles
III. Critical thinking
   A. The challenge of critical thinking
   B. Elements of critical thinking
      1. Component skills
      2. Domain-specific knowledge
      3. Metacognition
      4. Motivation
   C. Developing critical thinking: Instructional principles
IV. Transfer of learning
   A. General and specific transfer
   B. Factors affecting the transfer of learning
      1. Similarity between learning situations
      2. Depth of original understanding
      3. Learning context
      4. Quality and variety of examples and learning experiences
      5. Emphasis on metacognition

PRESENTATION OUTLINE

The suggested activities can be completed in small groups and discussed as a whole group, or they can be conducted as whole-class activities. We recommend that you promote as much discussion–both in small groups and with the whole class–as possible.

I. Problem solving
  A. Well-defined and ill-defined problems
  B. A problem solving model
    1. Identifying the problem
    2. Representing the problem
    3. Selecting a strategy
      a. Algorithms
      b. Heuristics
    4. Implementing the strategy
    5. Evaluating the results
  C. Expert-novice differences in problem-solving ability
    1. Developing expertise: The role of deliberate practice
  D. Helping learners become better problem solvers: Instructional principles
    1. Present problems in real-world contexts and take students' prior knowledge into account
    2. Capitalize on social interaction
    3. Provide scaffolding for novice problem solvers
      a. Analyzing worked examples
    4. Teach general problem-solving strategies
  F. Problem-based learning

Teaching Suggestions:

■ ***The suggestions in this section are designed is to help your students understand the characteristics of problem solving and what teachers can do to help learners become better problem solvers.***

Since **Episode 15 on DVD 1**: "Using a Problem-Solving Model: Finding Area in Elementary Math" is the opening case study of the chapter, you might want to introduce your study of problem solving with it. And, since the students got varying answers to the problem Laura Hunter presented, the episode generates a considerable amount of discussion.

1. After discussing the Laura Hunter lesson, continue the discussion of problem solving by displaying PP 9.1 "*Cases That Are and Are Not Problems*," which shows 6 brief incidents. Have the students identify the similarities and differences in the incidents.

2. Lead the students to conclude that examples 2, 3, 4, and 5 are problems, but that 1 and 6 are not problems. There is virtually no uncertainty about what to do about the flour, for example. You simply run to the store. The same is true for the situation in number 6. You simply write a check or go to an automated banking machine.

Examples 2 and 5 are well defined problems. The goal is clear (getting to your friends' house at the desired time, and getting Jerome to bring his book to class).

Examples 3 and 4 illustrate ill-defined problems. The goal isn't clear in either one, and no generally agreed upon strategy exists for moving toward a goal state.

3. **In discussing the problems point out that the line between well-defined and ill-defined problems can sometimes be blurred. (For example, wanting to know why Jerome consistently fails to bring his book to class is not well defined.) Also note that the existence of problems isn't cut and dried; they depend on the person and the situation. For instance, running out of flour might be a problem if it is late at night and the stores are closed, or the person is a guest from out of town and doesn't know there is a store nearby.**

■ *To help your students understand a general problem solving strategy:*

1. **Display PP 9.2 "*A General Problem-Solving Model.*" Tell the students to keep the general strategy in mind as you move through the steps in the process.**

2. **To illustrate this part of the problem solving process, again display PP 9.1 "*Cases That Are and Are Not Problems*" and focus on Example 3. Have the students identify the problem and report to the whole class. The "problems" they identify will vary, which will help them understand that identifying problems is often difficult.**

3. **To further illustrate the process of identifying problems as well as the role that domain-specific knowledge plays, display PP 9.3 "*The Druggists' Problem,*" and have the students identify the problem and suggest a solution. Even in this situation some of the students may have difficulty in identifying the problem, and many will lack the domain-specific knowledge in algebra needed to solve the problem.**

   Since some or your students might voice frustration, point out that their lack of experience in problem finding is the reason they have difficulty. Ask them how much experience they've had in identifying problems. Most will say very little, and acknowledging this factor should alleviate their frustration.

   The bottom of PP 9.3 "*The Druggist's Problem*" defines the problem and provides an equation that can be used to solve the problem.

■ *To help your students understand how problems can be represented and how algorithms and heuristics are used:*

1. **Represent the druggist's problem with a drawing of a beaker or graduated cylinder that illustrates the original 15% solution and another representing the 6% solution. Seeing the visual representation often helps learners work toward a solution.**

2. **The equation that appears at the bottom of PP 9.3 "*The Druggist's Problem*" is an algorithm. It is a standard way of solving percent mixture problems.**

3. **Ask the students to identify other examples of algorithms. Many exist, such as the algorithms for adding, subtracting, multiplying, and dividing numbers, simplifying algebraic expressions and many others.**

4. **Ask the students to what other form of content algorithms relate. (They are actually rules. The fact that they're arbitrary is illustrated by the fact that some children spontaneously create their own algorithms for addition and subtraction, for example.)**

■ *To help your students see how strategies are implemented and results are examined:*

1. **Have the students estimate the number of grams of the 6% solution that should be added to create the 10% solution. Ask them how many grams would seem to make sense. Do the same thing with Example 2 in PP 9.1 "*Cases That Are and Are Not Problems.*" Point out that estimating and then checking answers against the estimate is a powerful strategy for evaluating results in math.**

2. **Ask the students how they might evaluate the results in the case of an ill-defined problem, such as the curriculum evaluation problem in PP 9.1 or the problem with your old car (Example 4 in PP 9.1).**

■ *To help your students understand differences between experts and novices in their problem-solving abilities:*

1. **Display PP 9.4 "*Expert-Novice Differences in Problem-Solving Ability.*" Ask the students what theme they see illustrated in the descriptions of expert-novice differences.**

2. **The two most important factors are domain-specific knowledge and experience. You can point out that experts solve problems quickly, for example, because they've seen similar problems in the past, which allows them to use "Drawing Analogies" as a strategy. With experience they also acquire the disposition to evaluate their results, i.e., their metacognitive abilities improve. This discussion can then lead to the next section.**

3. **Pose the question, "How do learners acquire the domain-specific knowledge and experience needed to acquire expertise?" Deliberate practice is the primary way.**

4. **Point out that your approach to teaching the class is designed to provide them with the practice they need to acquire expertise. Offer examples of where you provide feedback, where you attempt to link what you're studying to topics you've already covered (to take existing knowledge into account), why you quiz frequently and discuss the results (to provide knowledge of results and feedback), and why you have them involved in the group problem-solving activities that you present.**

■ *To help your students understand how they can help learners become better problem solvers:*

1. **Display PP 9.5. "*Principles of Instruction for Promoting Problem-Solving Ability.*" Have them identify where Laura Hunter (in the case study on pages 271 and 272 of the chapter) applied each of the principles in her work with her students.**

2. **Point out that the "The Druggist's Problem" (PP 9.3) also illustrates the use of worked examples.**

3. **Point out that Laura Hunter's lessons are examples of problem-based learning.**

Here would be a good point to show or discuss **Episode 16 on DVD 2**: "Guiding Students' Problem Solving: Graphing in Second Grade."

II. The strategic learner
   A. Metacognition: The foundation of strategic learning
      1. Prior knowledge
      2. A repertoire of strategies
   B. Study strategies
      1. Note taking
      2. Using text signals
      3. Summarizing
      4. Elaborative questioning
      5. SQ3R
   C. Developing strategic learning in students: Instructional principles

Teaching Suggestions:

■ ***The suggestions in this section are designed to help your students understand the characteristics of effective strategy users.***

1. **Introduce this section by having the students identify as many strategies as they can think of that they use in their own study. Emphasize that the strategies they offer must be ones they actually use.**

2. **Have them describe differences in the strategies they use in class compared to the strategies they use when studying for tests and quizzes.**

3. **Ask them if they ever think about the strategies they use and how effective the strategies are. Ask them to describe specifically how they analyze the effectiveness of their strategies**

4. **Display PP 9.6 "*Characteristics of Effective Strategy Users*," and relate the information on it to what the students have reported.**

■ ***To help your students understand both basic study skills and sophisticated comprehension monitoring abilities:***

1. **Have the students again think about the strategies they use.**

2. **Relate effective and ineffective study skills to the concept of activity from Chapter 7. For example, many students highlight "passively," highlighting entire sections of the text and avoiding the decision about what is most important to highlight. Making a decision puts them in a more "active" role. Point out that even if they make an incorrect decision, the fact that they've thought about it will allow them to correct it based on class discussions or further reading. If they haven't thought about it however, they won't know. In any case, being active results in more meaningful learning.**

3. **Assign the students a section of the chapter (or another chapter), have them prepare some summaries of the sections and "self questions" related to the sections. (You might want the students to prepare the self questions and summaries on transparencies to allow them to be displayed.) Have some of the students display their results and discuss them with the class to identify the characteristics of effective self-questions and summaries.**

4. **Have the students work for a few minutes to identify the way this text capitalizes on SQ3R. Then display PP 9.7 "*Utilizing SQ3R with This Text*."**

5. **Display TM 9.8 "*Principles of Instruction for Developing Strategic Learning*." Have them identify where Donna Evans (in the case study on pages 281 and 282 of the chapter) applied each of the principles in her teaching.**

III. Critical thinking
   A. The challenge of critical thinking
   B. Elements of critical thinking
      1. Component skills
      2. Domain-specific knowledge
      3. Metacognition
      4. Motivation
   C. Developing critical thinking: Instructional principles

Teaching Suggestions:

■ ***The suggestions in this section are designed to help your students understand what "critical thinking" means and what teachers can do to promote it in their learners.***

1. **Display PP 9.9 "*Elements of Critical Thinking*," which identifies component skills, domain-specific knowledge, metacognition and motivation as the elements of thinking.**

2. **Have the class identify the component skills they used when you conducted the activity with identifying cases that are and are not problems, which was used to introduce the chapter.**

3. **Ask the students to identify other ways in which you've emphasized critical thinking in your instruction. Also, ask them what forms of metacognition you've promoted.**

4. **Ask the students to offer examples of *belief preservation* from their experiences in the real world. Ask them to also provide examples where people have not thought critically.**

5. **Display PP 9.10 "*Principles of Instruction for Promoting Critical Thinking*" and have the students identify one or more topics and describe how they might teach the topic to apply the principles. Have them present their ideas, and discuss the ideas with the class.**

IV. Transfer of learning
   A. General and specific transfer
   B. Factors affecting the transfer of learning
      1. Similarity between learning situations
      2. Depth of original understanding
      3. Learning context
      4. Quality and variety of examples and learning experiences
      5. Emphasis on metacognition

Teaching Suggestions:

■ ***The suggestions in this section of the chapter are designed to help your students understand what is meant by "transfer" and what can be done to promote it.***

1. **PP 9.11 "*Factors Affecting the Transfer of Learning*" identifies and illustrates the different factors affecting transfer. Begin this section by displaying PP 9.11 and then follow with the activities described in the sections below.**

2. **Point out that you are emphasizing *quality, variety,* and *context* more than the other factors, because they are the factors that teachers can most control.**

3. **Point out how you have attempted to capitalize on these factors in your teaching, and remind the students of the many examples that you use in your teaching. Some examples include:**
   - **PP 2.5 *An Example of Development in the Real World,* which illustrated Piaget's concepts in context.**
   - **PP 2.7 *An Example of Centering***
   - **PP 2.8 *An Example of Egocentrism***
   - **PP 2.9 *Measuring Thinking,* which illustrated preoperational, concrete operational, and formal operational tasks.**
   - **PP 2.10 *Preoperational Characteristics in Adults' Thinking,* which illustrated egocentrism and centering in adults.**

   You will be able to offer a variety of other examples from your teaching.

ENRICHMENT MATERIALS

TEACHER PREP WEBSITE

The *Teacher Prep* website an online resource for students and instructors. Both you and students can access the *Teacher Prep* website by going to http://www.prenhall.com/teacherprep. Enter your user name and password and click on "Log In." The *Teacher Prep* website includes video episodes, student and teacher artifacts, teacher and research resources, and information about licensing and beginning a teaching career. The *Teacher Prep* website is described in detail in the Media Guide.

The following articles are recommended by the *Exploring Further* section titled "Problem-Base Learning" on page 276 of the chapter.

Once into the *Teacher Prep* website access the articles by completing the following steps:
1. Click on "Research Resources" on the left panel of the screen, scroll down the middle of the page and again click on "Research Resources."
2. Go to "Classroom Processes" and click on "Instructional Methods."
3. Click on the following articles:
   Problem-Based Learning: As Authentic As It Gets, by W. Stepien and S. Gallagher (1993), Ref. No. 2288, and
   Problem Solved: How to Coach Cognition, by K. Krynock and L. Robb (1999), Ref. No. 2289.

These articles provide an overview and some examples of problem-based learning. The authors are strong advocates of the method, so they provide no critical review of the challenges involved in trying to implement it in classrooms. The articles do provide you with some additional information with respect to problem-based learning, which can give you some additional insights if you try to implement it in your classroom.

The following articles are recommended by the *Exploring Further* section titled "Teaching in Context" on page 289 of the chapter.

Once into the *Teacher Prep* website access the articles by completing the following steps:
1. Click on "Research Resources" on the left panel of the screen, scroll down the middle of the page and again click on "Research Resources."
2. Go to "Classroom Processes" and click on "Instructional Methods."
3. Click on the following article:
   Strategies for Mathematics: Teaching in Context, by M. Crawford and M Witte (1999), Ref. No. 2229

This article addresses the importance of context, experience, and application in promoting transfer of problem solving ability in math.

DISCUSSION STARTERS

You may choose to have your students discuss one or more of the following questions to further enrich their understanding of your learning activities.

1. Which of the different kinds of cognitive learning–concept learning, problem solving, or cognitive strategies–is most important for your content area or level? Least? Why?

2. There has been a long-time and on-going debate about the relative value of teaching students content, such as concepts, versus processes (e.g., study skills and critical thinking). Which should the schools emphasize more? Why? What do you predict will happen to this emphasis in the future?

3. How does the developmental level of the student (e.g., first grade versus high school) influence the answers to Question 2?

4. How will the increasing use of computers and technology in the future influence the answers to Question 2?

5. You are going to make a presentation to parents about your emphasis on transfer in your classroom. How would you explain and defend it from a research perspective? What strategies will you propose to use?

6. Some people have advocated placing greater emphasis on critical thinking through the introduction of a separate course on critical thinking. What advice do you have for them based upon the research in this chapter?

7. Much of the research and emphasis on problem solving has occurred in areas such as math where many of the problems are well defined. How might schools focus on problem solving using ill-defined problems to a greater extent than now typically occurs?

8. Research indicates that learners typically receive little formal instruction in the use of study strategies. Why is this the case? Are study strategies best taught within the context of a particular content area, such as history, or are they better taught "context-free?" Why do you think so?

BACKGROUND READINGS

Bruning, R., Schraw, G., Norby, M., & Ronning, R. (2004). *Cognitive psychology and instruction* (4th ed.). Upper Saddle River, NJ: Prentice Hall. This book devotes a chapter to an in-depth coverage of problem solving and critical thinking.

Gardner, H. (2000). *The disciplined mind: Beyond facts and standardized tests, the K–12 education that every child deserves.* New York: Penguin Books. Gardner describes how to translate current research on thinking into classroom practice.

Gaskill, P., & Murphy, P. K. (2004). Effects of a memory strategy on second-graders' performance and self-efficacy. *Contemporary Educational Psychology, 29*, 27–49. This article describes the influence of strategy instruction on the academic performance of young children.

Hofer, B. K., & Pintrich, P. R. (2002). *Personal epistemology: The psychology of beliefs about knowledge and knowing.* Mahwah, NJ: Erlbaum. This book describes the influence of personal epistemological beliefs on knowledge construction and their impact on critical thinking.

Mayer, R., & Wittrock, M. (1996). Problem-solving transfer. In D. Berliner, & R. Calfee (Eds.), *Handbook of educational psychology* (pp. 47–62). New York: Macmillan. This chapter provides an excellent overview of the issues involved in transfer of learning.

Schunk, D. (2004). *Learning theories: An educational perspective* (4th ed.). Upper Saddle River, NJ: Merrill/Prentice Hall. This book devotes a chapter each to problem solving and transfer.

Van Gelder, T. (2005). Teaching critical thinking: Some lessons from cognitive science. *College Teaching, 53*, 41–46. This article outlines many of the issues involved in attempting to help students become better critical thinkers.

FEEDBACK

Developing as a Professional: Praxis Practice: Feedback for Short-Answer Questions

The feedback that appears here is for the short-answer questions that follow the case study on pages 292 and 293 of the text. The feedback is also available to students on the companion website.

1. How effectively did Suzanne teach problem solving in her lesson? To what extent did she apply the instructional strategies for helping students become better problem solvers?

Suzanne did a generally good job of teaching problem solving with young children. She posed the situation and asked the children how they would solve the problem. In this way she provided some practice in identifying the problem and selecting a strategy for solving it. The learning-center work gave the students experience in applying their understanding of graphing to other problems.

Suzanne did a very good job of presenting her problem in a meaningful context, and she provided considerable scaffolding for the children who had difficulty with the process and the applications.

2. To what extent did Suzanne encourage critical thinking in her lesson? What could she have done to give students more practice in developing critical thinking abilities?

Suzanne did quite well at promoting critical thinking in her lesson. For example, she asked the students to make observations of the information in the graphs, and she asked the students to confirm their conclusions with observations (e.g., "How did you get that answer?" "Why is it not 24?").

She could have increased the emphasis on critical thinking by giving her students the chance to practice more of the basic processes. For instance, she might have posed questions, such as, "Suppose we went around the school and asked people what their favorite flavor of jelly bean is. What do you think they would say?" After the students predicted, she could ask them for the basis for their prediction (such as the information in their graph).

3. How effective would Suzanne's lesson have been for promoting transfer? What could Suzanne have done to increase the likelihood of transfer in her students?

Promoting transfer was one of the strengths of Suzanne's lesson. After she conducted the whole-group activity, she had the students work at a series of centers, each of which focused on gathering information and preparing bar graphs. In this way the students had a variety of high quality experiences, all of which were in realistic contexts.

Feedback for Online Case Book Questions

The feedback below is for the *Online Case Book* for Chapter 8 (references on page 274 of the chapter). Both you and the students can access the case study by going to www.prenhall.com/eggen, selecting Chapter 8, and clicking on *Online Case Book*.

You may choose to assign the online case as homework or you may want to discuss the case in class. Answers to these questions *do not* appear on the companion website, so students *do not* have access to the feedback.

Multiple-Choice Items

1. Of the following, which is the best description of the problems Vicki presented?
   a. All the problems Vicki presented were well defined.
   b. All the problems Vicki presented were ill defined.
   c. The problems in the first set were well defined, but the second problem (the one she divided into a trapezoid, rectangle, and triangle) was ill-defined.
   d. The problems were all well defined for someone with problem-solving expertise, but they were likely ill defined for Vicki's students.
   d. As you saw in the chapter, whether or not a problem is well defined is personal and contextual, meaning a problem that is well defined for one individual may be ill defined for another. Nancy not knowing the formula for the area of a triangle, and Jason's miscalculation are evidence that the problem was ill defined for Vicki's students.

2. Of the following instructional principles for helping students become better problem solvers, which did Vicki apply *most* effectively in her lesson?
   a. Present problems in real-world contexts, and take students' prior knowledge into account.
   b. Capitalize on social interaction.
   c. Provide scaffolding for novice problem solvers.
   d. Teach general problem-solving strategies.
   c. Vicki provided a considerable amount of scaffolding when she modeled a strategy for finding the area of an irregularly shaped figure, and she also guided the students in their efforts to solve the problem.

3. Of the following instructional principles for helping students become better problem solvers, which did Vicki apply *least* effectively in her lesson?
   a. Present problems in real-world contexts, and take students' prior knowledge into account.
   b. Capitalize on social interaction.
   c. Provide scaffolding for novice problem solvers.
   d. Teach general problem-solving strategies.
   a. In contrast with Laura Hunter, who attempted to teach her students to find the areas of irregularly shaped plane figures by finding the area of the carpeted portion of their classroom, Vicki presented her problems with no connection to anything in the real world.

Short-Answer Questions:

4. Using the instructional principles for helping students become better problem solvers as a basis, assess Vicki's lesson.

   Vicki applied some of the principles quite well, and others less well. She promoted a considerable amount of interaction in her lesson, and she did a good job of scaffolding the students' problem solving efforts. She didn't formally teach a general problem-solving strategy, but she offered a strategy for finding the areas of irregularly shaped plane figures. "Present problems in real-world contexts" is the principle she applied least effectively.

5. Assess the effectiveness of Vicki's lesson for promoting transfer.

   Providing a variety of high quality examples in context are the three factors influencing transfer that teachers can most control. (Learning context and quality and variety of examples are the factors.) Vicki provided adequate variety of examples. However, her examples were presented out of context, and having the students measure the figures in the homework assignment before finding the areas was likely somewhat problematic, since the students had no practice with measuring prior to the assignment. As a result they might get incorrect answers because of measuring errors and not because they didn't know how to solve the problems.

CLASSROOM EXERCISES

The classroom exercises that follow appear *only here* in the instructor's manual. Students do not have access to *either the questions or the answers.*

The purpose of keeping the exercises only in the instructor's manual is to allow you to use them as class discussion items, or for homework, if you should choose to do so.

Feedback for the exercises follows immediately.

1. Consider the following three examples:

- You're taking classes, and you live a considerable distance from campus. However, your car is about worn out, and you can't afford a new one, since you're going to school.
- You have been assigned to write a term paper for one of your classes. Your instructor has stated that you pick a topic that focuses on classroom applications of information processing theory and that you must include at least five references that support your applications.
- You and your significant other are planning to go to dinner, but about an hour before you're ready to go out s(he) falls asleep, since s(he) worked very late the previous night.

For each example, decide if it is or is not a problem, and if it is a problem, determine if it is well defined or ill defined. Explain in each case.

Use the following information for Items 2-5.

As you're studying the first section of this chapter, you say to yourself, "I'm not sure of the difference between a well-defined and an ill-defined problem. I'll try to write an answer to "Checking Your Understanding" question 1.1 to help me understand it better. . . . I'll look in the Student Study Guide too, to see if that will help."

2. What concept are you best demonstrating when you say to yourself, "I'm not sure of the difference between a well-defined and an ill-defined problem." Explain.

3. The concept that you're demonstrating when you say, "I'm not sure of the difference between a well-defined and an ill-defined problem," most relates to what theory of learning? Explain.

4. To what major section of the chapter—problem solving, the strategic learner, critical thinking, or transfer of learning–are your comments, "I'm not sure of the difference between a well-defined and an ill-defined problem. I'll try to write an answer to "Checking Your Understanding" question 1.1 to help me understand it better. . . . I'll look in the Student Study Guide too, to see if that will help" most closely related?

5. Your friend is also struggling with the idea, and she too wants to use "Checking Your Understanding 1.1 to help her, so she looks up the answer in Appendix B. Explain why your approach is better than hers.

6. Look at the following passage.

Jefferson, one rural **county** among several **counties**, has four schools—one high **school**, two elementary **schools**, and one middle **school**. Five of the **schools** are in Brookesville, the largest **city** in Jefferson county. **Schools** in the three **cities** nearest Brookesville are Brookesville's biggest rivals. The schools in all the **cities** hold an annual athletic and scholastic competition.

The two **women** advisors of the debate team and the **woman** who coached the softball team were proud of both the performance of the **students** from Big Tree High School and their appearance. (The school is named after a 600-year-old tree that stands prominently in a grove of oak trees near the school grounds.) One **student** took all-around honors, and four other students won medals. One **girl** and one **boy** were honored for their work in math, and two **boys** and two **girls** wrote exemplary essays. One essay was voted top of the competition. It described a **child** and how she helped several other **children** learn to cope with difficulty.

The students all looked the part of **ladies** and **gentlemen**. Each young **gentleman** wore a shirt and tie, and each young **lady** wore a dress or pant suit.

Explain why this passage is effective for promoting transfer of teaching the rules for forming plural nouns. Be very specific and refer directly to the passage in presenting your explanation.

7. On page 269 of the text, after the example with Holt and the boy, we say, "Situations like this are common in classrooms. Once students get an answer, they're satisfied, regardless of whether or not it makes sense." Is the tendency of students to accept any answer, regardless of whether or not it makes sense a well-defined or an ill-defined problem? Explain. Describe some steps that you might take to solve this problem. What heuristic is likely to be the most effective? Provide a rationale for your choice.

FEEDBACK FOR CLASSROOM EXERCISES

1. The first example is an ill-defined problem. Your goal isn't completely clear, and more than one acceptable strategy for reaching a solution exists. For instance, you might hope that your old car will remain serviceable for the remainder of the semester, you might try to arrange for another form of transportation, or a third or more possibilities might exist.

The second example is a well-defined problem. The requirements are clearly stated, and you merely need to meet the requirements.

The third example is not a problem. You can either let your partner sleep and skip dinner, or wake him or her up. You're not faced with a situation where you have a goal but lack an obvious way of achieving the goal.

2. You are demonstrating one characteristic of metacognition—knowing that you don't understand the idea.

3. Metacognition is an important part of information processing; it controls the cognitive processes to move information from one store to another.

4. Your comments most closely relate to the strategic learner. Writing an answer to a margin question and looking in the study guide are strategies designed to reach the goal of improved understanding.

5. By writing the answer, you put yourself in a more active role than does your friend.

6. The passage has high-quality examples in it. For instance, students don't have to know that "county" is singular, because it says "one rural county." Likewise, they don't have to know that "counties" is plural because it says "several counties." All the information the students need to understand the rules is in the passage.

The passage also has adequate variety. There are two different examples of each part of the rule in the passage.

The rules are embedded in the context of the passage.

The passage has all three—high-quality examples, adequate variety of examples, and context for examples.

7. This is an ill-defined problem. The problem is that learners tend to accept answers that make no sense, or they tend to not evaluate their solutions. The problem isn't as specific as, for example, finding the area of a room to determine how much carpet is necessary.

A means-ends analysis is likely to be the most effective heuristic. A series of subgoals could be identified, and efforts to reach each could be made in succession.

High levels of interaction will be the most effective teaching strategy.

CHAPTER 10: THEORIES OF MOTIVATION

CHAPTER OVERVIEW

This chapter begins by defining and comparing extrinsic and intrinsic motivation, which is followed by theoretical descriptions of motivation including an examination of behaviorist, cognitive and humanistic perspectives. The discussion then turns to specific theories of cognitive motivation, including expectancy x value theory, self-efficacy, goals, attribution theory and self-determination theory. The chapter closes with a discussion of affective factors in motivation, including self-worth theory, and arousal and anxiety. As students study this chapter, encourage them to think about their own motivation and factors that influence it.

CHAPTER OBJECTIVES

- Identify differences between extrinsic motivation, intrinsic motivation, and motivation to learn in classroom activities.
- Describe criticisms of behavioral views of motivation, and explain how rewards can be used to increase motivation to learn.
- Explain the basic premise of humanistic views of motivation and identify applications of humanistic motivation theory in classrooms.
- Describe the basic assumption on which cognitive motivation theories are based, and analyze applications of these theories in events in and outside of classrooms.
- Analyze applications of self-determination theory in classroom learning activities.
- Use self-worth theory and studies of arousal and anxiety to explain learner behavior.

POWERPOINT SLIDES

PP 10.1 Extrinsic and Intrinsic Motivation
PP 10.2 Theories of Motivation
PP 10.3 Principles of Instruction for Using Rewards in Classrooms
PP 10.4 An Illustration of Deficiency and Growth Needs
PP 10.5 Maslow's Hierarchy of Needs
PP 10.6 Principles of Instruction for Applying Humanistic Motivation Theory in Classrooms
PP 10.7 An Exercise in Cognitive Motivation
PP 10.8 Expectancy x value theory
PP 10.9 Factors Affecting Self-Efficacy
PP 10.10 The Influence of Self-Efficacy on Behavior and Cognition
PP 10.11 Goals, Motivation, and Achievement
PP 10.12 Effective and Ineffective Goals
PP 10.13 Analyzing Attributions and Self-Worth
PP 10.14 Principles of Instruction for Promoting Goals, Self-Efficacy and Positive Attributions in Students
PP 10.15 Psychological Needs According to Self-Determination Theory
PP 10.16 Teacher Behavior and Self-Determination
PP 10.17 Principles of Instruction for Developing Students' Self-Determination
PP 10.18 Motivation, Anxiety, and Performance
PP 10.19 Principles of Instruction for Accommodating Affective Factors in Motivation
PP 10.20 Praxis Practice: Feedback for Short-Answer Questions
PP 10.21 Feedback for Online Case Questions
PP 10.22 Classroom Exercises

VIDEO

DVD 2, Episode 17: "Applying Cognitive Motivation Theory: Writing Paragraphs in 5th Grade"
This episode illustrates two teachers attempting to begin their lesson with a demonstration that will attract students' attention.
This episode illustrates a 5th grade teacher involving her students in writing and evaluating paragraphs. In spite of having their paragraphs evaluated by their peers, the students are enthusiastic about displaying their work.

CHAPTER OUTLINE

I. What is motivation?
    A. Extrinsic and intrinsic motivation
    B. Motivation to learn
II. Behavioral views of motivation
    A. Using rewards in classrooms
    B. Criticisms of behavioral approaches to motivation
    C. Using rewards in classrooms: Instructional principles
III. Humanistic views of motivation
    A. Development of the whole person
        1. Maslow's hierarchy of needs
            a. Deficiency and growth needs
            b. Putting Maslow's work into perspective
        2. The need for positive regard: The work of Carl Rogers
    B. Humanistic views of motivation: Instructional principles
IV. Cognitive theories of motivation
    A. Expectancy x value theory
        1. Expectancy for success
        2. Factors influencing task value
            a. Intrinsic interest
            b. Importance
            c. Utility value
            d. Cost
    B. Self-efficacy: Beliefs about capability
        1. Factors influencing self-efficacy
        2. The influence of self-efficacy on motivation
        3. Developmental differences in self-efficacy
    C. Goals and goal orientation
        1. Learning and performance goals
        2. Goals and theories about the nature of intelligence
        3. Social goals
        4. Work-avoidance goals
        5. Goals, motivation, and achievement
        6. Using goals effectively
            a. Effective goal setting
            b. Goal monitoring
            c. Strategy use
            d. Metacognition
    D. Attribution theory
        1. Impact of attributions on learners
        2. Learned helplessness
        3. Attribution training
    E. Beliefs, goals, and attributions: Instructional principles
    F. Self-determination theory
        1. The need for competence
            a. Attributional statements
            b. Praise and criticism
            c. Emotional displays
            d. Offers of help
        2. The need for control
        3. The need for relatedness
    G. Assessment and learning: The role of assessment in self-determination
    H. Diversity in motivation to learn
    I. Developing students' self-determination: Instructional principles
V. Affective factors in motivation
    A. Self-worth theory
    B. Arousal and anxiety
    C. Accommodating affective factors in motivation: Instructional principles

PRESENTATION OUTLINE

The suggested activities can be completed in small groups and discussed as a whole group, or they can be conducted as whole-class activities. We encourage as much discussion–both in small groups and with the whole class–as possible.

I. What is motivation
   A. Extrinsic and intrinsic motivation
   B. Motivation to learn

Teaching Suggestions:

■ *The suggestions in this section are intended to help your students define motivation and understand the relationships between extrinsic and intrinsic motivation.*

1. **As an attention getter for this section ask students how many of them would study as hard as they now do if there were no tests, and if the class was ungraded. Many will admit that they study primarily for grades. Some will point out that potential employers focus heavily on grades.**

2. **Point out that studying for the purpose of getting high grades is extrinsic motivation; the studying is a means to an end–the end being the high grade.**

3. **Display PP 10.1 "*Extrinsic and Intrinsic Motivation*" and point out that extrinsic and intrinsic motivation are not mutually exclusive, and many learners display characteristics of both. (Some students will probably say that they study to both get high grades and understand the content.)**

4. **Emphasize that, as teachers, we are attempting to increase motivation to learn, and point out that intrinsic motivation often is not possible.**

II. Behavioral views of motivation
   A. Using rewards in classrooms
   B. Criticisms of behavioral approaches to motivation
   C. Using rewards in classrooms: Instructional principles

Teaching Suggestions:

■ *The suggestions in this section are intended to help your students understand behavioral approaches to motivation, together with some of the criticisms of this approach.*

1. **Display PP 10.2 "*Theories of Motivation*" and note that you will initially focus on behaviorist views of motivation.**

2. **Describe some of the common criticisms of behaviorist approaches to motivation.**

3. **Display PP 10.3 "*Principles of Instruction for Using Rewards in Classrooms.*" Have the students identify where Amanda Shah (in the case study on page 302 of the chapter) applied each of the principles in her teaching.**

   You might want to share some additional information with your students regarding the implementation of reinforcers to increase motivation. Stipek (2002) describes the "scarcity principle" which says, "anything available to all students is usually less desirable than something that only a few students can achieve" (p. 25). The fact that high grades are not available to all students, for example, is what makes them reinforcers for many students. For

students who don't have a history of high achievement, grades are ineffective reinforcers, and these are the students that most need to be motivated.

The scarcity principle is the basis for organizing exclusive clubs, sororities, fraternities, and other organizations or experiences which are unavailable to most people.
(The scarcity principle tends to not operate with young children in schools, however. They pay less attention to the tangible or symbolic reinforcement other children receive than do older students. As a result, common reinforcers affect young children's behavior more than they affect the behavior of older students.) [Source: Stipek, D. (2002). Motivation to learn (4th ed.). Needham Heights, MA: Allyn and Bacon.]

III. Humanistic views of motivation
- A. Development of the whole person
  1. Maslow's hierarchy of needs
     - a. Deficiency and growth needs
     - b. Putting Maslow's work into perspective
  2. The need for positive regard: The work of Carl Rogers
- B. Humanistic views of motivation: Instructional principles

Teaching Suggestions:

■ *To help students understand humanistic views of motivation:*

1. **Display PP 10.4 "*An Illustration of Deficiency and Growth Needs.*" Have the students answer the question and provide an explanation for their choice. Many students select Choice c, others will select Choice b, and a few will select Choice d. Have them give their reasons. Then share the information at the bottom of the slide.**

2. **Display PP 10.5 "*Maslow's Hierarchy of Needs*" as the students work.**

3. **Have the students identify several implications of Maslow's work for teachers. Require that they offer concrete examples in their implications. (You might also remind the students of the link between Maslow's work and humanistic views of motivation. The "whole person" is readily observable in Maslow's hierarchy.)**

4. **Display PP 10.6 "*Principles of Instruction for Applying Humanistic Motivation Theory in Classrooms.*" Have the students identify where Kathy Brewster (in the case study on page 305) applied each of the principles in her work with her students.**

IV. Cognitive theories of motivation
- A. Expectancy x value theory
  1. Expectancy for success
  2. Factors influencing task value
     - a. Intrinsic interest
     - b. Importance
     - c. Utility value
     - d. Cost
- B. Self-efficacy: Beliefs about capability
  1. Factors influencing self-efficacy
  2. The influence of self-efficacy on motivation
  3. Developmental differences in self-efficacy
- C. Goals and goal orientation
  1. Learning and performance goals
  2. Goals and theories about the nature of intelligence
  3. Social goals
  4. Work-avoidance goals
  5. Goals, motivation, and achievement

6. Using goals effectively
   a. Effective goal setting
   b. Goal monitoring
   c. Strategy use
   d. Metacognition

D. Attribution theory
   1. Impact of attributions on learners
   2. Learned helplessness
   3. Attribution training

E. Beliefs, goals, and attributions: Instructional principles

Teaching Suggestions:

■ ***The purpose of the suggestions in this section is to help students understand the basic assumptions in cognitive motivation theory.***

1. **Present the problem on PP 10.7 "*An Exercise in Cognitive Motivation*" to the students.**

2. **Have the students answer the question. Take a class poll to determine the number of students that think the water level will be higher, the number that think it will be lower, and the number that think it will be the same with the jar on the bottom as with the jar on the board. After several have offered their answers and their explanations for the answers, make a comment, such as the following, "Okay, very good everyone. Now, let's move on." Someone in the class is likely to ask, "Wait, what is the answer?" You can then explain that the reason you had them do the problem and not give them the answer was to illustrate that they would be dissatisfied with having done the problem and not know what the answer was. Then can point out that this illustrates people's intrinsic need to understand events and "how the world works." This is the basic premise of cognitive theories of motivation.**

   (The water level is lower with the jar in the water. While the jar is on the board it displaces 200 ml of water (its weight)(water weighs one gram for each milliliter), but when it is at the bottom of the tub it only displaces 40 ml of water (its volume), so the water level is lower.)

3. **Ask the students how they feel when they do a paper and don't get any feedback on it, take a quiz and don't discuss the results, and other examples. In each case the "need to know," is illustrated.**

■ ***To help students understand the characteristics of four cognitive theories of motivation–expectancy x value theory, self-efficacy, goal theory, and attribution theory:***

1. **Display PP 10.8 "*Expectancy x value theory.*" Have them offer additional examples of each of the factors influencing task value.**

   Emphasize that the reason you promote involvement, use real-world examples, and personalize the content for them is that they have all been identified as ways of increasing intrinsic interest, which is one of factors that increases task value according to expectancy x value theory.

2. **Display PP 10.9 "*Factors Affecting Self-Efficacy.*" then, display PP 10.10 "*The Influence of Self-Efficacy on Behavior and Cognition,*" and emphasize that your approach frequent assessment, detailed feedback, high-quality examples, and modeling–is intended to help them be successful on challenging tasks which will increase their self-efficacy.**

3. **Display PP 10.11 "*Goals, Motivation, and Achievement.*" Have the students give some additional examples of learning goals, performance-approach and performance-avoidance goals, and social goals.**

4. **Display PP 10.12 "*Effective and Ineffective Goals*" and have the students explain why each is effective or ineffective.**

5. **Display PP 10.13 "*Analyzing Attributions and Self-Worth.*" Have the students answer each of the questions. (Tell them that you will discuss Items 4 and 6 a little later.)**

6. **Display PP 10.14 "*Principles of Instruction for Promoting Goals, Self-Efficacy and Positive Attributions in Students.*" Have them identify where Kathy Brewster (in the case study on pages 318 and 319) applied each of the principles in her teaching.**

F. Self-determination theory
  1. The need for competence
    a. Attributional statements
    b. Praise and criticism
    c. Emotional displays
    d. Offers of help
  2. The need for control
  3. The need for relatedness

G. Assessment and learning: The role of assessment in self-determination

H. Diversity in motivation to learn

I. Developing students' self-determination: Instructional Principles

Teaching Suggestions:

■ ***The purpose in the following suggestions is to help students understand self-determination theory.***

1. **Display PP 10.15 "*Psychological Needs According to Self-Determination Theory.*" Explain that competence helps organisms survive in the world. Note also how stressed people become when they're out of control. Relate the need for competence and control to Piaget's concept of equilibrium.**

2. **Point out that you're treating self-determination theory apart from the other cognitive theories, because it has aspects of humanistic views of motivation in it. Ask the students to identify these aspects (the need for relatedness, which is similar to Maslow's need for belonging).**

3. **Display PP 10.16 "*Teacher Behavior and Self-Determination.*" Have the students explain how the teacher's behavior could detract from students' self-determination.**

4. **Display PP 10.17 "*Principles Of Instruction for Developing Students' Self-Determination.*" Have the students identify where Elaine Goodman (in the case study beginning on page 324) applied each of the principles in her teaching.**

Here would be a good point to show or discuss **Episode 17 on DVD 2**: "Applying Cognitive Motivation Theory: Writing Paragraphs in 5th Grade."

V. Affective factors in motivation
   A. Self-worth theory
   B. Arousal and anxiety
   C. Accommodating affective factors in motivation: Instructional principles

Teaching Suggestions:

■ *The purpose of these suggestions is to help students understand self-worth theory and the influence of emotional arousal on motivation.*

1. **Display PP 10.13 "*Analyzing Attributions and Self-Worth*" again. Focus on Billy's behavior and have the students look again at Items 4 and 6 and explain Billy's behavior based on self-worth theory.**

2. **Display PP 10.18 "*Motivation, Anxiety, and Performance.*" Have them decide if their performance is likely to increase, decrease, or remain unchanged in each of the three examples. (Feedback is provided at the bottom of the page.) Point out that this research has important implications for them as students. Since anxiety can increase performance on well-practiced tasks, the better they understand the content they're studying, the less likely anxiety will detract from their performance.**

3. **Display PP 10.19 "*Principles of Instruction for Accommodating Affective Factors in Motivation.*" Have the students go back to the case studies in the chapter and identify where the teachers applied each of the principles.**

ENRICHMENT MATERIALS

TEACHER PREP WEBSITE

The *Teacher Prep* website an online resource for students and instructors. Both you and students can access the *Teacher Prep* website by going to http://www.prenhall.com/teacherprep. Enter your user name and password and click on "Log In." The *Teacher Prep* website includes video episodes, student and teacher artifacts, teacher and research resources, and information about licensing and beginning a teaching career. The *Teacher Prep* website is described in detail in the Media Guide.

The following articles are recommended by the *Exploring Further* section titled "Applying Goal Theory with At-Risk Students" on page 316 of the chapter.

Once into the *Teacher Prep* website access the articles by completing the following steps:

1. Click on "Research Resources" on the left panel of the screen, scroll down the middle of the page and again click on "Research Resources."
2. Go to "Classroom Processes" and click on "Instructional Methods."
3. Click on the following article:
   Using Motivational Theory with At-Risk Children, by R. Callopy and T. Green (1995), Ref. No. 2294

This article describes one elementary school's efforts to create a learning-focused versus a performance focused environment and help students adopt learning goals instead of performance goals.

ADDITIONAL EXPLORING FURTHER SUGGESTIONS

Page 303 of the chapter suggests that students to go the *Exploring Further* module of Chapter 10 for a more detailed discussion of Freud's psychoanalytic theories.

Page 323 of the chapter suggests that students to go the *Exploring Further* module of Chapter 10 for a more detailed discussion of self-determination theory.

Page 218 of the chapter suggests that students to go the *Exploring Further* module of Chapter 7 for a discussion of levels of processing, an alternative view of meaningful encoding.

DISCUSSION STARTERS

You may choose to have your students discuss one or more of the following questions to further enrich their understanding of your learning activities.

1. How could motivation in the schools be improved through modifications in the present grading system? In attempting to answer this question use as many concepts from the chapter as possible.

2. Defend and justify one of these two polar positions: "Take care of learning and motivation takes care of itself," and "All learning begins with motivation."

3. Does our current emphasis on extrinsic motivation (e.g., grades, prizes, etc.) damage students' intrinsic motivation? If so, what concrete steps can teachers take to remedy the problem? If not, how could the use of these extrinsic motivators be made more effective?

4. Is competition good or bad for classroom motivation? What information from the chapter supports your conclusion?

5. A teacher is assigned to teach the same class but has high-ability, college-bound students in one and low-ability, poorly motivated students in the other. What specifically should the teacher do differently in the two classes?

6. How does the age and developmental level of students affect motivation in the classroom? Specifically, what would you do differently if you were teaching first graders versus high school students?

7. How do culture and SES influence motivation? What can teachers do to make this influence a positive one?

BACKGROUND READINGS

Brophy, J. (2004). *Motivating students to learn* (2nd ed.). Mahwah, NJ: Erlbaum. Boston: McGraw Hill.
This book explains motivation to learn and includes two chapters dealing with issues involved in the motivation of low achievers and students who are alienated from school.

Good, T., & Brophy, J. (2003). *Looking in classrooms* (9th ed.). Boston: Allyn & Bacon.
Good and Brophy include a chapter on motivation in this popular book that applies theories and concepts to classroom practice.

Graham, S., & Weiner, B. (1996). *Theories and principles of motivation.* In D. Berliner, & R. Calfee (Eds.), Handbook of educational psychology (pp. 63–84). New York: Macmillan.
This chapter provides a conceptual and historical perspective on theories of motivation.

Pintrich, P., & Schunk D. (2002). *Motivation in education: Theory, research, and applications* (2nd ed.) Upper Saddle River, NJ: Prentice Hall.
This book provides the most up-to-date, comprehensive, and applicable presentation of motivation presently available.

Ryan, R., & Deci, E. (2000). Intrinsic and extrinsic motivations: Classic definitions and new directions. *Contemporary Educational Psychology, 25*, 54–67.
This paper describes the complex relationships between extrinsic and intrinsic motivation and learner autonomy.

Stipek, D. (2002). *Motivation to learn* (4th ed.) Upper Saddle River, NJ: Prentice-Hall.
This readable book provides a reasonably comprehensive description of motivation.

FEEDBACK

Developing as a Professional: Praxis Practice: Feedback for Short-Answer Questions

The feedback that appears here is for the short-answer questions that follow the case study on page 332 of the text. The feedback is also available to students on the companion website.

1. With respect to humanistic views of motivation, assess the extent to which Damon helped students meet the deficiency needs and contribute to the growth needs in Maslow's hierarchy.

Damon's instruction was less than effective for meeting the needs described in Maslow's hierarchy. For example, his comment, ". . . so that doesn't make sense . . .," is not likely to make students feel safe in their attempts to answer. And, safety is preceded only by survival in Maslow's deficiency needs. Further, he lectured, and the content of his lecture was mostly a list of facts, which would not appeal to students' intellectual achievement needs.

2. With respect to expectancy x value theory, how effectively did Damon promote intrinsic interest in the topic?

Expectancy x value theory suggests that students are motivated to engage in an activity to the extent they expect to succeed in it times the value they place on the success. Intrinsic interest is one of the factors that increases task value. Personalizing content, using concrete examples, and promoting high levels of involvement increase intrinsic interest. In contrast with Kathy Brewster who personalized the topic with the "crusade" to prevent the school from eliminating extracurricular activities, Damon presented facts about the Crusades in a lecture. The lecture was delivered in the abstract, and the students were generally uninvolved. Further, his comment, "I know that learning dates and places isn't the most pleasant stuff, but you might as well get used to it because that's what history is about," would also be likely to detract from intrinsic interest.

3. Assess Damon's effectiveness in applying self-determination theory with his students.

Self-determination theory is grounded in the belief that learners have innate needs for competence, control (autonomy), and relatedness. Learners' needs for competence are met when they get evidence that their competence is increasing. Damon's comment to Clifton, "No, no, remember that Columbus sailed in 1492, which was before 1500, so that doesn't make sense," communicates that Clifton lacked competence. Also he praised Liora for her performance (identifying the correct date) but made no comment about her understanding, which also gave her no feedback about her competence.

Learners' perceptions of control are enhanced when the teacher promotes high levels of student participation in learning activities, emphasizing effort and de-emphasizing ability in promoting success, and using assessments that emphasize deep understanding of content. Damon primarily lectured, so student participation was low; he focused on ability with statements such as, "Let's give these sharp ones with the A's a run for their money;" and his assessments focused on factual information. Each detracts from students' self determination.

4. Assess Damon's effectiveness in accommodating students' needs to preserve feelings of self-worth.

According to self-worth theory, people try to preserve perceptions of high ability, because ability is so strongly valued in our society. By displaying the grades on the board, and making comments like, "Let's give these sharp ones with the A's a run for their money," he made demonstrations of ability a priority. In addition, his comment, "This wasn't that hard a test," would tend to detract even further from the self-worth of the students who didn't do well.

A more effective approach would be to de-emphasize students' performance, instead emphasizing and modeling effort attributions as Kathy Brewster did in her interactions with her students.

Feedback for Online Case Book Questions

The feedback below is for the *Online Case Book* for Chapter 7 (referenced on page 329 of the chapter). Both you and the students can access the case study by going to www.prenhall.com/eggen, selecting Chapter 10, and clicking on *Online Case Book.*

You may choose to assign the online case as homework or you may want to discuss the case in class. Answers to these questions *do not* appear on the companion website, so students *do not* have access to the feedback.

Multiple-Choice Questions

1. Based on research examining behaviorist approaches to motivation, which of the following is the best assessment of Mrs. Jones' approach to working with Adam?

   a. It is likely to increase Adam's motivation to learn because her system of giving tallies contributes to an orderly learning environment, and an orderly learning environment contributes to motivation.
   b. It is likely to decrease Adam's motivation to learn, since research indicates that behaviorist approaches to motivation are ineffective.
   c. It is likely to decrease Adam's motivation to learn, because research indicates that punishment or the threat of punishment always detracts from motivation to learn.
   d. It is likely to decrease Adam's motivation to learn, because research indicates that behaviorist approaches are most effective when students are praised for genuine accomplishment.
   d. Research indicates that rewards that reflect genuine accomplishment can increase motivation to learn. Mrs. Jones' system of giving tallies could create an orderly learning environment if they were given consistently. Her inconsistency would likely detract from Adam's equilibrium (choice a). Behaviorist approaches to motivation can be effective if rewards reflect genuine accomplishment, so choice b isn't a true statement. The use of punishment isn't effective but to say that the threat of punishment is always ineffective isn't a valid statement (choice c).

2. One of the instructional principles for applying humanistic views of motivation in classrooms as a basis says "Provide students with unconditional positive regard by separating their behaviors from their intrinsic worth." Of the following statements Mrs. Jones made, which is most inconsistent with this principle.

   a. "Adam, Sanchia just told me that you spit on her. . . . We don't behave that way."
   b. "We wonder about people who would spit on someone else."
   c. "You will be receiving a tally."
   d. "Sometimes you need to just shake it off. That's part of life. . . . Now, go back into the classroom."
   b. Saying "We wonder about people who would spit on someone else," implies a flaw in Adam as a human being, or with Adam's character. This runs counter to the notion of unconditional positive regard.

3. Using self-determination theory as a basis, which of the following is the best assessment of Adam's encounter with Mrs. Jones?

   a. It will enhance his feelings of competence since being able to "shake it off" will make him feel more competent.
   b. It will detract from his feelings of autonomy, since Mrs. Jones' inconsistency and arbitrariness in administering tallies would detract from Adam's sense of control over his environment.
   c. It will enhance his feelings of relatedness, since Mrs. Jones talked to him about the note, which indicated that she was taking a personal interest in him.
   d. It will detract from Adam's feelings of competence, since being accused of spitting without direct evidence will make Adam feel incompetent.
   b. A predictable environment contributes to feelings of autonomy and control. Arbitrariness detracts from those feelings.

Short-Answer Items

1. Assess Mrs. Jones' interactions with Adam based on humanistic views of motivation.

With respect to Maslow's hierarchy, Mrs. Jones' rather loud pronouncement, "Adam, Sanchia just told me that you spit on her. . . . We don't behave that way," is likely to detract from Adam's feelings of safety," and safety is only preceded by survival in Maslow's description of deficiency needs. In addition, the statement, "We wonder about people who would spit on someone else," does not demonstrate unconditional positive regard. Mrs. Jones' handling of the incident is not an effective application of humanistic views of motivation.

2. Assess Mrs. Jones' interactions with Adam based on the general principles of cognitive motivation theory.

People's needs to understand their experiences is at the heart of cognitive motivation theory. This need can be explained with Piaget's concept of equilibrium; people want the world to make sense to them.

Mrs. Jones' comment, "Well, that's the way it goes sometimes. . . . Sometimes you need to just shake it off. That's part of life," makes Adam's world seem arbitrary and capricious to him, which is disequilibrating. Had she seen this alleged incident herself and confirmed that Adam did indeed commit the act, the situation would have been completely different. It would have been predictable for him, and the consequence—getting a "tally"—would have been understandable.

CLASSROOM EXERCISES

The classroom exercises that follow appear *only here* in the instructor's manual. Students do not have access to *either the questions or the answers.*

The purpose of keeping the exercises only in the instructor's manual is to allow you to use them as class discussion items, or for homework, if you should choose to do so.

Feedback for the exercises follows immediately.

1. Humanistic thinkers were critical of the reductionist nature of behaviorism and psychoanalysis. Predict how humanistic thinkers would react to cognitive psychology, and particularly information processing.

2. Humanistic views of motivation emphasize the "whole person." Explain how the "whole person" is illustrated in Maslow's hierarchy.

3. Both White (1959) and Connell and Wellborn (1991) suggest that "competence" is a basic human need. Offer an explanation as to why competence might be a basic need. What concept from Piaget's work is closely related to the need for competence. Explain how the concept is related.

4. Two students are equally successful on a task, but the teacher praises only one of them. Suppose someone observes this happen. Which of the two students does the observer assume has higher ability?

5. Suppose two students fail, and one is criticized. Which of the two will the observer conclude has higher ability?

6. Suppose learners have an entity view of ability. Are they more likely to adopt learning goals or performance goals? Why would they be likely to have this goal orientation?

7. Do affective needs precede or follow intellectual needs? (Give an example of an affective need. Give an example of an intellectual need.) On what basis do you make your conclusion about which precedes the other? On what theoretical view of motivation are you basing your conclusion about which precedes the other?

8. Time is perhaps the most powerful indicator of caring that exists. Explain why giving someone else your time would be such an important indicator.

9. In the chapter we saw that teachers' expectations influence the amount of emotional support they provide, the effort they expend to promote learning and the demands they place on learners, their questioning, and the feedback and evaluations they provide (See Table 10.6 in this chapter). Research also indicates that expectations influence teachers' behaviors in terms of the: 1) attributional statements they make to students about their performance (the explanations teachers offer for success or failure), 2) the way they use praise and criticism, 3) their emotional displays, and 4) their offers of help. Describe the differences in the way a teacher would respond to a high expectation student compared to a low expectation student for each of these four areas.

10. What is the teacher trying to accomplish in the following incident?

I just want to remind you that we agreed to begin our presentations on genetics on Monday, so we need to sign up today. You all know what you have to do in your presentations. For those of you who chose to write a report on genetics instead, remember we discussed that your report must contain at least two common examples of genetic traits, one example of a trait that isn't genetic but is commonly thought to be, and one example in which scientists now think genetics may play a part but aren't sure. Your report is also due on Monday.

11. Consider the relationship between attributions and self-efficacy. Suppose a student is high in self-efficacy and fails at a task. How will her attributions compare to a student who is low in self-efficacy?

Now suppose the student is successful. How will her attributions compare to a low self-efficacy student who is also successful.

FEEDBACK FOR CLASSROOM EXERCISES

1. Advocates of humanistic views would argue that both behaviorists and cognitive theorists tend to dehumanize education in the sense that neither behaviorist techniques, such as programmed learning, nor cognitive approaches, such as discovery learning take into account how students feel about themselves or about learning, teachers, and schooling. The "human" side of learning isn't emphasized enough.

2. The physical person is illustrated in the first two levels, survival and safety. Safety is also often interpreted to mean emotional safety as well, so the emotional person is interpreted by some to be illustrated in the second level. The social person is illustrated through belonging, and the personal, emotional person is illustrated through self-esteem. The intellectual and aesthetic persons are illustrated in the growth needs, and the entire person is illustrated through self-actualization.

3. Increasing competence allows individuals to effectively adapt to the environment. The ability to adapt is a basic need. Effective adaptation keeps an individual at equilibrium. In fact, Piaget suggested that adaptation was the process learners used to arrive at and maintain equilibrium.

Competence motivation is closely related to Piaget's concept of equilibrium; as schemes develop, competence increases and equilibrium is easier to achieve and maintain.

4. The observer is likely to conclude that the one not praised has higher ability. Praise is usually associated with effort, so the one praised is assumed to have exerted the greater effort, and since effort and ability are viewed as inversely related, the observer is likely to conclude that the praised student is lower in ability.

5. It is likely that the one criticized will be assumed to have higher ability. Criticism is associated with lack of effort, so it is assumed that the one criticized didn't try as hard, and therefore must be higher in ability. If he or she wasn't higher in ability, the teacher wouldn't have criticized him or her.

6. They would be more likely to adopt performance goals. Performance goals, such as performing better than peers, allow them to demonstrate high ability. A person with an entity view of ability would be more likely than a person with an incremental view of ability to want to demonstrate high ability.

7. An example of an affective need would be to feel welcome in the class. An intellectual need would be to feel like you understand proofs in geometry, for example. Maslow' hierarchy would suggest that affective needs precede intellectual needs. This is based on humanistic views of motivation.

8. The most significant aspect of time is that we all have the same amount of it. This being the case, it communicates that the person is important enough to allocate time to. If people had different amounts of time, giving time would be less significant.

9. Teachers tend to make statements that attribute success to high ability and failure to lack of effort for high- expectation learners, whereas they tend to attribute failure to lack of ability for low-expectation learners. They tend to praise low-expectation learners more for success than they do high-expectation learners, particularly on easy tasks. They tend to criticize high-expectation learners more for failure. They tend to express sympathy to low expectation learners and anger to high-expectation learners, particularly when they perceive high expectation learners as not exerting effort. They tend to offer low-expectation learners help more readily than high-expectation learners.

10. The teacher is likely attempting to address learners' needs for autonomy.

11. High self-efficacy students tend to attribute failure to lack of effort or use of ineffective strategies, whereas students low in self-efficacy tend to attribute failure to lack of ability (Bruning et al., 1999). High self-efficacy students tend to attribute success to effort and ability, whereas low self-efficacy students tend to attribute success to luck, task difficulty, or other external factors.

CHAPTER 11: MOTIVATION IN THE CLASSROOM

CHAPTER OVERVIEW

This chapter presents a model that applies the theories of motivation presented in Chapter 10. The chapter begins with a discussion of learning-focused compared to performance-focused classrooms. It then describes strategies for promoting learner self-regulation. The chapter continues with discussions of teacher characteristics and classroom climate variables that increase learner motivation, and it closes with a discussion of instructional factors that enhance motivation to learn.

CHAPTER OBJECTIVES

- Explain the differences between a learning-focused and a performance-focused classroom.
- Describe strategies that can be used to develop learner self regulation and explain different levels of student self-regulation.
- Identify the personal characteristics of teachers who increase students' motivation to learn, and analyze these characteristics in classroom activities.
- Analyze teachers' behaviors using the climate variables as a basis, and describe the relationships between the climate variables and the categories in the TARGET model.
- Identify examples of teachers implementing the instructional variables in learning activities.

POWERPOINT SLIDES

PP 11.1 Comparisons of Learning-Focused and Performance-Focused Classrooms
PP 11.2 A Model for Promoting Learner Motivation
PP 11.3 An Application of Self-Regulation
PP 11.4 Instructional Principles for Increasing Learner Self-Regulation
PP 11.5 Demonstrating Personal Qualities That Increase Learner Motivation
PP 11.6 Characteristics of Caring Teachers
PP 11.7 Applying the Model For Promoting Student Motivation
PP 11.8 Answers for Applying the Model
PP 11.9 Principles of Instruction for Applying Climate and Instructional Variables in Your Classroom
PP 11.10 Praxis Practice: Feedback for Short-Answer Questions
PP 11.11 Feedback for Online Case Questions
PP 11.12 Classroom Exercises

VIDEO

DVD 2, Episode 18: **DVD 2**: "Studying Arthropods in the Fifth Grade."
The episode illustrates a teacher, DeVonne Lampkin, attempting to increase her students' interest by using real-world examples to study the concept *arthropods*.

This video is also the chapter opening case study.

CHAPTER OUTLINE

I. Class structure: Creating a learning-focused environment
II. Self-regulated learners: Developing student responsibility
   A. Developing self-regulation: Applying Self-Determination Theory
   B. Helping students develop self-regulation: Instructional principles
III. Teacher characteristics: Personal qualities that increase student motivation to learn
   A. Personal teaching efficacy: Beliefs about teaching and learning
   B. Modeling and enthusiasm: Communicating genuine interest
   C. Caring: Meeting the need for belonging and relatedness
      1. Communicating caring
   D. Teacher expectations: Increasing perceptions of competence
   E. Demonstrating personal qualities that increase motivation: Instructional principles
IV. Climate variables: Creating a motivating environment
   A. Order and safety: Classrooms as secure places to learn
   B. Success: Developing learner self-efficacy
   C. Challenge: Increasing perceptions of competence and self-determination
   D. Task Comprehension: Increasing perceptions of autonomy and value
   E. The TARGET Program: Applying goal theory in classrooms
V. Instructional variables: Developing interest in learning activities
   A. Introductory focus: Attracting students' attention
   B. Personalization: Links to students' lives
   C. Involvement: Increasing intrinsic motivation
      1. Using open-ended questioning to increase involvement
      2. Using hands-on activities to promote involvement
   D. Feedback: Meeting the need to understand
   E. Applying the climate and instructional variables in your classroom: Instructional principles
   F. Assessment and learning: Using feedback to increase interest and self-efficacy
   G. Learning Contexts: Motivation to learn in the urban classroom
      1. The impact of teachers
         a. Caring
         b. Order and safety
         c. Involvement
         d. Challenge

PRESENTATION OUTLINE

The suggested activities can be completed in small groups and discussed as a whole group, or they can be conducted as whole-class activities. We encourage as much discussion–both in small groups and with the whole class–as possible.

I. Class structure: Creating a learning-focused environment

Teaching Suggestions:

■ *The suggestions in this section are designed to help your students understand the differences between a learning-focused and performance-focused classroom, as well as the variables in the Model for Promoting Student Motivation.*

1. **To introduce the section display PP 11.1 "*Comparisons of Learning-Focused and Performance-Focused Classrooms.*" PP 11.1 outlines the characteristics that differentiate the two types of classrooms. Have the students identify some things teachers can do to promote a learning-focused versus a performance-focused classroom. Require that students offer specific and concrete suggestions.**

2. **Point out the reasons for some of your practices, such as:**
   - **Emphasizing that the focus in the course is learning.**
   - **De-emphasizing grades by putting their quiz scores on the last page of their quizzes instead of on the front page.**
   - **Telling them to not share their scores with each other.**
   - **Modeling an incremental view of ability**
   - **Avoiding any comparisons of student performance, such as displaying grades or arrays of scores on quizzes.**

3. **Display PP 11.2 "*A Model for Promoting Learner Motivation,*" which outlines the variables in the Model for Promoting Motivation. Point out that is will be the framework for the study of the chapter.**

Since **Episode 18 on DVD 2**: "Studying Arthropods in the Fifth Grade," is the opening case study for this chapter, you might want to either show or discuss the lesson and the extent to which is was motivating for the students as an introduction to the chapter.

II. Self-regulated learners: Developing student responsibility
   A. Developing self-regulation: Applying Self-Determination Theory
   B. Helping students develop self-regulation: Instructional principles

Teaching Suggestions:

■ *The purpose of these suggestions is to help students understand how self-regulation can be developed in learners.*

1. **Display PP 11.3 "*An Application of Self-Regulation.*" Have the students identify the characteristics of self-regulated learners in the vignette.**

2. **Discuss the students' responses. The following are some possible conclusions.**
   i. **Selena demonstrates metacognition when she says, "But, all the quizzes are application. Just memorizing the definitions won't work."**
   ii. **Selena sets the goal of doing and understanding all the items on the practice quiz in the study guide, as well as those on the website.**

iii. Selena monitors progress toward her goal with her chart.
iv. Selena adapts her strategy; if she doesn't understand some of the items on the practice quizzes, she goes in a sees her instructor.

3. Display PP 11.4 "*Instructional Principles for Increasing Learner Self-Regulation.*" Have the students identify where Sam Cook (in the case study beginning on page 339) applied each of the principles in his teaching.

III. Teacher characteristics: Personal qualities that increase student motivation and learning
  A. Personal teaching efficacy: Beliefs about teaching and learning
  B. Modeling and enthusiasm: Communicating genuine interest
  C. Caring: Meeting the need for belonging and relatedness
    1. Communicating caring
  D. Teacher expectations: Increasing perceptions of competence
  E. Demonstrating personal qualities that increase motivation: Instructional principles

Teaching Suggestions:

■ *These suggestions are intended to help students understand teacher characteristics that promote motivation.*

1. Display PP 11.5 "*Demonstrating Personal Qualities That Increase Learner Motivation.*" Have the students identify where DeVonne Lampkin (in the case study beginning on page 346) demonstrated each of these qualities.

2. To emphasize the importance of caring, display PP 11.6 "*Characteristics of Caring Teachers.*" Further emphasize the relationship between caring, respect, and holding students to high standards. Refer the students to the quote at the bottom of page 344, for an additional source.

IV. Climate variables: Creating a motivating environment
  A. Order and safety: Classrooms as secure places to learn
  B. Success: Developing learner self-efficacy
  C. Challenge: Increasing perceptions of competence and self-determination
  D. Task Comprehension: Increasing perceptions of control and value
  E. The TARGET Program: Applying goal theory in classrooms

V. Instructional variables: Developing interest in learning activities
  A. Introductory focus: Attracting students' attention
  B. Personalization: Links to students' lives
  C. Involvement: Increasing intrinsic motivation
    1. Using open-ended questioning to increase involvement
    2. Using hands-on activities to promote involvement
  D. Feedback: Meeting the need to understand
  E. Applying the climate and instructional variables in your classroom: Instructional principles
  F. Assessment and learning: Using feedback to increase interest and self-efficacy
  G. Learning contexts: Motivation to learning in the urban classroom
    1. The impact of teachers
      a. Caring
      b. Order and safety
      c. Involvement
      d. Challenge

Teaching Suggestions:

■ ***The purpose in these suggestions is to help students understand how the climate and instructional variables can be applied in classrooms.***

1. **Display PP 11.7 "*Applying the Model For Promoting Student Motivation.*" Have the students identify the variable from the Model for Promoting Motivation for each implication and then circle the theory that best supports the implication and variable. PP 11.8 "*Answers for Applying the Model*" provides answers for the exercise.**

   The following provides some additional information for the items.
   1. **Page 309 of Chapter 10 describes the link between *involvement* and expectancy x value theory.**
   2. **Page 350 of Chapter 11 describes the relationship between *task attraction* and self-determination theory.**
   3. **Page 309 of Chapter 10 also describes the link between *personalization* expectancy x value theory.**
   4. **Page 348 of Chapter 11 describes the relationship between *order and safety* and humanistic views of motivation. (You might also note that order and safety increases perceptions of autonomy, which is a basic need according to self-determination theory.)**
   5. **Page 349 of this chapter describes the link between *safety* and self-efficacy.**
   6. **Page 357 of this chapter discusses the relationship between feedback and attribution theory.**
   7. **Page 311 of Chapter 10 discusses the influence of *modeling* on self-efficacy.**
   8. **Page 353 of the chapter points out that *introductory focus* attempts to capitalize on the motivating effects of curiosity and novelty, and page 321 of Chapter 10 describes the relationship between self-determination theory and the motivating effects of curiosity.**
   9. **Page 345 of this chapter describes the relationship between teacher expectations and self-determination theory. (You might also refer the students to the quote on page 344, which suggests that holding students to high standards is evidence of caring.)**

2. **Display PP 11.9 "*Principles of Instruction for Applying Climate and Instructional Variables in Your Classroom.*" Have the students identify where David Crawford (in the case study beginning on page 357) applied the principles in his work with his students.**

3. **Have the students discuss reasons why *Caring* , *Order and safety, Involvement,* and *Challenge* are so important in urban environments.**

4. **The Classroom Exercises for this chapter provide an additional opportunity for the students to apply the Model for Promoting Student Motivation in the context of a classroom case study.**

ENRICHMENT MATERIALS

TEACHER PREP WEBSITE

The *Teacher Prep* website an online resource for students and instructors. Both you and students can access the *Teacher Prep* website by going to http://www.prenhall.com/teacherprep. Enter your user name and password and click on "Log In." The *Teacher Prep* website includes video episodes, student and teacher artifacts, teacher and research resources, and information about licensing and beginning a teaching career. The *Teacher Prep* website is described in detail in the Media Guide.

The following article is recommended by the *Exploring Further* section titled "High-Stakes Testing and Student Motivation to Learn" on page 359 of the chapter.

Once into the *Teacher Prep* website access the articles by completing the following steps:
1. Click on "Research Resources" on the left panel of the screen, scroll down the middle of the page and again click on "Research Resources."
2. Go to "Classroom Processes" and click on "Assessment."
3. Click on the following article:
   The Effects of High-Stakes Testing on Student Motivation and Learning, by A. Amrein and D. Berliner (2003), Ref. No. 1725.

This research report begins with the questions: Do high-stakes testing policies lead to increased student motivation to learn? And do these policies lead to increased student learn? This article then provides a critical examination of the impact of high-stakes on students' motivation to learn, student dropout rates, and student learning.

The following article is recommended by the *Exploring Further* section titled "What Urban Students Say About Good Teaching" on page 361 of the chapter.

Once into the *Teacher Prep* website access the articles by completing the following steps:
1. Click on "Research Resources" on the left panel of the screen, scroll down the middle of the page and again click on "Research Resources."
2. Go to "Classroom Processes" and click on "Instructional Methods."
3. Click on the following article:
   What Urban Students Say About Good Teaching, by D. Corbett and B. Wilson (2002), Ref. No. 1667.

This article provides a detailed look at urban students' perceptions of good teachers in a variety of areas. It contains a number of quotes from students.

ADDITIONAL EXPLORING FURTHER SUGGESTIONS

Page 349 of the chapter suggests that students to go the *Exploring Further* module of Chapter 11 for a discussion of the American Psychological Association's learner-centered principles.

DISCUSSION STARTERS

You may choose to have your students discuss one or more of the following questions to further enrich their understanding of your learning activities.

1. Respond to the following assertion: "My job as a teacher is to plan to promote learning. Motivation is a student's responsibility."

2. Should teachers be held accountable for increasing the motivation of students who are alienated from school or are disinterested in school?

3. To what extent should motivation be part of teachers' planning?

4. Teachers are encouraged to promote self-regulation in students. Does this include allowing students to set their own learning goals?

5. Which is more important, intrinsic motivation, or motivation to learn? Why do you think so?

6. Is it possible to increase learner motivation in a performance-focused classroom? Why or why not?

7. Describe the characteristics of students for which a learning-focused classroom is most important.

BACKGROUND READINGS

Alder, N. (2002). Interpretations of the meaning of care: Creating caring relationship in urban middle school classrooms. *Urban Education, 37*(2), 241–266.
This article emphasizes the importance of caring in urban environments and what teachers can do to communicate that they care about their students.

Brophy, J. (2004). *Motivating students to learn* (2nd ed.). Mahwah, NJ: Erlbaum. Boston: McGraw Hill.
This book explains motivation to learn and includes two chapters dealing with issues involved in the motivation of low achievers and students who are alienated from school.

Bruning, R., Schraw, G., Norby, M., & Ronning, R. (2004). *Cognitive psychology and instruction* (4th ed.). Upper Saddle River, NJ: Prentice Hall.
This text provides additional information on personal teaching efficacy and self-regulation, as well as other topics related to motivation.

Good, T., & Brophy, J. (2003). *Looking in classrooms* (9th ed.). Boston: Allyn & Bacon.
Good and Brophy provide a detailed discussion of teacher expectations and their influence on learner motivation and behavior.

Pintrich, P., & Schunk D. (2002). *Motivation in education: Theory, research, and applications* (2nd ed.) Upper Saddle River, NJ: Prentice Hall.
This book provides the most up-to-date, comprehensive, and applicable presentation of motivation presently available.

Ryan, R., & Deci, E. (2000). Intrinsic and extrinsic motivations: Classic definitions and new directions. *Contemporary Educational Psychology, 25*, 54–67.
This paper describes the complex relationships between extrinsic and intrinsic motivation and learner autonomy.

Stipek, D. (1996). Motivation and instruction. In D. Berliner, & R. Calfee (Eds.), *Handbook of educational psychology* (pp. 85–113). New York: Macmillan.
This chapter provides information about classroom applications of motivation theory.

Stipek, D. (2002). *Motivation to learn* (4th ed.) Upper Saddle River, NJ: Prentice-Hall.
This readable book presents a reasonably comprehensive look at motivation.

FEEDBACK

Developing as a Professional: Praxis Practice: Feedback for Short-Answer Questions

The feedback that appears here is for the short-answer questions that follow the case study on pages 363 and 364 of the text. The feedback is also available to students on the companion website.

1. Feelings of safety are essential for student motivation to learn. Assess the extent to which DeVonne's students felt safe in her classroom.

It appears that DeVonne's students felt very safe in her class. This conclusion is based on the fact that they knew that their paragraphs were going to be openly evaluated by their peers, yet they were eager to have them displayed, as indicated by comments like "I want to go next! I want to go next!" and "Are we going to get to do ours tomorrow?" Further, they were eager to have their paragraphs displayed and evaluated in spite of the fact that Justin was given a fairly low rating on his paragraph.

2. Assess DeVonne's application of the instructional variables in her classroom.

DeVonne provided introductory focus by saying that they were going to practice composing good paragraphs and reviewing the characteristics of paragraphs that were well-written. Her introductory focus was enhanced with her example with computers and television displayed on the overhead. She personalized the task by emphasizing that their paragraphs could be about any topic. The students were actively involved as they constructed their paragraphs and when they assessed those that were displayed. The assessments provided feedback for both the student whose paragraph was being displayed and the class as a whole. Each of the instructional variables was demonstrated in the lesson.

3. In spite of the fact that they were having their paragraphs publicly evaluated, DeVonne's students were enthusiastic about displaying their work. Offer an explanation for their enthusiasm.

The students' enthusiasm can be explained with both teacher characteristics and climate variables. DeVonne was enthusiastic, caring, and had positive expectations for her students. With respect to the climate variables, her class was orderly, and, as we saw in item 1, the students felt very safe. In addition, she explained the writing task clearly, which increased task comprehension, and the assignment provided opportunities for both challenge and success.

4. DeVonne's students' backgrounds are very diverse, and she teaches in an urban school. Assess her classroom environment for learners from urban contexts.

Research suggests that teachers who are successful with urban learners are enthusiastic, supportive, and have high expectations. They also create lessons that connect to students' lives and have high rates of involvement. DeVonne possessed each of these teacher characteristics, her lesson connected to students' lives by allowing them to write on a topic of their choice, and they were actively involved throughout the lesson.

Feedback for Online Case Book Questions

The feedback below is for the *Online Case Book* for Chapter 7 (referenced on page 361 of the chapter). Both you and the students can access the case study by going to www.prenhall.com/eggen, selecting Chapter 11, and clicking on *Online Case Book.*

You may choose to assign the online case as homework or you may want to discuss the case in class. Answers to these questions *do not* appear on the companion website, so students *do not* have access to the feedback.

Multiple-Choice Questions:

1. At the beginning of his lesson Tony said, "We've all been doing really well, so I'm going to kick it up a notch and see how good at thinking you've become." Of the following, the variable in the model form promoting student motivation that Tony is most attempting to apply is:

   a. personal teaching efficacy.
   b. challenge.
   c. personalization.
   d. involvement.
   b. By saying, "I'm going to kick it up a notch and see how good at thinking you've become," Tony is challenging the students.

2. Tony wrote the following words on the board

get	fight
mat	hope

The following dialogue then took place:

Tony:	Look at the words I've written on the chalkboard. Tell me something about them. . . . Sonya?
Sony:	They're all words.
Tony:	Indeed they are. . . . What else? . . . Pat?
Pat:	Those have three letters (pointing to the words in the left column).
Tony:	Yes, good! . . . Something else. . . . Sheldon?
Sheldon:	The ones on the right begin with different letters.

Of the following, variable in the model for promoting student motivation that Tony is best applying in this dialogue is:

   a. modeling.
   b. task comprehension.
   c. personalization.
   d. success.
   d. Tony used open-ended questions in this dialogue, and, since open-ended questions allow a variety of acceptable responses, they promote success.

3. The following dialogue took place near the end of the lesson.

Tony:	Now let's put this together and try and state it in a rule. . . . I'll get you started.... When adding 'ing' to words . . . Trang?
Trang:	You double the consonant at the end if the vowel sound is short, but you don't if the vowel sound is long."
Tony:	Very well done, Trang. You've identified the relationship between vowel sounds and spelling when adding 'ing'.

Of the following, variable in the model for promoting student motivation that Tony is best applying in this dialogue is:

a. modeling.
b. positive expectations.
c. involvement.
d. feedback.

d. In saying, "Very well done, Trang. You've identified the relationship between vowel sounds and spelling when adding 'ing'," Tony is providing Trang with specific feedback about his response.

Short-Answer Questions:

4. Assess Tony's application of the climate variables in the model for promoting student motivation in his lesson. Provide specific evidence from the case study in making your assessment.

Tony did a good job of promoting success and a good job of creating challenge in his lesson. He used open-ended questions extensively, which virtually ensures that students will be successful. And, since the students were uncertain about the outcome of the lesson, a sense of curiosity and challenge that could be engaging was created. It also appeared that the classroom environment was safe and orderly. Task comprehension was the variable least evident in the lesson. He did say, "We're going to see how good at thinking you've become. I'm going to write some words on the board and I want you to observe and compare them carefully," which was a form of task comprehension, but the purpose of the lesson wasn't emphasized.

5. Assess Tony's application of the instructional variables in the model for promoting student motivation in his lesson. Provide specific evidence from the case study in making your assessment.

By saying "We're going to see how good at thinking you've become. I'm going to write some words on the board and I want you to observe and compare them carefully. Then we'll see if we can find a pattern in them. . . . Okay," he established introductory focus for his lesson. He also used open-ended questions extensively, which is effective for promoting involvement. His feedback was mostly in the form of general praise, since the students were primarily responding to open-ended questions. Personalization was the instructional variable that he applied least effectively. The words were somewhat abstract and distant from the students' experiences.

6. Assess the effectiveness of Tony's lesson for promoting motivation to learn in urban students. Provide specific evidence from the case study in making your assessment.

Tony's application of success and challenge would be effective for urban students. And, his examples contained all the information the students needed to understand the rule. The primary weakness in his lesson for urban students (and for students in general) is the fact that he taught the rule out of the context of a written passage, such as a short essay. The relevance of content for their lives is particularly important for urban students, and the relevance of the topic was not apparent. Further, if he wanted to the students to be able to use the rule in their writing, presenting the rule on the context of a written paragraph would have been a more effective way to present the rule.

CLASSROOM EXERCISES

The classroom exercises that follow appear *only here* in the instructor's manual. Students do not have access to *either the questions or the answers*.

The purpose of keeping the exercises only in the instructor's manual is to allow you to use them as class discussion items, or for homework, if you should choose to do so.

Feedback for the exercises follows immediately.

A synthesis of Kathy Brewster's lesson on the Crusades (in the case study in Chapter 10) is shown below. Read the case study and answer the questions that follow.

1. "We better get moving," Susan urged Jim as they approached the door of Kathy Brewster's classroom. "The bell is gonna ring, and you know how Brewster is about this class. She thinks it's SO important."
2. "Did you finish your homework?" Jim asked and then stopped himself. "What am I talking about? You've done your home in every class since I first knew you."
3. "I don't mind it that much. . . . It bothers me when I don't get something, and sometimes it's even fun. My dad helps me. He says he wants to keep up with the world," Susan responded with a laugh.
4. "In some classes, I just do enough to get a decent grade, but not in here," Jim responded. "I used to hate history, but Brewster sorta makes you think. It's actually interesting the way she's always telling us about the way we are because of something that happened a zillion years ago. . . . I never thought about this stuff in that way before."
5. "Gee, Mrs. Brewster, that assignment was impossible," Harvey grumbled as he walked in.
6. "That's good for you," Kathy smiled back. "I know it was a tough assignment, but you need to be challenged. It's hard for me, too, when I'm studying and trying to put together new ideas, but if I hang in, I feel like I can usually get it."
7. "Aw, c'mon, Mrs. Brewster. I thought you knew everything."
8. "I wish. I have to study every night to keep up with you people, and the harder I study, the smarter I get," Kathy continued with a smile. "And, . . . I feel good about myself when I do."
9. "But you make us work so hard," Harvey continued in feigned complaint.
10. "Yes, but look how good you're getting at writing," Kathy smiled again, pointing her finger at him. "I think you hit a personal best on your last one. You're becoming a very good writer."
11. "Yeh, yeh, I know," Harvey smiled on his way to his desk, ". . . and being good writers will help us in everything we do in life," repeating a rationale the students continually hear from Kathy.
12. Kathy turned to Jennifer as she walked in, and said quietly, "I pulled your desk over here, Jenny," motioning to a spot in the middle of the second row. "You've been a little quiet lately. . . . I almost considered calling your Mom, to see if everything's okay," and she touched Jennifer's arm, motioning her to the spot.
13. She finished taking roll and then pulled down a map in the front of the room. "Let's look again at the map and review for a moment to see where we are. We began our discussion of the Crusades yesterday. What was significant about them? . . . Greg?"
14. "You came in with pictures of Crusaders and asked us to imagine what it'd be like to be one of them. . . . Antonio said he didn't think he'd like iron underwear," Greg grinned as the rest of the class giggled.
15. "All right, that's true." Kathy smiled back. "Now, how did we start the lesson? . . . Kim?"
16. ". . ."
17. "Remember, we started by imagining that we all left Lincoln High School and that it was taken over by people who believed that all extracurricular activities should be eliminated. We then asked what we should do about it. What did we decide we should do?"
18. "We decided we'd talk to them . . . and try and change their minds," Kim responded hesitantly.
19. "Right. Exactly, Kim. Very good. We said that we would be on a 'crusade' to try to change their minds.
20. "Now, what were the actual Crusades all about? . . . Selena?"
21. ". . . The Christians wanted to get the Holy Land back from the Muslims."
22. "About when was this happening?"

23. "I . . . I'm not sure."
24. "Look up at our time line."
25. ". . . Oh, yeah, about 1100," Selena answered peering at the time line.
26. "Good, and why did they want them back? . . . Becky?"
27. "The . . . Holy Lands were important for the Christians. I suppose they just wanted them because of that."
28. "Yes. Good, Becky," Kathy smiled. "Indeed, that was a factor. What else? . . . Anyone?"
29. After surveying the class and seeing uncertainty on students' faces, Kathy said, "You might not see what I'm driving at. . . . Let's look at this," and she then displayed a map that illustrated the extent of Muslim influence in the Middle East, North Africa, and Europe.
30. "What do you see here? . . . Cynthia?"
31. Cynthia scanned the map for several seconds and then said, "It looks like the Muslims are getting more and more territory."
32. "Yes, very good. So, what implication did this have for the Europeans?"
33. "They probably were scared . . . like afraid the Muslims would take over their land," Scott volunteered.
34. "That's a good thought, Scott," Kathy responded. "They certainly were a military threat. In fact, the conflict occurring in Bosnia is a present-day reminder of the clash between Christians and Muslims. How else might they have been threatening?"
35. "Maybe . . . economically," Brad added. "You're always telling us how economics rules the world."
36. "Brilliant, Brad," Kathy laughed. "Indeed, economics was a factor. In fact, this is a little ahead of where we are, but we'll see that the military and economic threats of the Muslims, together with the religious issue, were also factors that led to Columbus's voyage to the New World. . . . Think about that. The Muslims in 1000 A.D. have had an influence on us here today."
37. "Now," Kathy said, "let's get back on track. Why do we study the Crusades? Like, who cares, anyway? . . . Toni?"
38. "They were important in Europe, . . . it affected its development in the Middle Ages, like fashion and war strategies, . . . all the way up to today. The Renaissance wouldn't have been the same without them."
39. "Excellent, Toni! Very good analysis. Now, for today's assignment, you were asked to write a paragraph answering the question, 'Were the Crusades a success or a failure?' You could take either position. We want to learn how to make and defend an argument, so the quality of your paragraph depends on how you defended your position, not on the position itself. Remember, this is a skill that goes way beyond a specific topic like the Crusades. This applies in everything we do.
40. "So, let's see how we made out. Go ahead. . . . Nikki?"
41. "I said they were a failure. They didn't . . ."
42. "Wait a minute!" Joe interrupted. "How about the new fighting techniques they learned?"
43. "Joe," Kathy began firmly, "what is one of the principles we operate on in here?"
44. "We don't have to agree with someone . . . but we have to listen. . . . Sorry."
45. "Go on, Nikki," Kathy continued.
46. "That's okay," Nikki continued nodding to Joe. "It seemed to me that militarily, at least, they failed because the Europeans didn't accomplish what they were after . . . to get the Holy Land back for Christianity," Nikki said. "There were several Crusades, and after only one did they get sort of a foothold, and it only lasted a short time, like about 50 years, I think."
47. "Okay. That's good, Nikki," Kathy responded. "You made your point and then supported it. That's what I wanted you to do in your paragraph."
48. "Now, go ahead, Joe. You were making a point," Kathy said, turning back to him.
49. "I said they were a success because the Europeans learned new military strategies that they used on the Natives . . . here, in the Americas, and they were good at it. If it hadn't been for the Crusades, they probably wouldn't have learned the techniques, . . . at least not for a long time. Then, only the Japanese knew the attacking techniques the Crusaders learned when they went to the Middle East. It even changed our ideas about like guerrilla fighting."
50. "Also good, Joe," Kathy responded, nodding. "This is exactly what we're after. Nikki and Joe took opposite points of view in their paragraphs, but they each provided several details to support their positions. Again, we're more concerned with the support you provide than the actual position you take.
51. "Let's look at one more," she went on. "What was your position, Anita?"

52. "I said they . . . were a success," Anita responded. "Europe, you know, like Western Europe took a lot from their culture, their culture in the Middle East. Like, some of the spices we eat today first came to Europe then."
53. "Now isn't that interesting!" Kathy waved energetically. "See, here's another case where we see ourselves today finding a relationship to people who lived 1,000 or more years ago. That's what history is all about."
54. "Brewster loves this stuff," David whispered to Kelly, smiling slightly.
55. "Yeah," she replied. "History has never been my favorite subject, but some of this stuff is actually kind of neat."
56. "Okay. One more," Kathy continued, "and we'll move on."
57. The class reviewed another example, and then Kathy told the students to revise their paragraphs in light of what they had discussed that day and to turn in a final product the following day. "Remember, think about what you're doing when you make your revisions," she emphasized. "Read your paragraph after you write it, and ask yourself, 'do I actually have evidence here, or is it simply an opinion?' . . . The more aware you are when you write, the better you work will be."
58. When the period was nearly over, Kathy said, "Excuse me, but the bell is about to ring. Just a reminder, group presentations on the Renaissance are Wednesday and Thursday. You decide what groups will be on each day. For those who chose to write the paper on the Middle Ages, remember we agreed that they should be due next Friday."

Identify the variable in the Model best illustrated by each of the following combinations of paragraphs. Remember, it is the combinations of the paragraphs. Do not focus on a single paragraph in each case (unless only a single paragraph is identified, as in Item 3 [paragraph 12]).

For example, paragraphs 6–8 best illustrate Teacher modeling and enthusiasm.

Now, you identify the variable for the following combinations of paragraphs. Be sure to provide a rationale for your choice in each case.

1. 1–11

2. 5–6

3. 12

4. 7–19

5. 22–25

6. 30–31 (Identify two different variables for these paragraphs.)

7. 37–38

8. 40–43

9. 50

10. 53–54

FEEDBACK FOR CLASSROOM EXERCISES

1. Paragraphs 1–11: Teacher Expectations
Evidence for Kathy' s high expectations exists in the students' responses, " ...you know how Brewster is about this class. She thinks it's SO important." (1); ". ..Brewster sorta makes you think," (4); and "But you make us work so hard." (9)

2. Paragraphs 5–6: Challenge
Kathy even uses the word "challenge" in (6).

3. Paragraph 12: Caring
Kathy demonstrates a personal interest in Jennifer by moving her to the middle of the row.

4. Paragraphs 17–19: Personalization
Kathy personalizes the Crusades by using their "crusade" to prevent the elimination of extracurricular activities as a metaphor for their topic.

5. Paragraphs 22–25: Success
Kathy provides a prompt which allows Selena to answer correctly.

6. Paragraphs 30–31: Involvement/Success
Using open-ended questions is a technique for promoting involvement, and they also ensure success. (Either or both answers would be acceptable.)

7. Paragraphs 37–38: Task Comprehension
Kathy wants the students to understand the reasons for studying the Crusades.

8. Paragraphs 40–43: Order and Safety
Kathy creates a safe environment by admonishing Joe for interrupting Nikki.

9. Paragraph 50: Feedback
Kathy provides information about the extent to which goals are being reached.

10. Paragraphs 53–54: Modeling and enthusiasm
Kathy demonstrates her own genuine interest in the topic.

CHAPTER 12: CREATING PRODUCTIVE LEARNING ENVIRONMENTS
Classroom Management

CHAPTER OVERVIEW

This chapter is the first of two focusing on the creation of productive learning environments with emphasize on the creation and maintenance orderly classrooms. The chapter begins with a discussion of planning for orderly classrooms, the preparation and teaching of rules and procedures, and communication with parents. It continues with a discussion of management interventions from both cognitive and behaviorist perspectives. The chapter closes with a discussion of serious management problems and school violence.

CHAPTER OBJECTIVES

- Describe the relationships between classroom management, the complexities of classrooms, and motivation and learning.
- Analyze the planning components for creating productive learning environments in examples of classroom activities.
- Explain how effective communication with parents helps meet classroom management goals and why communication with parents who are members of cultural minorities is particularly important.
- Describe effective interventions in cases of learner misbehavior.
- Describe teachers' legal responsibilities and the steps involved in responding to acts of violence and aggression.

POWERPOINT SLIDES

PP 12.1 The Importance of Classroom Management
PP 12.2 The Goals of Classroom Management
PP 12.3 Planning for an Orderly Classroom
PP 12.4 Learner Characteristics Affecting Classroom Management
PP 12.5 Sample Classroom Procedures,
PP 12.6 Principles of Instruction for Creating and Teaching Rules
PP 12.7 Examples of Teachers' Rules
PP 12.8 Teaching Children Procedures
PP 12.9 Guidelines for Beginning the School Year
PP 12.10 Beginning the School Year
PP 12.11 Involving Caregivers in Their Children's Education
PP 12.12 Guidelines for Successful Interventions
PP 12.13 Cognitive Interventions
PP 12.14 A Behavioral Management System
PP 12.15 An Intervention Continuum
PP 12.16 Praxis Practice: Feedback for Short-Answer Questions
PP 12.17 Feedback for Online Case Questions
PP 12.18 Classroom Exercises

VIDEO

DVD 2, Episode 19: "Establishing and Practicing Classroom Rules"
This episode illustrates a teacher establishing a set of rules with her students and reviewing the rules several days later.

CHAPTER OUTLINE

I. The importance of well-managed classrooms
  A. Public and professional concerns
  B. The complexities of classrooms
    a. Classroom events are multidimensional and simultaneous
    b. Classroom events are immediate
    c. Classroom events are unpredictable
    d. Classroom events are public
  C. Influence on motivation and learning
  D. Goals of classroom management
    1. Developing learner responsibility
    2. Creating a positive classroom climate
    3. Maximizing time and opportunity for learning
II. Planning for productive classroom environments
  A. Accommodating student characteristics
  B. Arranging the physical environment
    1. Arranging desks
    2. Personalizing your classroom
  C. Organizing for Instruction
  D. Creating and teaching rules: Instructional principles
    1. Teaching rules and procedures
    2. Beginning the school year
    3. Monitoring rules
  E. Learning Contexts: Classroom management in urban environments
    1. Caring and supportive teachers
    2. Clear standards for acceptable behavior
    3. High structure
    4. Effective instruction
III. Communication with parents
  A. Benefits of communication
  B. Involving parents: Instructional principles
  C. Communication with parents: Accommodating learner diversity
    1. Economic, cultural, and language barriers
    2. Involving minority parents
IV. Intervening when misbehavior occurs
  A. Guidelines for successful interventions
    a. Demonstrate withitness
    b. Preserve student dignity
    c. Be consistent
    d. Follow-through
    e. Keep interventions brief
    f. Avoid arguments
  B. Cognitive interventions
    1. Verbal-nonverbal congruence
    2. I-messages
    3. Logical consequences
  C. Behavioral interventions
    1. Designing and maintaining a behavioral management system
  D. An intervention continuum
    1. Praising desired behavior
    2. Ignoring inappropriate behavior
    3. Using indirect cues
    4. Using desists
    5. Applying consequences
V. Serious management problems: Violence and aggression
  A. School violence and aggression
    1. Responding to aggression against peers
    2. Responding to bullying
    3. Responding to defiant students
  B. Long-term solutions to violence and aggression

PRESENTATION OUTLINE

The suggested activities can be completed in small groups and discussed as a whole group, or they can be conducted as whole-class activities. We encourage as much discussion–both in small groups and with the whole class–as possible.

I. The importance of well-managed classrooms
   A. Public and professional concerns
   B. The complexities of classrooms
      a. Classroom events are multidimensional and simultaneous
      b. Classroom events are immediate
      c. Classroom events are unpredictable
      d. Classroom events are public
   C. Influence on motivation and learning
   D. Goals of classroom management
      1. Developing learner responsibility
      2. Creating a positive classroom climate
      3. Maximizing time and opportunity for learning
II. Planning for productive classroom environments
   A. Accommodating student characteristics
   B. Arranging the physical environment
      1. Arranging desks
      2. Personalizing your classroom
   C. Organizing for Instruction
   D. Creating and teaching rules: Instructional principles
      1. Teaching rules and procedures
      2. Beginning the school year
      3. Monitoring rules
   E. Learning Contexts: Classroom management in urban environments
      1. Caring and supportive teachers
      2. Clear standards for acceptable behavior
      3. High structure
      4. Effective instruction

Teaching Suggestions:

■ *The purpose in the following suggestions is to help your students understand the importance of orderly classrooms, together with the process of planning an effective classroom management system.*

1. **To check students' perceptions and informally assess their backgrounds with respect to classroom management, have them identify some of the characteristics of effective managers. To help them in their thinking ask them to think about some of their previous teachers. Discuss their results. Record some of their suggestions so that you can refer back to them as you examine the content of the chapter.**

2. **Display PP 12.1 "*The Importance of Classroom Management*" and have the students offer their reactions to the information in it.**

3. **Display PP 12.2 "*The Goals of Classroom Management*" and emphasize that—ultimately—each of the goals is designed to increase learning. Point out that each—instructional time, engaged time, and academic learning time—is more strongly correlated with learning than is the one preceding it.**

■ *To help your students understand the processes involved in planning for classroom management:*

1. **Display PP 12.3 "*Planning for an Orderly Classroom*" illustrates the elements that should be considered in planning for rules and procedures, and PP 12.4 "*Learner Characteristics Affecting Classroom Management*" identifies some of the learner attributes that should be considered.**

2. **To illustrate some additional procedures, display PP 12.5 "*Sample Classroom Procedures,*" which outlines some examples of procedures at the elementary as well as the middle, junior high, and secondary levels.**

3. **Display PP 12.6 "*Principles of Instruction for Creating and Teaching Rules.*" Using the principles, have the students generate lists of rules that they would use in their classrooms. Discuss their decisions as a whole group. Display PP 12.7 "*Examples of Teachers' Rules*" as some additional examples taken from the real world, and have the students assess the extent to which they are consistent with the principles.**

> Here would be a good point to show or discuss **Episode 19 on DVD 2**: "Establishing and Practicing Classroom Rules."

4. **To illustrate the way effective teachers teach their procedures and rules, display PP 12.8 "*Teaching Children Procedures.*" Have students look at the example, and then have them describe specifically what the teacher did to teach the procedures. They should notice that she used concrete examples to illustrate the procedure. You might also remind them that Martha was using a form of direct modeling, which was designed to teach the children new behaviors, which is a link to the content of social cognitive theory in Chapter 6.**

■ *To help your students understand the importance of beginning the school year effectively and how rules and procedures are monitored:*

1. **Display PP 12.9 "*Guidelines for Beginning the School Year.*" Ask the students to use social cognitive theory to explain why the beginning of the year is so important. Included in their responses should be the fact that the beginning establishes expectations for the kinds of behaviors that will be reinforced.**

2. **Display PP 12.10 "*Beginning the School Year,*" as an application exercise, and have the students compare the way the two teachers began their year.**

III. Communication with parents
   A. Benefits of communication
   B. Involving parents: Instructional principles
   C. Communication with parents: Accommodating learner diversity
      1. Economic, cultural, and language barriers
      2. Involving minority parents

Teaching Suggestions:

■ *The suggestions in this section are intended to help your students understand the importance of communication with parents, particularly those coming from diverse backgrounds.*

1. **Display PP 12.11 "*Involving Caregivers in Their Children's Education,*" which outlines some of the issues related to involving parents, as well as some suggestions for trying to increase**

parental involvement. Discuss the suggestions and what teachers might do to improve school-home communication.

2. **Even though teachers try to communicate with parents and other caregivers, some remain reluctant to get involved in school activities. Have the students brainstorm some additional ways to try and involve parents and other caregivers.**

IV. Intervening when misbehavior occurs
   A. Guidelines for successful interventions
      a. Demonstrate withitness
      b. Preserve student dignity
      c. Be consistent
      d. Follow-through
      e. Keep interventions brief
      f. Avoid arguments
   B. Cognitive interventions
      1. Verbal-nonverbal congruence
      2. I-messages
      3. Logical consequences
   C. Behavioral interventions
      1. Designing and maintaining a behavioral management system
   D. An intervention continuum
      1. Praising desired behavior
      2. Ignoring inappropriate behavior
      3. Using indirect cues
      4. Using desists
      5. Applying consequences

Teaching Suggestions:

■ ***The purpose of the suggestions in this section is to help your students understand basic approaches to intervention.***

1. **Display PP 12.12 "*Guidelines for Successful Interventions*" which provides examples of each of the interventions.**

■ ***To help your students understand cognitive interventions:***

1. **Ask the students to explain why verbal-nonverbal congruence, I-messages, and logical consequences are cognitive versus behaviorist.**

2. **They should conclude that the assumption involved in each is that the learner is an active, thinking being. If verbal and nonverbal behaviors are inconsistent, for example, a learner's equilibrium is disrupted by the inconsistency. They won't react to the verbal directive, as behaviorism would predict; rather they react to their perception of the true meaning of the message, which is a cognitive explanation.**

3. **Display PP 12.13 "*Cognitive Interventions*," which provides examples of each of the cognitive interventions.**

■ ***To help your students understand behaviorist interventions:***

1. **Display PP 12.14 "*A Behavioral Management System*" which illustrates one teacher's behavioral management system. You might display PP 12.14 and have the students discuss its strengths and weaknesses. Remind the students that behavioral management systems are somewhat controversial, but many teachers in the field continue to design and use them successfully.**

2. **The Online Case referenced on page 395 of the chapter provides another example of a behaviorist management system.**

3. **Since many schools and teachers may expect beginning teachers to be able to design a behavioral management system, you may want to have students design a system of their own. In the process, remind them that they can incorporate characteristics that promote responsibility by providing rationales for the rules they design and allowing student input into the rules. (They won't be able to solicit student input in this activity, of course, but they can have this notion in mind as they prepare their rules.)**

■ *To help your students apply effective interventions in their own teaching:*

1. **Display PP 12.15 "*An Intervention Continuum*" and have the students explain each of the points on the continuum from both a cognitive and a behaviorist perspective. As a simple example, from a cognitive perspective, praise is feedback that helps the students understand what is appropriate. From a behaviorist perspective, praise is a positive reinforcer. From a cognitive perspective consequences should be logical and connected to the act, and from a behaviorist perspective, they're punishers than are intended to eliminate the behavior.**

2. **As an application exercise have the students compare the effectiveness of Judy Harris' and Janelle Powers's management (the case studies at the beginning and the end of the chapter respectively).**

   Some of the conclusions students should make include:
   - **Janelle could have been better organized by having the students complete a warmup activity while she took roll.**
   - **Judy demonstrated withitness and overlapping, whereas Janelle did not**
   - **Judy had well established routines, and Janelle did not.**
   - **Janelle's communication did not utilize "I-message"s.**
   - **Judy better maintained lesson momentum in spite of interventions than did Janelle.**

V. Serious management problems: Violence and aggression
   A. School violence and aggression
      1. Responding to aggression against peers
      2. Responding to bullying
      3. Responding to defiant students
   B. Long-term solutions to violence and aggression

Teaching Suggestions:

■ *The purpose in the following suggestions is to help your students put serious management problems into perspective.*

1. **Remind the students that while violence and aggression make dramatic headlines, the incidents are in reality very infrequent. Tell them that in the case of a violent incident that they should break up the incident, if possible, and then get help immediately.**

ENRICHMENT MATERIALS

TEACHER PREP WEBSITE

The *Teacher Prep* website an online resource for students and instructors. Both you and students can access the *Teacher Prep* website by going to http://www.prenhall.com/teacherprep. Enter your user name and password and click on "Log In." The *Teacher Prep* website includes video episodes, student and teacher artifacts, teacher and research resources, and information about licensing and beginning a teaching career. The *Teacher Prep* website is described in detail in the Media Guide.

The following article is recommended by the *Exploring Further* section titled "Time Management" on page 373 of the chapter.

Once into the *Teacher Prep* website access the articles by completing the following steps:
1. Click on "Research Resources" on the left panel of the screen, scroll down the middle of the page and again click on "Research Resources."
2. Go to "Classroom Processes" and click on "Classroom Management."
3. Click on the following article:
   Time Management, by J Queen, J. Burrell, and S. McManus (2001), Ref. No. 1558.

This excerpt offers planning suggestions designed to help teachers use their time efficiently and maximize the amount of time available for instruction.

The following article is recommended by the *Exploring Further* section titled "Improving Home-School Communication" on page 388 of the chapter.

Once into the *Teacher Prep* website access the articles by completing the following steps:
1. Click on "Research Resources" on the left panel of the screen, scroll down the middle of the page and again click on "Research Resources."
2. Go to "Classroom Processes" and click on "Classroom Management."
3. Click on the following article:
   Building Cultures with a Parent-Teacher Conference, by B. Quinoz, P. Greenfield, and M. Alchech (1999), Ref. No. 537.

This article offers a Latina mother's perspective on a parent-teacher conference. It also outlines potential cross-cultural conflicts about values, describes strategies teachers can use to help prevent or eliminate these conflicts.

The following articles are recommended by the *Exploring Further* section titled "Conflict Resolution" on page 400 of the chapter.

Once into the *Teacher Prep* website access the articles by completing the following steps:
1. Click on "Research Resources" on the left panel of the screen, scroll down the middle of the page and again click on "Research Resources."
2. Go to "Classroom Processes" and click on "Classroom Management."
3. Click on the following articles:
   Changing the Way Kids Settle Conflicts, by G. Holden (1997), Ref. No. 219;
   Down with Put-Downs, by M. Lundeberg, J. Emmett, P. Osland, and N. Lindquist (1997), Ref No. 243; and
   Helping Students Avoid Risky Behavior, by C. Sullivan-DeCarlo, K. DeFalco, and V. Roberts (1998), Ref. No. 272.

Each of these articles offers strategies for helping students learn to deal with conflict in positive ways.

ADDITIONAL EXPLORING FURTHER SUGGESTIONS

Page 371 of the chapter suggests that students to go the *Exploring Further* module of Chapter 12 for a more detailed discussion of Jacob Kounin's work.

Page 395 of the chapter suggests that students to go the *Exploring Further* module of Chapter 12 for a discussion of Assertive Discipline.

DISCUSSION STARTERS

You may choose to have your students discuss one or more of the following questions to further enrich their understanding of your learning activities.

1. Have classroom management issues changed over the last 10 years? Fifteen years? Twenty years? Why do you think so?

2. To what extent is effective classroom management a function of teachers' personalities compared to teachers' knowledge? Provide a rationale for your position.

3. We discussed rules and procedures from cognitive and behaviorist views. How would they be designed based on humanistic views of learners?
4. Effective management has been called a "necessary but not sufficient" component of effective teaching. Explain the "necessary" and "not sufficient" parts of this expression.

5. Suppose some high school teachers are moving to elementary schools. What advice would you give them for modifying their existing management plans? What about teachers making the transition the other way?

6. To what extent does classroom management involve moral decisions, both on the part of the teacher and on the part of the students? Use Kohlberg's theory to support your answer.

7. A concerned parent at the beginning of the school year wants to know if you think that Assertive Discipline is an effective way to manage classrooms. How would you answer the parent?

8. How might learners' cultural and SES backgrounds influence the way you manage your classroom? In answering this question choose and describe a specific location where you anticipate you will be teaching.

BACKGROUND READINGS

Charles, C. M., & Senter, G. W. (2005). *Building classroom discipline* (8th ed.). Boston: Allyn & Bacon. This short, readable book describes several "models" of classroom management. These models offer a succinct overview of several experts' views on approaches to effective management and discipline.

Doyle, W. (1986). *Classroom organization and management.* In M. Wittrock (Ed.), Handbook of research on teaching (3rd ed., pp. 392–431). New York: Macmillan.
The chapter, almost a classic, provides a wide-ranging, research-based discussion of effective management issues at both the elementary and secondary school levels.

Emmer, E., Evertson, C., & Worsham, M. (2003). *Classroom management for secondary teachers* (6th ed.). Upper Saddle River, NJ: Prentice Hall. Based on the practices of effective managers at the secondary level, this book is a source of practical ideas for secondary teachers.

Evertson, C., Emmer, & Worsham, M. (2003). *Classroom management for elementary teachers* (6th ed.). Needham Heights, MA: Allyn & Bacon.
This practical and readable text translates the research literature on management in elementary classrooms into concrete suggestions.

Good, T., & Brophy, J. (2003). *Looking in classrooms* (9th ed.). New York: Addison-Wesley Longman.
This well known text includes two detailed chapters on classroom management.

Hong, S., & Ho, H. (2005). Direct and indirect longitudinal effects of parental involvement on student achievement: Second-order latent growth modeling across ethnic groups. *Journal of Educational Psychology, 97*(1), 32–42.
This article examines the effects of parental involvement on student achievement and identifies factors that influence the achievement.

Weinstein, C. S., & Mignano, A. J., Jr. (2003). *Elementary classroom management: Lessons from research and practice* (3rd ed.). New York: McGraw-Hill.
This popular book offers a variety of practical suggestions for teachers in elementary schools.

FEEDBACK

Developing as a Professional: Praxis Practice: Feedback for Short-Answer Questions

The feedback that appears here is for the short-answer questions that follow the case study on pages 401 and 402 of the text. The feedback is also available to students on the companion website.

1. Analyze Janelle's planning for classroom management.

   Janelle's planning for classroom management was quite ineffective. For example, in contrast with Judy Harris at the beginning of the chapter, Janelle's students were expected to sit quietly while she called the roll, went to the file cabinet to get out her transparencies, and finished arranging her materials. The result was "dead" time for students, during which disruptions occurred, and lost instructional time for Janelle.

2. Evaluate the effectiveness of Janelle's management interventions.

   Several problems existed in Janelle's management interventions. First, she demonstrated lack of withitness when she admonished Leila for blurting out "Stop it Damon." Janelle initially 'caught' the wrong one and allowed the incident to disrupt the learning activity to a greater extent than did Judy. Janelle also allowed her encounter with Howard and Manny to disrupt the momentum of her lesson. Janelle's nonverbal behavior also didn't communicate that she was "in charge," or that she meant it when she intervened. For example, she glanced up from her papers to admonish Howard and Manfred, and she again "looked up" in response to a hum of voices around the classroom. Also, requiring Manfred to read the rule aloud in front of the class was a form of power play that did nothing to improve the classroom climate, and her comment, "You've been bugging me all week . . ." was inconsistent with recommendations of experts to criticize the behavior and not the student.

3. The chapter stressed the interdependence of management and instruction. Analyze the relationship between management and instruction in Janelle's class. Include both strengths and weaknesses in the relationship.

   Janelle's instruction would have been more effective if it had been more interactive and developed with more supporting materials such as maps and globes. This would have allowed her to involve students more, which usually results in fewer management problems. Janelle's management was also less effective than it might have been. She wasn't well-organized and she didn't communicate as clearly and assertively as she might have to be effective. In addition, she was slightly less "withit" than what would have been desirable and she allowed her interventions with the students to disrupt the momentum and smoothness of her lesson, resulting in more problems with management.

   Some suggestions for improvement include the following: First, Janelle would have been more effective if she had been better organized. A beginning-of-class warm-up activity would have helped her better use her time and would also have eliminated "dead" time at the beginning of the lesson during which management problems can occur. Also, her materials should have been ready and waiting, so she didn't have to spend time arranging them while students were supposed to sit quietly. Her verbal and nonverbal channels of communication weren't quite congruent, so her admonishments of students weren't as credible as they might have been, and her interaction with Howard implied a character flaw rather than simple inappropriate behavior. Finally, allowing her intervention with Howard and Manfred to disrupt the flow of her lesson further detracted from the smooth management of her students.

Feedback for Online Case Book Questions

The feedback below is for the *Online Case Book* for Chapter 7 (referenced on page 395 of the chapter). Both you and the students can access the case study by going to www.prenhall.com/eggen, selecting Chapter 12, and clicking on *Online Case Book.*

You may choose to assign the online case as homework or you may want to discuss the case in class. Answers to these questions *do not* appear on the companion website, so students *do not* have access to the feedback.

Multiple-Choice Items

1. Of the following, which *goal* of classroom management is best illustrated by Erika individually greeting each of her students as they come in the door of her classroom?
   a. Developing learner responsibility
   b. Creating a positive classroom environment
   c. Maximizing time available for learning
   d. Maximizing opportunity for learning
   b. The discussion of positive classroom climate in the chapter says, "An essential element of a positive classroom climate is a caring teacher who communicates respect and concern for others." Erika's greeting communicated caring and respect.

2. In the case study you saw that "the students, who are chattering among themselves, quickly stop as they see Erika move to the front of the room to begin the day's math lesson." Of the following aspect of *effective organization*, the students' behavior best illustrates which of the following?
   a. Starting on time
   b. Preparing materials in advance
   c. Establishing routines and procedures
   d. Other actions that increase instructional time
   c. The students stopped their chattering without being told, which suggests that a routine is well established.

3. Of the following, which best describes Erika's approach to classroom management?
   a. It was primarily a cognitive approach to management, because the students understood the routines and procedures that they followed to keep the classroom a productive learning environment.
   b. It was primarily a behaviorist approach because Erika had rules displayed at the front of the room.
   c. It was primarily a cognitive approach, because the students behaved responsibly when they came into the classroom.
   d. It combined cognitive and behaviorist approaches, because it was based on a combination of understanding and rewards.
   d. It combined cognitive and behaviorist approaches because the students understood the routines and procedures and accepted responsibility for following them, which is cognitive, and they also were given rewards for acceptable behavior, which is behaviorist.

Short-Answer Questions:

4. Using the principles for creating and teaching rules as a basis, assess Erika' classroom rules.
   Erika's rules were quite effective. They were stated positively, she only had four rules, and they were stated clearly enough to be understandable.

5. Assess Erika's ability to capitalize on the interdependence of instruction and classroom management.
   We don't have a great deal of evidence to assess Erika's ability to capitalize on the interdependence of management and instruction, but based on the evidence we have, she integrated the two quite effectively. She was well organized, she used her time well, she emphasized understanding, and she provided the students with detailed feedback on the quiz problems that were difficult. Each contributes to a productive learning environment.

CLASSROOM EXERCISES

The classroom exercises that follow appear *only here* in the instructor's manual. Students do not have access to *either the questions or the answers.*

The purpose of keeping the exercises only in the instructor's manual is to allow you to use them as class discussion items, or for homework, if you should choose to do so.

Feedback for the exercises follows immediately.

1. In the chapter we talked about the concept of follow-through, meaning the teacher must follow through to be certain that misbehavior stops when she intervenes. Suppose the teacher asks students to stop misbehaving, but doesn't follow through. Explain what the likely outcomes of failing to follow through would be based on social cognitive theory. Explain for the target students and also explain for other students.

2. Behavioral approaches to classroom management can be effective because clearly specified consequences for breaking and following rules reduce the need for split second decisions by the teacher. Using information processing as a basis, explain why reducing the need for making split second decisions is helpful for teachers. Again using information processing theory as a basis, explain why would making "split second" decisions be easier for an expert than for a novice teacher?

3. Duranna Hamilton greets her students with a smile at the classroom door. "How's your new little sister?" she asks Devon, whose mother recently had a baby girl.

"Be ready today," she smiles and whispers to Cassie as she comes in. "I've been watching you, and you've been a little quiet lately, so I'm going to call on you today. . . . Be ready," she smiles again and ushers Cassie into the room with a touch on her shoulder.

As she is ushering Cassie to her seat, she says, "Rico and Steve," in response to the students' whispering after the bell stops ringing. "One of the rules we all agreed on was 'Be ready to work as soon as the bell stops ringing.'"

Duranna watches them carefully, and the boys quickly stop.

Identify the three guidelines for successful interventions that were best illustrated in the vignette. Explain.

4. Think about the study of psychosocial development in Chapter 3. How would Erikson explain the disruptive behavior of a low-achieving fifth grader? Using Erikson's work as a guide, explain what you might do to help the student.

5. Learners in obedience-oriented classrooms see rules in an absolute "do it or else" frame of reference, whereas learners in responsibility-oriented classrooms learn to obey rules because they understand that we agree upon the rules, and the rules exist to protect their rights and the rights of others. To which of Kohlberg's stages do each of these orientations most closely relate?

6. Read the case study and respond to the question that follows. (This is a real-world example of an encounter between a student and a teacher.) (The paragraphs are numbered for your reference.)

1. Adam is a bright but active and talkative sixth grader who periodically blurts out answers in class before his classmates have a chance to respond. He also has a habit of putting pens in his mouth. Mrs. Jones, his teacher uses a classroom management system in which students get "tallies" for misbehavior. She usually gives students one warning if they break a rule, which is then followed by giving a "tally," although students will occasionally get tallies for a first infraction. Receiving three or more tallies in a one-week period results in a half hour of detention.

2. Adam is periodically warned about his blurting out answers, and he then stops doing so for several days. He, and other students, periodically receive tallies, but rarely receive three in a week, wanting to avoid the possibility of detention.
3. As the students are making the transition from the learning activity to seatwork, Mrs. Jones announces quite loudly, "Adam, Sanchia just told me that you spit on her. . . . We don't behave that way, and we particularly don't spit on each other. You will be receiving a tally."
4. The students, somewhat startled by Mrs. Jones' announcement look around at Adam and Sanchia, but they quickly settle down and begin their seatwork, and the rest of the day proceeds without incident.
5. "Mom!" Adam nearly screams as he walks into the house after school that day. "Mrs. Jones is so terrible and so mean. She is so unfair," he continues nearly out of control.
6. "Wait, . . . calm down, honey," Suzanne, his mother, says, putting her arm around him and attempting to sooth his feelings. "Tell me what happened."
7. "I'm just working, and out of the blue Mrs. Jones announces in front of the whole class that I spit on Sanchia, and that I have a tally."
8. "Are you sure you were 'just working'?" Suzanne probes. "Did you spit on Sanchia?"
9. "No, no, no, . . . Mom, I really didn't."
10. "You must have don't something," Suzanne continues to probe. "Sanchia wouldn't just make that up out of the clear blue."
11. They talk at length, and during the discussion it comes out that Adam did indeed have his pen in his mouth and "I maybe pointed it at Sanchia,"
12. "Did it have saliva on it?"
13. "I don't know . . . maybe," Adam confesses. "But, Mom, it's terrible unfair. I got a tally once for tattling, and now Sanchia says I spit at her, when I didn't really do it, and I get a tally. It just isn't fair. Why didn't she get a tally for tattling?"
14. Suzanne considers the incident, talks to a friend, and decides to write Mrs. Jones a note inquiring about her tally system and how it's administered. In the note Suzanne questions Mrs. Jones giving Adam a tally when she didn't see the incident–she only used the other student's word, and she also questions the inconsistency in giving tallies.
15. Upon receiving the note, Mrs. Jones calls Adam out in the hall before class and says, "What's this all about? I got a note from your mom about the tally you received for spitting on Sanchia."
16. "But, Mrs. Jones," Adam protests. "I didn't spit on her. I swear, . . . I didn't."
17. "Well, that's the way it goes sometimes," Mrs. Jones responds. "Sometimes you need to just shake it off. That's part of life. . . . Now, go back into the classroom. We're about to start."
18. "Do I still have the tally?"
19. "Yes."

Identify at least four things Mrs. Jones did in the encounter with Adam that were ineffective, specify the paragraphs in which the ineffective behavior is illustrated, and explain why they were ineffective. .

For example:

1. She gave Adam a tally based on Sanchia's accusation rather than her own observation. As a result, Adam felt screwed. (In Adam's perception, he didn't spit on her. She shouldn't have given him a tally unless she observed the infraction. [This also demonstrates a lack of "withitness."])

Now, identify at least three more:

FEEDBACK FOR CLASSROOM EXERCISES

1. Social cognitive theory would suggest that failing to follow through would result in an increase in the undesired behavior. Misbehaving students expect to be admonished for their misbehavior. The nonoccurrence of these consequences act as reinforcers, which results in an increase in the misbehaviors.

The nonoccurrence of expected punishers act as vicarious reinforcers for the rest of the students, and they also become more likely to misbehave.

2. Split-second decisions require working memory space. Eliminating the split-second decisions frees working memory space that can be devoted to other aspects of learning and teaching.

Making split-second decisions is easier for experts because more of their knowledge is automatic, so they have more working memory space that can be devoted to making the decision.

3. Duranna first demonstrated withitness by quickly recognizing that Rico and Steve were talking inappropriately. second, by watching them carefully until they stopped, she demonstrated follow through, and third, she kept the intervention brief. It is likely that she demonstrated the guidelines as well, but we don't have evidence for them in the vignette.

4. Erikson's work would suggest that the fifth grader is disruptive because he or she hasn't achieved a sense of industry that results from success on worthwhile tasks. While difficult, the key is genuine accomplishment on tasks the student perceives as challenging.

5. The first orientation most closely relates to Stage 1. "Do it or else," implies punishment for disobedience. A responsibility orientation is related to Stage 5. When "we agree upon" the rules, they become social contracts. If there wasn't an implied agreement, rules existing to protect everyone's rights implies Stage 3.

6. First, Mrs. Jones is inconsistent in her administering of tallies. (paragraph 1 and paragraph 13)

Second, Mrs. Jones confronts Adam about Suzanne's note. (paragraph 15). The issue of the note was between Mrs. Jones and Suzanne, not Mrs. Jones and Adam.

Third, Mrs. Jones teaches Adam that the world is arbitrary and capricious, rather than orderly and sensible, with the comment, "Well, that's the way it goes sometimes. Sometimes you need to just shake it off. That's part of life." (paragraph 17). Cognitive approaches to management emphasize learner understanding, which can lead to them accepting responsibility for controlling their own behavior. A capricious environment detracts from this understanding.

CHAPTER 13: CREATING PRODUCTIVE LEARNING ENVIRONMENTS
Principles and Models of Instruction

CHAPTER OVERVIEW

This chapter continues the discussion of the development and maintenance of productive learning environments, with emphasis on the interdependence of effective instruction and orderly classrooms. The chapter begins with an examination of the types of teacher knowledge needed to produce as much learning as possible. It continues with the teacher thinking that is involved in planning instruction, implementing learning activities, and assessing student understanding. The chapter then turns to the abilities, called essential teaching skills, that we expect to see in all teachers regardless of topic or grade level, and closes with a discussion of the relationship of assessment to the planning and implementation of effective learning activities.

CHAPTER OBJECTIVES

- Describe the steps involved in planning for instruction, and identify an additional step when planning in a standards-based environment
- Identify examples of essential teaching skills in learning experiences, and analyze the role of feedback in promoting learning.
- Explain the relationships between essential teaching skills and models of instruction, and analyze the components of different models.
- Identify the characteristics of effective assessments, and explain the relationships between effective assessments and essential teaching skills.

POWERPOINT SLIDES

PP 13.1 Planning for Instruction
PP 13.2 A Taxonomy for Learning, Teaching, and Assessing
PP 13.3 Essential Teaching Skills
PP 13.4 Characteristics of Effective Questioning
PP 13.5 Characteristics of Effective Praise
PP 13.6 Direct Instruction
PP 13.7 Characteristics of Effective Homework
PP 13.8 Strengths and Weaknesses of Lectures
PP 13.9 Lecture Discussion
PP 13.10 Guided Discovery
PP 13.11 Characteristics of Cooperative Learning
PP 13.12 Capitalizing on Diversity with Cooperative Learning
PP 13.13 Instructional Alignment
PP 13.14 Praxis Practice: Feedback for Short-Answer Questions
PP 13.15 Feedback for Online Case Questions
PP 13.16 Classroom Exercises

VIDEOS

DVD 2, Episode 20: "Analyzing Instructional Alignment"
This episode illustrates a fifth-grade teacher introducing her students to the Civil War.

DVD 2, Episode 21: "Essential Teaching Skills in An Urban Environment"
This episode illustrates a teacher's attempts to demonstrate each of the essential teaching skills that are presented in the chapter. (This is the chapter's opening case study.)

DVD 2, Episode 22: "Guided Discovery in An Elementary Classroom"
This episode illustrates a fourth-grade teacher using the guided discovery model to teach her students the concept *Haiku* poetry.

CHAPTER OUTLINE

I. Planning for instruction
  A. Selecting topics
  B. Preparing learning objectives
    1. Objectives in the cognitive domain
    2. A taxonomy for cognitive objectives
  C. Preparing and organizing learning activities
    1. Task analysis: A planning tool
  D. Planning for assessment
  E. Instructional alignment
  E. Planning in a standards-based environment
II. Implementing instruction: Essential teaching skills
  A. Attitudes
  B. Organization
  C. Communication
    1. Knowledge of content: Its role in clear communication
  D. Focus: Attracting and maintaining attention
  E. Feedback
    1. Praise
    2. Written feedback
  F. Questioning
    1. Questioning Frequency
    2. Equitable distribution
    3. Prompting
    4. Wait-time
    5. Cognitive levels of questions
  G. Review and closure
  H. Learning contexts: Instruction in urban environments
    1. Attitudes
    2. Questioning
    3. Feedback
III. Models of instruction
  A. Direct instruction
      a. Introduction and review
      b. Developing understanding
      c.. Guided practice
      d. Independent practice
      e. Homework
  B. Lecture and lecture-discussion
    1. Lectures
    2. Overcoming the weaknesses of lectures: Lecture-discussions
  C. Guided discovery
      a. Introduction and review
      b. The open-ended phase
      c. The convergent phase
      d. Closure
  D. Cooperative learning
    1. Introducing cooperative learning
    2. Cooperative learning strategies
  E. Cooperative learning: A tool for capitalizing on diversity
IV. Assessment and learning: Using assessment as a learning tool

PRESENTATION OUTLINE

The suggested activities can be completed in small groups and discussed as a whole group, or they can be conducted as whole-class activities. We encourage as much discussion–both in small groups and with the whole class–as possible.

I. Planning for instruction
  A. Selecting topics
  B. Preparing learning objectives
    1. Objectives in the cognitive domain
    2. A taxonomy for cognitive objectives
  C. Preparing and organizing learning activities
    1. Task analysis: A planning tool
  D. Planning for assessment
  E. Instructional alignment
  E. Planning in a standards-based environment

Teaching Suggestions:

■ ***The following suggestions are intended to help your students understand the processes involved in planning for instruction.***

Showing or discussing **Episode 20 on DVD 2**: "Analyzing Instructional Alignment" would be a good way to introduce the chapter.

1. **Begin your discussion by showing Episode 20 on DVD 2: "Analyzing Instructional Alignment."**

2. **After showing the episode, have the students rate the quality of the instruction on a scale of 5 (excellent) to 1 (poor). Then ask the students to provide a rationale for their ratings. This process will provoke considerable discussion, since the ratings will vary quite dramatically, with some students rating the lesson a 4 or 5, and others rating the lesson a 1 or 2. Then, have the students identify the following:**
   - **The teacher's stated goals.**
   - **What the teacher did in the actual lesson.**
   - **The teacher's seatwork assignment.**
   - **The teacher's homework assignment.**

3. **After the students have identified each of the components above, ask them how well the components relate to each other. They will see that the components are essentially unrelated, i.e., the learning activity didn't point to her stated goals, she had the students write an essay about the words on the board, but she had not discussed the words, and her homework assignment was essentially unrelated to anything else in the lesson.**

4. **Introduce the notion of instructional alignment and the students will see that the teacher's instruction was not aligned.**

5. **Now turn to the processes involved when teachers plan for instruction, and ask the students what teachers first consider when they begin planning. You will get a variety of responses. Display PP 13.1 "*Planning for Instruction*" use your own instruction as an example of the processes. Emphasize what you do to ensure that your instruction is aligned.**

6. **Display PP 13.2 "*A Taxonomy for Learning, Teaching, and Assessing*." Have the students classify some of your objectives into one of the cells of the taxonomy table. Remind them that**

an important function of the taxonomy table is to make teachers aware of the need to have objectives that would be classified into cells other than factual knowledge-remember.

7. **Remind the students of the affective and psychomotor domains, and remind them that the Exploring Further section of the chapter provides information for these domains.**

II. Implementing instruction: Essential teaching skills
  A. Attitudes
  B. Organization
  C. Communication
    1. Knowledge of content: Its role in clear communication
  D. Focus: Attracting and maintaining attention
  E. Feedback
    1. Praise
    2. Written feedback
  F. Questioning
    1. Questioning Frequency
    2. Equitable distribution
    3. Prompting
    4. Wait-time
    5. Cognitive levels of questions
  G. Review and closure
  H. Learning contexts: Instruction in urban environments
    1. Attitudes
    2. Questioning
    3. Feedback

Teaching Suggestions:

■ ***The purpose of the suggestions in this section is to help your students understand the essential teaching skills.***

1. **Display PP 13.3 "*Essential Teaching Skills*" and briefly discuss them with students. This will also give you the chance to remind students of your attempts to model the information presented in the text, since your class will be a concrete example of a number of the essential teaching skills.**

Showing or discussing **Episode 21 on DVD 2**: "Analyzing Instructional Alignment" would be a good way to demonstrate the essential teaching skills.

2. **Have the students identify where Scott demonstrated each of the essential teaching skills in his lesson. List Scott's behavior and the skill he demonstrates on the board for sake of emphasis.**

3. **As you discuss Scott's lesson, display PP 13.4 "*Characteristics of Effective Questioning*" which summarizes effective questioning techniques. Have the students assess Scott's questioning.**

4. **Display PP 13.5 "*Characteristics of Effective Praise*," and have the students assess Scott's use of praise.**

5. **To reduce some of the concerns the students will have about getting the "right answer," remind them that your goal is for them to see and understand the essential teaching skills in context and that a great deal of overlap of the skills exists in the real world.**

6. **Have the students identify essential teaching skills in your teaching. This will help personalize the topic for them. They will quickly identify examples, such as you starting your class on time, having your materials ready, providing focus when you use the overhead or PowerPoint slides, developing your lessons with questioning and so on.**

7. **The classroom exercises at the end of this chapter gives the students additional practice with identifying the essential teaching skills in the context of a lesson.**

III. Models of instruction
- A. Direct instruction
  - a. Introduction and review
  - b. Developing understanding
  - c.. Guided practice
  - d. Independent practice
  - e. Homework
- B. Lecture and lecture-discussion
  - 1. Lectures
  - 2. Overcoming the weaknesses of lectures: Lecture-discussions
- C. Guided discovery
  - a. Introduction and review
  - b. The open-ended phase
  - c. The convergent phase
  - d. Closure
- D. Cooperative learning
  - 1. Introducing cooperative learning
  - 2. Cooperative learning strategies
- E. Cooperative learning: A tool for capitalizing on diversity

Teaching Suggestions:

■ *The purpose of the suggestions in this section is to help your students understand and be able to use different models of instruction*

1. **Point out that models of instruction are prescriptive approaches to teaching that are designed to help students acquire a deep understanding of specific forms of knowledge.**

■ *To help the students understand direct instruction:*

1. **Display PP 13.6 "*Direct Instruction,*" which illustrates the phases of direct instruction and their related cognitive learning components. Have the students identify each of the phases in Sam Barnett's lesson (in the case study on pages 423-425 of the chapter).**
2. **Display PP 13.7 "*Characteristics of Effective Homework.*" Note that you attempt to be consistent with these characteristics with your own homework.**

■ *To help the students understand lecture-discussion and how the instructional model overcomes the weaknesses of lectures:*

1. **Display PP 13.8 "*Strengths and Weaknesses of Lectures*" and point out that lecture discussion is designed to overcome the weaknesses of lectures.**

2. **Display PP 13.9 "*Lecture Discussion*" and have the students identify each of the phases in Diane Anderson's lesson (in the case study on pages 428 and 429 of the chapter).**

■ *To help the students understand guided discovery:*

1. **Display PP 13.10 "*Guided Discovery*" and have the students assess the extent to which Scott Sowell (in Episode 21 of DVD 2) implemented each of the phases in his lesson.**

Here would be a good point to show or discuss **Episode 22 on DVD 2**: "Guided Discovery in An Elementary Classroom."

2. **Have the students assess the extent to which the teacher (Jenny Newhall) in Episode 22 of DVD 2 implemented each of the guided discovery phases in her lesson.**

3. **Have the students describe how Scott Sowell or Jenny Newhall could have modified their lessons to use the direct instruction model instead of guided discovery.**

■ *To help the students understand cooperative learning:*

1. **Display PP 13.11 "*Characteristics of Cooperative Learning*." Have the students describe how these characteristics are embedded in each of the cooperative learning strategies discussed in the chapter.**

2. **Display PP 13.12 "*Capitalizing on Diversity with Cooperative Learning*," to demonstrate how cooperative learning can be a tool for accommodating diversity. Have the students describe how Maria Sanchez (in the case study beginning on page 433) capitalized on the suggestions in PP 13.12.**

IV. Assessment and Learning: Using assessment as a learning tool

Teaching Suggestions:

■ *The purpose of the suggestions in this section is to help your students understand the role of assessment in promoting learning.*

1. **Discuss the students' thinking in Scott's lesson, as presented on page 436 of the text, and emphasize the need for assessment in promoting learning.**

2. **Again, remind the students that promoting learning is the reason you quiz frequently and provide detailed feedback about their responses. Note that feedback is one of the most important essential teaching skills.**

3. **Relate frequent assessment and feedback to your study of motivation in Chapters 10 and 11. Assessment and feedback provide information about increasing competence and self-efficacy, both essential for motivation to learn.**

4. **Summarize the chapter by displaying PP 13.13 "*Instructional Alignment*" and have the students identify which of the examples are aligned and which are not. Have them assess the extent to which Scott's instruction was aligned.**

ENRICHMENT MATERIALS

TEACHER PREP WEBSITE

The *Teacher Prep* website an online resource for students and instructors. Both you and students can access the *Teacher Prep* website by going to http://www.prenhall.com/teacherprep. Enter your user name and password and click on "Log In." The *Teacher Prep* website includes video episodes, student and teacher artifacts, teacher and research resources, and information about licensing and beginning a teaching career. The *Teacher Prep* website is described in detail in the Media Guide.

The following articles are recommended by the *Exploring Further* section titled "Making Cooperative Learning Equitable" on page 434 of the chapter.

Once into the *Teacher Prep* website access the articles by completing the following steps:
1. Click on "Research Resources" on the left panel of the screen, scroll down the middle of the page and again click on "Research Resources."
2. Go to "Classroom Processes" and click on "Instructional Methods."
3. Click on the following articles:
   Making Cooperative Learning Equitable, by E. Cohen (1998), Ref. No. 2240
   Varying Instructional Strategies, by M. Goethals, R. Howard, and S. Sanders (2004), Ref. No. 1936

The first article examines some of the issues that arise when socially dominant and socially isolated students work together in cooperative learning groups together with the causes of the inequality. It then goes on to offer suggestions for overcoming these obstacles.

The second article identifies some of the benefits of cooperative learning but also points out that it isn't appropriate for all learning situations and that instructional strategies need to be varied.

ADDITIONAL EXPLORING FURTHER SUGGESTIONS

Page 408 of the chapter suggests that students to go the *Exploring Further* module of Chapter 13 for a discussion of the original taxonomy developed in 1956 by Bloom et al., commonly described as "Bloom's Taxonomy."

Page 409 o the chapter suggests that students to go the *Exploring Further* module of Chapter 13 for a discussion of objectives in the affective and psychomotor domains.

Page 411 of the chapter suggests that students to go the *Exploring Further* module of Chapter 13 for access to standards created by different professional organizations.

Page 429 of the chapter suggests that students to go the *Exploring Further* module of Chapter 13 to see a discussion of Ausubel's theory of meaningful verbal learning.

Page 431 of the chapter suggests that students to go the *Exploring Further* module of Chapter 13 to see a discussion and illustration of *inquiry* as an instructional model.

DISCUSSION STARTERS

You may choose to have your students discuss one or more of the following questions to further enrich their understanding of your learning activities.

1. Which of the different types of knowledge expert teachers possess are most important for elementary teachers? Middle and junior high school teachers? Secondary teachers?

2. What would be the advantages of moving to a longer school year (e.g., 240 versus 180 days?) What disadvantages would there be? Weighing these advantages and disadvantages, what would be your recommendation?

3. What are the major barriers to instructional time in the classroom? What concrete steps can teachers take to maximize instructional time?

4. What can teachers do to maximize student engaged time? How do the strategies teachers might use vary in elementary, middle and junior high, and secondary schools?

5. What differences exist in the planning process for teachers in elementary schools, middle and junior high schools, and secondary schools?

6. Are each of the essential teaching skills equally important in elementary, middle and junior high, and high schools? If not, explain the differences.

7. Is assessment equally important for elementary, middle and junior high and secondary teachers? If not, describe the differences.

BACKGROUND READINGS

Anderson, L., & Krathwohl, D. (Eds.).(2001). *A taxonomy for learning, teaching, and assessing: A revision of Bloom's taxonomy of educational objectives*. New York: Addison Wesley Longman.
As the title suggests, this book provides a revision of the famous Bloom's taxonomy

Borko, H., & Putnam, R. (1996). Learning to teach. In D. Berliner & R. Calfee (Eds.), *Handbook of educational psychology* (pp. 673–708). New York: Simon & Schuster.
This chapter describes in detail the processes involved in learning to teach.

Calderhead, J. (1996). Teachers: Beliefs and knowledge. In D. Berliner & R. Calfee (Eds.), *Handbook of educational psychology* (pp. 709–725). New York: Macmillan.
This chapter provides a detailed description of the influence of beliefs on teachers' classroom behavior.

Eggen, P., & Kauchak, D. (2006). Strategies and models for teachers (5th ed.). Boston: Allyn & Bacon.
This book describes a number of instructional models, each grounded on cognitive learning theory

Kauchak, D., & Eggen, P. (2007). Learning and teaching: Research-based methods (5th ed.). Boston: Allyn & Bacon.
This book describes the processes involved in planning and implementing instruction and assessing learning in detail.

Marzano, R. (2003). What works in schools. Alexandria, VA: Association for Supervision and Curriculum Development.
This book provides an overview of current research on effective teaching.

McDougall, D., & Granby, C. (1996). How expectation of questioning method affects undergraduates' preparation for class. *Journal of Experimental Education, 65,* 43–54.
This article documents the effectiveness of teacher questioning and equitable distribution on college students' preparedness for their classes.

Shuell, T. (1996). Teaching and learning in a classroom context. In D. Berliner & R. Calfee (Eds.), *Handbook of educational psychology* (pp. 726–764). New York: Simon & Schuster.
This chapter provides additional research support for the essential teaching skills.

Shulman, L. (1986). Those who understand: Knowledge growth in teaching. *Educational Researcher, 15*(2), 4–14.
This article provides the framework for the concept of pedagogical content knowledge.

FEEDBACK

Developing as a Professional: Praxis Practice: Feedback for Short-Answer Questions

The feedback that appears here is for the short-answer questions that follow the case study on pages 438 and 439 of the text. The feedback is also available to students on the companion website.

1. Describe the types of teacher knowledge Judy displayed in the lesson. Provide evidence from the case study to support your conclusions.

Judy displayed each of the types of teacher knowledge in planning and implementing her lesson. First, her knowledge of content allowed her to structure the lesson so that students could see similarities and differences in the four geographic areas.

Judy's pedagogical content knowledge was demonstrated by her ability to represent the abstract relationships between the geography and economy of the different regions in a way that illustrated patterns, which the students could then identify.

General pedagogical knowledge involves an understanding of general principles of instruction and classroom management. Judy's lesson was clearly focused and she moved the students between groupwork and whole-class instruction quickly and smoothly. She also demonstrated general pedagogical knowledge in developing the entire lesson with questioning. Finally, she demonstrated knowledge of learners and learning by realizing that students need to be actively involved in learning activities, and Judy involved her students with her groupwork and questioning.

2. Describe Judy's thinking as she planned the lesson. Identify at least three decisions that she made as she planned.

Planning typically involves several decisions. First, Judy had to decide that the topic—identifying relationships between geography and economy of different geographical regions—was an important topic to study. Second, Judy decided that her learning objective would be for students to describe the effect of geography on the economy of a region. Third, she had to make a decision about how the learning activity would be prepared. She decided that she would have the students gather information about the regions, organize the information in a matrix and then analyze the information. She also decided that she would use a combination of groupwork and whole-class discussion in her learning activity.

3. Analyze Judy's instructional alignment. Offer any suggestions that you might have that would have increased the alignment of the lesson.

Alignment refers to the connections between learning objectives, instructional activities, and assessment. Judy's learning objective was for students to understand the relationships between geography and the economy of different regions in the country. Since her learning activity focused on these relationships, her objective and learning activity were aligned. We'll examine the alignment of her assessment discuss evaluation alignment below in the Document-Based Analysis question.

4. Analyze Judy's application of the essential teaching skills in her lesson. Which did she demonstrate most effectively? Which did she demonstrate least effectively?

Judy demonstrated several of the essential teaching skills in her lesson. First, she demonstrated a positive approach to the lesson with appropriately high expectations. She was well organized. She began the lesson immediately after the bell rang, she had the chart already displayed on the wall of her room, and students moved back and forth from small-group to whole-group activities quickly and smoothly.

Judy's communication was clear. She used clear language, and the lesson was thematic and led to a point (connected discourse). We didn't see explicit transition signals in the lesson, nor was emphasis apparent.

The chart that Judy and the students had prepared provided a good form of sensory focus. Introductory focus wasn't evident in the lesson.

Judy's questioning was quite good. She called on a variety of students, called on girls and boys about equally, called on students by name, and assured success with open-ended questions and prompting.

Because of the way the lesson was organized, much of Judy's feedback was a simple acknowledgement of students' observations, and her closure was quite brief, because the period was nearing an end. She would need to do a careful review the next day to ensure that the students had encoded the information clearly into long term memory.

Feedback for Online Case Book Questions

The feedback below is for the *Online Case Book* for Chapter 7 (referenced on page 420 of the chapter). Both you and the students can access the case study by going to www.prenhall.com/eggen, selecting Chapter 7, and clicking on *Online Case Book.*

You may choose to assign the online case as homework or you may want to discuss the case in class. Answers to these questions *do not* appear on the companion website, so students *do not* have access to the feedback.

Multiple-Choice Items

Multiple-Choice Questions:

1. Look at paragraphs 4–7 of the case study. Of the following, which essential teaching skill is best illustrated by these paragraphs?
    a. Personal teaching efficacy
    b. Modeling
    c. Organization
    d. Focus
    a. In saying, "My kids didn't score as well as I would have liked on the fractions part of the SAT last year, and I swore that they were going to do better this year," and "I don't care. I'm pushing them harder. I think I could have done a better job last year, so I swore I was really going to be ready for them this time," Shirley demonstrated that she believed she was capable of getting the students to achieve regardless of constraints.

2. Look at paragraphs 10–13 of the case study. Of the following, which essential teaching skill is best illustrated by these paragraphs?
    a. Modeling
    b. Organization
    c. Focus
    d. Closure
    b. Shirley began her math lesson within a minute of the time math was scheduled, she had her transparency with the problems on it prepared and ready to be displayed, and the students had their math books out and were waiting when she began, which indicated that they were used to the routine.

3. Look at paragraphs 14, 16, 19, 21, 27, 29, and 34. Of the following, which essential teaching skill is best illustrated by these paragraphs?
    a. Personal teaching efficacy
    b. Communication
    c. Focus
    d. Equitable distribution
    d. Shirley called on a different student in each of these paragraphs, so she distributed her questions to the students as equally as possible.

Short-Answer Questions:

4. What was Shirley's learning objective? Into what cell of the taxonomy table you studied in the chapter would the objective be classified? Was her instruction aligned? Explain.

Shirley's learning objective was for her students to understand the concept equivalent fractions. Since equivalent fractions is a concept, the learning objective would be classified into the cell where conceptual knowledge intersects with understand. Her learning activity focused on equivalent fractions, and her seatwork assignment, which also served as a form of assessment required the students to find equivalent fractions. Because of the consistency between her objective, learning activity, and seatwork assignment, her instruction was aligned.

5. Analyze Shirley's planning. Describe the way she thought about the lesson and the decisions she made in planning it.

Shirley's goal was for her students to be able to add fractions with unlike denominators. As part of a subject matter task analysis, she realized that they first needed to understand equivalent fractions, so this was the focus of her first lesson, which would then be followed with a lesson or lessons on adding fractions with unlike denominators.

Shirley decided that she would use the cardboard drawings to illustrate equivalent fractions. The examples were high quality because all the information the students needed to understand the concept was illustrated in the examples.

She then made decisions about the sequence of her lesson. She began with a review followed by one of her most concrete and obvious examples, followed by examples that were more complex. Her ability to design examples in this way is evidence of her pedagogical content knowledge.

CLASSROOM EXERCISES

The classroom exercises that follow appear *only here* in the instructor's manual. Students do not have access to *either the questions or the answers*.

The purpose of keeping the exercises only in the instructor's manual is to allow you to use them as class discussion items, or for homework, if you should choose to do so.

Feedback for the exercises follows immediately.

Read the following case study and answer the questions that follow.

1. Kathy Johnson is a fifth-grade teacher with 27 students, about half of whom are classified as placed at risk in her class from mostly low to middle income families in an urban midwestern city. Four of her students have learning disabilities, and two are classified as behaviorally disordered. A veteran of six years, she typically schedules her day as follows:

8:15– 9:15	Math
9:15–10:45	Language Arts
10:45–11:00	Break
11:00–11:30	Social Studies
11:30–12:00	Lunch
12:00–1:25	Reading
1:25–1:35	Break
1:35–2:00	Science
2:00–2:45	Resource (Art, music, P.E., computer)

2. In social studies Kathy has begun a unit on the on the Northern and Southern Colonies prior to the Civil War.
3. As the students file into the room from their break, they see a large chart displayed at the front of the room that appears as follows:

	People	Land and Climate	Economy
Northern States	Small towns Religious Valued education Cooperative	Timber covered Glacial remains Poor soil Short growing season Cold winters	Syrup Rum Lumber Shipbuilding Fishing Small farms
Southern States	Aristocratic Isolated Social class distinction	Fertile soil Hot weather Long growing season	Large farms Tobacco Cotton Unskilled workers Servants and slaves

4. Kathy is standing at the doorway as her students enter the room. She smiles and jokes with them as they pass by, and reminds them of what they're about to do with comments, such as, "Look carefully at the chart at the front of the room, and see if you can find anything interesting about it and how the north and south were different?"

5. At 11:02 the students have their social studies books on their desks, Kathy has moved to the front of the room and she begins, "We began talking about the Northern and Southern Colonies yesterday. Let's see what we remember. . . .Where are they compared to where we live?. . . Lorenda?"
6. ". . . They're over here," Lorenda answers, motioning to the right with her hand.
7. "Yes, they're generally east of us," Kathy adds, as she walks quickly and points to the map at the side of the room identifying the general location of the colonies relative to their location with a wave of her hand.
8. "And about how long ago are we talking about, a few years or a long time? . . . Greg?"
9. ". . . A long time. Like when our great, great, great, great grandfathers and grandmothers might have lived."
10. "Yes, very good," Kathy smiles and nods. "We're talking about time during the early and middle 1800s."
11. "We also talked about some important ideas, like 'Economy,'" Kathy continues. "What do we mean by economy?. . . Carol?"
12. ". . . It's . . . like . . . the way they make their money, like when we said that the economy here is based on manufacturing, like making cars and parts for cars and stuff," Carol responds uncertainly.
13. "Very good description, Carol," Kathy nods. "You identified auto manufacturing as an important part of our economy, and that's a good example."
14. "Now, look here," Kathy directs, pointing to the column marked 'Economy.' "We see that the economy for the two groups of colonies is very different. Today we want to see what some of these specific differences are and why the two economies are so different. So, remember as we go through the lesson that we're talking about the way the colonies made their money, and we're trying to figure out why it is so different. . . . Everybody ready?" Kathy surveys the class. "Good. Let's go."
15. She then begins, "What are some of the differences we see in the economies for the two regions? . . . Ann Marie?"
16. ". . ."
17. "What do you notice about the farms in the two colonies?"
18. ". . . The farms were much bigger in the Southern Colonies than they were in the Northern Colonies."
19. "OK, Good observation," Kathy nods energetically. "Now why might that have been the case? . . . Jim?"
20. ". . ."
21. ". . . Would you like me to repeat the question?" Kathy asks, knowing that Jim hasn't heard her.
22. "Yes," Jim responds quickly, with a look of relief.

[Kathy continues guiding the students' analysis of the information on the chart, in the process finding relationships between the geography, climate, and economy. When students are unable to answer she rephrases her questions and provides cues to help them along. She then has them consider why the economy of their city might be the way it is. We return to her lesson now.]

23. "You have done very well, everyone," she smiles, pointing her finger in the air for emphasis. "Now, everyone, get with your partner, take two minutes and write two or three summary statements about what we've learned here today. . . . Quickly now, get started.

[The students start buzzing, pointing at the chart, and one of the two in each pair begin writing. In some cases they stop, crumple their papers and begin again. As they work, Kathy walks among them offering encouragement and periodic suggestions.]

24. At the end of two minutes Kathy announces, "One more minute, and we're going to look at what you wrote."
25. After another minute she begins, "OK, let's see what you've got. What did you and Linda say, David?"
26. ". . . We said that the weather and the land had a lot to do with the way the different colonies made their money."
27. "Excellent! That's a good one. How about someone else.. . . Danielle, how about you and Tony?"

[Kathy has several other pairs offer their summary statements, they further develop the statements as a whole group, and then Kathy collects the papers.]

28. At 11:28 she announces, "Almost lunch time. Please put away your papers."
29. The students quickly put their books, papers, and pencils away, glance around their desks for any waste paper, and are sitting quietly at 11:30.

Identify the Essential Teaching Skill best illustrated by each of the following paragraph or sets of paragraphs in the case study. (The paragraphs in the case study are numbered for your reference.) In each case, where appropriate, identify both the skill and the subskill. For example, if you select Organization, also include "Starting on Time" or "Preparing Materials in Advance" or Established Routines if one of the subskills is represented more than any other. Your answer would then be, for example, "Organization-Established Routines."

Explain your choice in each case.

1. 2–5
2. 5–13
3. 14
4. 15–18
5. 23–27
6. 5 and 28
7. 5, 8, 11, 15, 19
8. 7, 13, 19
9. In 19 Kathy called on Jim, knowing that he wasn't listening (as we see in 20 and 21). Is this [calling on a student who isn't paying attention] effective teaching strategy? Why do you think so, or why do you think not?
10. Look at the type of questions Kathy asked in 15 and 17. What kind of questions are these. Give at least three reasons why they're effective.

FEEDBACK FOR CLASSROOM EXERCISES

1. Organization—Materials prepared in advance, and starting on time.

Kathy had her chart prepared in advance a displayed in front of the room as the students walked in, and she began her instruction two minutes after it was scheduled to begin.

2. Review—Beginning of class review.

Kathy reviewed the time when the events occurred and checked the students' perception of terms such as economy.

3. Focus—Introductory Focus.

Kathy's comment, "So, remember as we go through the lesson that we're talking about the way the colonies made their money, and we're trying to figure out why it is so different. . . . ," provided a conceptual umbrella for the lesson.

4. Questioning—Prompting.

When Ann Marie wasn't able to answer, Kathy prompted her by saying, "What do you notice about the farms in the two colonies?"

5. Review and Closure—Closure.

Kathy had the students summarize the information, and they discussed the students' conclusions as a class.

6. Organization

Of the 30 minutes allocated to social studies, Kathy used 26 in her lesson.

7. Questioning—Equitable Distribution.

Kathy called on individual students by name, and she asked the question first and identified the person to respond after the question had been asked.

8. Feedback.

Kathy provided the students with information about the quality of their responses in each of these paragraphs.

9. Yes, this is an effective technique. It draws the student back into the lesson in a non-punitive way.

10. These are open-ended questions. Some reasons they're effective include:

a. They're safe, and they ensure student success, since a variety of answers are acceptable.
b. They're easy to ask, so they take some pressure off the teacher.
c. They're excellent as prompts when students aren't initially able to answer. (This is how Kathy used them in helping Ann Marie to respond.)
d. They're effective for cultural minorities and non-native English speakers, who sometimes aren't used to the fast-paced drill-type questioning that goes on in classrooms.

CHAPTER 14: LEARNING, INSTRUCTION, AND TECHNOLOGY

CHAPTER OVERVIEW

This chapter provides an overview of educational technology with an emphasis on its relationship to learning and instruction in classrooms. It begins with a short section on defining technology and then links technology to different theories of learning. Next follows a major section on different instructional uses of technology. The final section examines different ways that technology can be used to support teachers in their different professional roles.

CHAPTER OBJECTIVES

- Identify different views of technology in descriptions of classroom support materials.
- Explain how different theories of learning are applied to technology use in classrooms.
- Describe ways that different forms of technology are used to support instruction and identify the learning theories that support these forms of technology.
- Explain how word processing, the Internet, and assistive technology can increase learning.
- Identify different ways that technology can be used to make teachers' work more effective.

POWERPOINT SLIDES

PP 14.1 Learning from an Information Processing Perspective
PP 14.2 Software Design and Our Information Processing System
PP 14.3 Issues in the Use of Word Processing
PP 14.4 Principles of Instruction for Using Technology in Classrooms
PP 14.5 Praxis Practice: Feedback for Short-Answer Questions
PP 14.6 Feedback for Online Case Questions
PP 14.7 Classroom Exercises

VIDEOS

DVD 2, Episode 23: "Laptops for Data in Fifth Grade"
This episode illustrates a teacher using laptop computers to store and manipulate information in a fifth-grade learning activity attract students' attention.

DVD 1, Episode 24: "Using PowerPoint in the Classroom"
This episode illustrates the use of PowerPoint as a tool for presenting information in a world history class.

CHAPTER OUTLINE

I. What is technology?
II. Technology and learning
    A. Behaviorism and technology
    B. Technology and cognitive learning theory
        1. Information processing
            a. Attracting attention and creating accurate perceptions
            b. Managing the resources of working memory
            c. Promoting encoding into long-term memory
            d. Managing processing with metacognitive skills
        2. Constructivism and technology
    C. Social cognitive theory and technology
III. Technology and Instruction
    A. Drill-and-practice software
    B. Tutorials
        1. Multimedia & hypermedia
        2. Strengths of tutorials
        3. Weaknesses of tutorials
    C. Simulations
        1. Benefits of simulations
            a. Time alteration
            b. Safety
            c. Expense
        2. Simulations as problem solving tools
    D. Databases & spreadsheets
        1. Databases
        2. Spreadsheets
    E. Word processing: Using technology to teach writing
        1. Issues in the use of word processing technologies
    F. Internet-based technologies
        1. The Internet in problem-based learning
        2. The Internet as a communication tool
        3. Advantages & disadvantages of Internet communication
    G. Distance education
    H. Exploring diversity: Employing technology to support learners with disabilities
        1. Adaptations to computer input devices
        2. Adaptations to output devices
    I. Using technology in the classroom: Instructional principles
        1. Using technology in classrooms: Findings from research
IV. Teacher support applications of technology
    A. Preparing instructional materials
        1. PowerPoint: Planning for presentation options
    B. Classroom assessment
        1. Planning & constructing tests
        2. Administering tests
        3. Scoring and interpreting tests
        4. Maintaining student records
    C. Communicating with Parents

PRESENTATION OUTLINE

The suggested activities can be completed in small groups and discussed as a whole group, or they can be conducted as whole-class activities. We encourage as much discussion—both in small groups and with the whole clas—as possible.

I. What Is Technology?

Teaching Suggestions:

■ ***The purpose of this section of the chapter is to introduce two differing views of technology in education.***

1. **Share with your students your own views of technology—why you use what you do and what obstacles exist to greater technology usage.**

2. **Ask how teachers' and students' roles change in hardware and process views of technology usage.**

3. **Discussion Starter Question #1 asks which view of technology--hardware or process–is more prevalent in the schools and why.**

> Here would be a good point to show or discuss **Episode 23 on DVD 2**: "Laptops for Data in Fifth Grade."

4. **Discuss the questions asked in Episode 23, particularly the question as to whether or not the question of whether or not the educational benefits of using the technology justifies the cost.**

II. Technology and learning
   A. Behaviorism and technology
   B. Technology and cognitive learning theory
      1. Information processing
         a. Attracting attention and creating accurate perceptions
         b. Managing the resources of working memory
         c. Promoting encoding into long-term memory
         d. Managing processing with metacognitive skills
      2. Constructivism and technology
   C. Social cognitive theory and technology

Teaching Suggestions:

■ ***The purpose of the activities in this section of the chapter is to help students understand how different theories of learning result in different applications of educational technology.***

1. **Begin the section by reviewing the major theories of learning in Chapters 6, 7, and 8. Emphasize differences between the different theories in terms of their definition of learning, and learner and teacher roles.**

2. **Extending Your Knowledge 1 asks students to identify the major advantages and disadvantages of a behaviorist perspective on learning from technology.**

3. **Display PP 14.1 "*Learning from an Information Processing Perspective*," and use it as a frame of reference to discuss PP 14.2 "*Software Design and Our Information Processing System*."**

4. **Extending Your Knowledge question 2 examines the crucial role of working memory in learning from technology.**

5. **Check out a sport-related DVD or video from any local library. Use it to show how modeling and observational learning are central to Social Cognitive Theory. Discuss how a teacher might apply Social Cognitive Theory in the classroom.**

III. Technology and Instruction
- A. Drill-and-Practice Software
- B. Tutorials
  1. Multimedia & hypermedia
  2. Strengths of tutorials
  3. Weaknesses of tutorials
- C. Simulations
  1. Benefits of simulations
     - a. Time alteration
     - b. Safety
     - c. Expense
  2. Simulations as problem solving tools
- D. Databases & Spreadsheets
  1. Databases
  2. Spreadsheets

Teaching Suggestions:

■ ***The purpose of the suggestions in this section is to help students understand the different ways that technology can be used to promote learning.***

1. **Bring in a sample of a drill-and-practice software so students can see how it works. Discuss the different ways it provides feedback and deals with motivation issues. Discuss how teachers could integrate drill-and-practice software in the classroom.**

2. **Locate a tutorial in your school's media lab or borrow one from a local school district. Share with students and explore the different ways tutorials use multimedia and hypermedia.**

3. **Ask students to locate additional tutorials on the Internet. Ask them to report on their main features as well as strengths and weaknesses.**

4. **If available, bring in the board games *Monopoly* or *Clue*. Ask how many have played these. Analyze how they are simulations. Discuss the advantages and disadvantages of these non-tech simulations.**

5. **Share a simulation with the class (*Oregon Trail* is an excellent one). If a media lab is available, have students actually participate in the simulation. Afterwards, debrief and talk about what they learned from it.**

6. **Discuss the relative advantages and disadvantages of using simulations at the beginning and end of a unit.**

7. **To demonstrate the different uses of a database, gather some actual data from the class and place it in a database. One way to do this is to ask what they typically eat for the three meals in a day and divide the data out by age or gender. Favorite recreation activities or television programs are other options. Discuss the advantages and disadvantages of databases and how they could be used in the classroom.**

8. Bring in an actual database from either your own research or a colleague's. Discuss how it relates to the larger goals of the study and how it helps make finding trends and patterns easier.

E. Word Processing: Using Technology to Teach Writing
   1. Issues in the use of word processing technologies
F. Internet based technologies
   1. The Internet in problem-based learning
   2. The Internet as a communication tool
   3. Advantages & disadvantages of Internet communication
G. Distance Education

Teaching Suggestions:

■ *The purpose of the suggestions in this section is to help students understand the*

1. Ask if any of your students remember writing without word processing. Discuss how word processing influences your own professional life.

2. Present PP 14.3 "*Issues in the Use of Word Processing*" and have the students offer their perspectives related to the issues.

3. Use this as an opportunity to review all the resources that are available on this book's Companion Website. Ask which students have used which features and ask them to share their experiences.

4. Refer students to the ASCD/Merrill Website at www.prenhall.com/teacherprep. Walk them through the resources they can find on this website.

5. Encourage students to use the Message Board connected to this text. Ask students who have used it to share their experiences.

6. Share with students the various efforts at distance education in your department or college.

7. Bring in an instructor who has developed a distance learning course and have them walk students through the course. Ask them to discuss their own experiences as an instructor/developer.

H. Exploring Diversity: Employing Technology to Support Learners with Disabilities
   1. Adaptations to computer input devices
   2. Adaptations to output devices
I. Technology in the classroom: Instructional principles
   1. Using technology in classrooms: Findings from research

Teaching Suggestions:

■ *The purpose of the suggestions in this section is to help students understand the*

1. Enlist the assistance of an instructor in your special education department to talk about different technology adaptations in your area.

2. Ask a special educator from a local school distract to come in and discuss the technology resources in their district.

3. Discuss your own experiences with using technology in your classroom, including successes and challenges. Explain how your use of technology has changed over time.

4. **Display PP 14.4 "*Principles of Instruction for Using Technology in Classrooms.*" Have the students identify where Jacinta Lopez (in the case study beginning on page 464 of the chapter) applied the principles in her teaching.**

IV. Teacher Support Applications of Technology
   A. Preparing Instructional Materials
      1. PowerPoint: Planning for presentation options
   B. Classroom Assessment
      1. Planning & constructing tests
      2. Administering tests
      3. Scoring and interpreting tests
      4. Maintaining student records
   C. Communicating with Parents

Teaching Suggestions:

■ ***The purpose of the activities in this section of the chapter is to illustrate the different ways that technology can make instructors' tasks easer and more efficient.***

1. **Discuss and demonstrate the different technology tools that come with this text. Explain how different tools like the test bank can make your job easier.**

2. **Bring in a commercial assessment software program (e.g. Create a Test, Test Writer, Test Generator, etc.). Walk students through the various features found in the software.**

3. **Borrow the assessment software from a text used in the public schools (most science and math series have these). Walk students through the features and explain how they can be used to produce better assessment products.**

Here would be a good point to show or discuss **Episode 24 on DVD 2**: "Using PowerPoint in the Classroom."

ENRICHMENT MATERIALS

TEACHER PREP WEBSITE

The *Teacher Prep* website an online resource for students and instructors. Both you and students can access the *Teacher Prep* website by going to http://www.prenhall.com/teacherprep. Enter your user name and password and click on "Log In." The *Teacher Prep* website includes video episodes, student and teacher artifacts, teacher and research resources, and information about licensing and beginning a teaching career. The *Teacher Prep* website is described in detail in the Media Guide.

The following article is recommended by the *Exploring Further* section titled "Plagiarism" on page 459 of the chapter.

Once into the *Teacher Prep* website access the articles by completing the following steps:
1. Click on "Research Resources" on the left panel of the screen, scroll down the middle of the page and again click on "Research Resources."
2. Go to "Classroom Processes" and click on "Technology."
3. Click on the following article:
   Cut and Paste 101: Plagiarism and the Net, by L. Renard (1999), Ref. No. 235

This article describes the recently discovered problem of plagiarism from the Internet and what teachers can do to combat this problem.

The following articles are recommended by the *Exploring Further* section titled "Teacher Support Applications of Technology" on page 467 of the chapter.

Once into the *Teacher Prep* website access the articles by completing the following steps:
1. Click on "Research Resources" on the left panel of the screen, scroll down the middle of the page and again click on "Research Resources."
2. Go to "Classroom Processes" and click on "Instructional Methods."
3. Click on the following articles:
   How can I use E-mail for professional purposes? by P. Ertmer, C. Hruskocy and D. Woods (2000), Ref. No. 113
   How can I use the Web as a lesson planning bank?, by P. Ertmer, C. Hruskocy and D. Woods (2000), Ref. No. 424, and
   How can I use the web as a research tool? by P. Ertmer, C. Hruskocy and D. Woods (2000), Ref. No. 425

These articles describe different ways to use technology to increase your instructional effectiveness.

ADDITIONAL EXPLORING FURTHER SUGGESTIONS

Page 449 of the chapter suggests that students to go the *Exploring Further* module of Chapter 14 for a discussion of television as a form of symbolic modeling and its influence on people's behavior.

Page 454 of the chapter suggests that students to go the *Exploring Further* module of Chapter 14 for a more detailed discussion of the Jasper Series.

DISCUSSION STARTERS

You may choose to have your students discuss one or more of the following questions to further enrich their understanding of your learning activities.

1. Which view of technology—hardware or process—is more prevalent in the schools? Why is this the case? What could be done to improve the balance?

2. In what areas of the curriculum is technology used as a way of delivering instruction most useful? Least? Why?

3. What are the advantages and disadvantages of using technology to deliver instruction, such as drill-and-practice or PowerPoint presentations? In what areas and at what levels is this use of technology most effective?

4. Should Internet filtering occur at the national or local level? What are the advantages and disadvantages of each approach?

5. What can teachers do to overcome students' uneven access to computers at home? What can they do at the school or district level?

6. What is the biggest obstacle to more effective technology use in schools? What can beginning teachers realistically do to address this problem?

BACKGROUND READINGS

Clark, R. C., & Mayer, R. E. (2003). *e-learning and the science of instruction: Proven guidelines for consumers and designers of multimedia learning.* San Francisco: Pfeiffer/Wiley.
This book provides an excellent overview of cognitive technology design efforts, with an emphasis on information processing. Lots of examples make this a very readable book.

Cuban, L. (2001). *Computers in the classroom: Oversold and underused.* Cambridge, MA: Harvard University Press.
This contains an excellent critique of the technology movement with a realistic look at classroom uses.

Dabbagh, N., & Bannan-Ritland, B. (2005). *Online learning.* Upper Saddle River, NJ: Pearson.
This volume is an up-to-date overview of basic principles of online learning.

Forcier, R. & Descy, D. (2005). *The computer as an educational tool: Productivity and problem solving* (4th ed.). Upper Saddle River, NJ: Merrill/Prentice Hall.
This is one of the more comprehensive and current text on computers in education, with excellent classroom applications.

Jonassen, D., Howland, J., Moore, J., Marra,R. (2003). *Learning to solve problems with technology* (2nd ed.) Upper Saddle River, NJ: Merrill/Prentice Hall.
This book provides an excellent overview of constructivist applications of technology, and is well written with lots of classroom examples.

Morrison, G. R., & Lowther, D. L. (2002). *Integrating computer technology into the classroom* (2nd ed.). Upper Saddle River, NJ: Merrill/Prentice Hall.
This is a well written and practical text that focuses on applying computers to classroom learning.

Newby, T., Stepich, D., Lehman, J., & Russell, J. (2006). *Instructional technology and teaching and learning* (3rd ed.). Upper Saddle River, NJ: Merrill/Prentice Hall.
This book provide a comprehensive overview of educational technology.

Picciano, A. (2001). *Distance learning.* Upper Saddle River, NJ: Pearson.
This volume provides a comprehensive examination of distance learning from multiple perspectives including the instructor, students, and the support services needed to make distance learning work.

Roblyer, M. (2006). *Integrating educational technology into teaching* (4th ed.). Upper Saddle River, NJ: Merrill/Prentice Hall.
This is one of the most current and comprehensive books that exist on the various facets of educational technology.

FEEDBACK

Developing as a Professional: Praxis Practice: Feedback for Short-Answer Questions

The feedback that appears here is for the short-answer questions that follow the case study on page 469 of the text. The feedback is also available to students on the companion website.

1. How does Callie's experience with the Internet compare with other teachers'? What do experts suggest to remedy this problem?

   Callie's experience is a common problem that teachers encounter in using the Internet. The broad array of information is often overwhelming to students. Experts recommend structuring access to Internet sites b: 1) limiting the number of options, 2) providing specific suggestions about how to use specific Internet sites, and 3) providing instructional scaffolding in the form of handouts and questions.

2. How was Callie's experience with her students' word processing capabilities similar to other teachers'? What options does Callie have to remedy this problem?

   Research suggests that word processing can improve students' writing but that proficient word processing skills are necessary for this to occur. One effective way to develop students' word processing skills is through the use of tutorials that adapt instruction to student skill levels.

3. Callie wanted to teach her students to learn to organize the different kinds of information they gathered about pets. What technology tool could Callie use to teach her students to do this, and how should she introduce this tool to students?

   Databases are an effective tool to organize and display different kinds of information. In introducing databases to her students, Callie needs to carefully explain the logic behind them and how their capabilities can be used to organize data.

Feedback for Online Case Book Questions

The feedback below is for the *Online Case Book* for Chapter 7 (referenced on page 463 of the chapter). Both you and the students can access the case study by going to www.prenhall.com/eggen, selecting Chapter 14, and clicking on *Online Case Book.*

You may choose to assign the online case as homework or you may want to discuss the case in class. Answers to these questions *do not* appear on the companion website, so students *do not* have access to the feedback.

Multiple-Choice Items

1. Carl's use of technology in his unit on westward expansion was most nearly grounded in which of the following theories of learning?
   a. Behaviorism
   b. Information processing
   c. Constructivism
   d. Social cognitive theory
   c. Simulations are technology applications that are grounded in constructivist views of learning.

2. Of the following, which is the most likely reason that Karl's students had problems with important names, dates, and places associated with westward expansion?

a. The students were initially overwhelmed in trying to imagine what it would be like to plan such a lengthy and involved trip.
b. Karl did too much group work, so the students weren't prepared for the quiz.
c. The topic was not relevant to the students' everyday lives.
d. Karl's quiz was not aligned with his learning activity.
d. Based on the information in the case study, Karl's students focused on aspects of planning and conducting a trip to help them better understand the experiences the original pioneers had. The lesson didn't emphasize names, places, and dates.

3. Which of the principles for using technology in classrooms (page 462 of the chapter) did Karl apply most effectively in his unit?

a. Begin planning by specifying learning objectives.
b. Use technology only when it helps students meet your learning objectives.
c. Ensure that your expertise with technology allows you to support students when they struggle.
d. Carefully monitor students as they use technology.
c. The statement in the case study: "Karl has used the simulation repeatedly in the past, and he can predict where the students are likely to have difficulties," indicates that he has expertise with the technology.

Short-Answer Questions:

1. What other forms of technology could Karl have used to help his students see similarities and differences between a journey in an 1840's covered wagon and a camping trip in a modern automobile?

Databases and spreadsheets are both suited for organizing and presenting large amounts of information in an organized and systematic fashion. In doing this, Karl could also teach students about how databases and spreadsheets work and their different applications in various subject matter areas.

2. Using the instructional principles for using technology in classrooms as a basis, provide an assessment of Karl's use of technology in his unit.

Karl applied the principles quite effectively. He applied the first—planning with a clear learning objective in mind (for the students to better understand the hardships pioneers encountered with they sought new lands in the west). The use of the simulation helped his students reach the objective, and in this way he applied the second principle. As you saw in item 3, he had expertise with the technology, and he monitored the students.

The primary problem with his lesson was the fact that his assessment was not aligned with his learning objective and learning activity.

CLASSROOM EXERCISES

The classroom exercises that follow appear *only here* in the instructor's manual. Students do not have access to *either the questions or the answers.*

The purpose of keeping the exercises only in the instructor's manual is to allow you to use them as class discussion items, or for homework, if you should choose to do so.

Feedback for the exercises follows immediately.

Read the following case study and answer the questions that follow it.

Maria Villenas, a middle-school health teacher in an inner-city school, sits at her desk during her planning period.

"How can I make this unit on nutrition come alive for my students?" she thinks as she gazes at the mound of planning materials on her desk. "I know last year's lecture almost put them and me to sleep."

"I know," she thinks. "They love thinking about themselves and finding out how they're similar and different from their friends. I'll have them keep a food journal for a week, and then we'll see if we can organize the class's eating habits into a chart or graph. That should give them practice in using the computer to organize information as well as with working in groups. Hmm, I'll need to check the district's curriculum guidelines for nutrition to make sure I'm still covering all the bases."

With these thoughts in mind, Maria prepares the following lesson plan.

LESSON PLAN
Topic: Food and Nutrition
Goals

1. Students will understand the role of calories in their diet.
2. Students will understand the Food Guide Pyramid and apply it to their diets.
3. Students will be able to analyze diets in terms of calories and the major food groups.

Procedures

1. Introduce concept of calories. Have students read section in text on calories. Students will complete worksheet in small groups. Discuss as a whole-group activity.
2. Display food pyramid transparency. Explain differences between carbohydrates, proteins, and fats. Illustrate with common foods. Use Think–Pair–Share to categorize additional foods. Check categorization in whole group.
3. Introduce journaling assignment. Take first 5 minutes of class each day to allow time for students to edit and answer questions.

Follow-up

1. Check on availability of software to do spreadsheets.
2. Explain and demonstrate how to use computer to analyze and graph data.
3. Form research groups to analyze data. Make sure equal numbers of high-ability and low-ability students and boys and girls are in each group. Assign rotating roles so boys and high-ability students don't do everything.
4. Make sure research groups have plenty of research time to complete assignments, as many students don't have computers at home to work on.
5. Plan for group presentations.

Assessment

1. Test on basic concepts (check last year's and update).
2. Group presentation.

"Whew," Maria sighs. "This is going to be a lot of work, and it'll take time, but it should be a fun learning experience—for them and me."

1. Did Maria's lesson plan reflect a hardware or process view of technology use? Explain.

2. Did Maria's lesson focus more on problem solving or problem-based learning? Explain.

3. Evaluate Maria's lesson in terms of instructional alignment.

FEEDBACK FOR CLASSROOM EXERCISES

1. Maria's lesson plan reflected a process view of technology because her use of technology was integrated into the lesson.

2. Maria's lesson focused more on problem-based learning because her goals were more divergent and open-ended. Had her lesson focused on the computation of total calories expended, for example, it would have been more oriented to problem solving.

3. Maria's lesson was aligned. She considered learning goals first, then thought of how technology could further those goals, and also checked to see if her goals matched the district's curricular goals.

CHAPTER 15: ASSESSING CLASSROOM LEARNING

CHAPTER OVERVIEW

This chapter begins by defining and outlining the functions of assessment and describing measurement, evaluation, validity and reliability. These descriptions are followed by a discussion of teachers' assessment patterns together with an examination of reliable and valid traditional assessment items.

The chapter then turns to a discussion of alternative assessment, including the design of performance assessments, evaluation methods with performance assessments, and portfolio assessments.

The discussion of alternative assessment is followed by effective assessment practices, which involve preparing students for assessment, including test-taking strategies and test anxiety, administering assessments, analyzing results, and bias in assessment. The chapter closes with a discussion of grading and reporting.

CHAPTER OBJECTIVES

- Identify examples of basic assessment concepts, such as formal and informal assessments, validity, and reliability in classroom activities.
- Analyze assessment items based on criteria used to create effective assessments, and explain how rubrics can increase the validity and reliability of essay items.
- Describe applications of different forms of alternative assessments.
- Explain applications of effective assessment practices.
- Describe the components and decisions involved in designing a total assessment system

POWERPOINT SLIDES

PP 15.1 The Relationship Between Validity and reliability
PP 15.2 Teachers' Assessment Patterns
PP 15.3 Characteristics of Teacher-Made Tests
PP 15.4 Principles of Instruction for Constructing Valid Test Items
PP 15.5 Guidelines for Preparing Multiple-Choice Items
PP 15.6 Guidelines for Preparing and Scoring Essay Items
PP 15.7 Sample Rubric for Paragraph Structure
PP 15.8 Designing Performance Assessments
PP 15.9 Rating Scale for Content Representations
PP 15.10 Effective Assessment Practices
PP 15.11 Definitions of Values for Rating Scale
PP 15.12 The Total Assessment System
PP 15.13 Praxis Practice: Feedback for Short-Answer Questions
PP 15.14 Feedback for Online Case Questions
PP 15.15 Classroom Exercises

VIDEO

DVD 2, Episode 25: "Using Assessment in Decision Making."
This video lesson illustrates a fifth grade teachers' use of assessment as a basis for making decisions about instruction. (It is the opening case study of the chapter.)

CHAPTER OUTLINE

I. Classroom assessment
   A. Functions of classroom assessment
      1. Formal and informal assessment
      2. The need for formal assessment
   B. Validity: Making appropriate assessment decisions
   C. Reliability: Consistency in assessment
II. Traditional assessment strategies
   A. Teachers' assessment patterns
   B. Constructing valid test items: Instructional principles
      1. Multiple choice
         a. The stem
         b. Distracters
         c. Assessing higher level learning
      2. Matching items
      3. True-false items
      4. Completion items
      5. Essay items: Measuring complex outcomes
      6. Using rubrics
   C. Commercially prepared test items
III. Alternative assessment
   A. Performance assessments
   B. Designing performance assessments: Instructional principles
      1. Specifying the performance
      2. Selecting the focus of assessment
      3. Structuring the evaluation setting
      4. Designing evaluation procedures
         a. Systematic observation
         b. Checklists
         c. Rating scales
   C. Portfolio assessment: Involving students in alternative assessment
   D. Putting traditional and alternative assessment into perspective
IV. Effective assessment practices: Instructional principles
   A. Planning for assessment
      1. Tables of specifications: Increasing validity through planning
   B. Preparing students for assessments
      1. Teaching test-taking strategies
      2. Reducing test anxiety
      3. Specific test-preparation procedures
   C. Administering assessments
   D. Analyzing results
V. Grading and reporting: The total assessment system
   A. Designing a grading system
      1. Formative and summative assessments
      2. Norm-referenced and criterion-referenced grading systems
      3. Traditional and alternative assessments
      4. Homework
   B. Assigning grades: Increasing learning and motivation
      1. Points or percentages
   C. Learning contexts: Assessment in urban classrooms

PRESENTATION OUTLINE

The suggested activities can be completed in small groups and discussed as a whole group, or they can be conducted as whole-class activities. We encourage as much discussion—both in small groups and with the whole class—as possible.

I. Classroom assessment
   A. Functions of classroom assessment
      1. Formal and informal assessment
      2. The need for formal assessment
   B. Validity: Making appropriate assessment decisions
   C. Reliability: Consistency in assessment

Teaching Suggestions:

■ *To help your students understand classroom assessment and concepts of validity and reliability:*

You might want to begin your discussion by showing or discussing **Episode 25 on DVD 2**: "Using Assessment in Decision Making." This episode illustrates the role of assessment in making instructional decisions.

1. Introduce the topic by referring your students to the way you've assessed them in this class, which will be real and concrete for them. Describe the process by which it has evolved, its structure, and its evolution over time. While acknowledging that one function of assessment is to provide a basis for assigning grades, emphasize that your primary goal in assessment is to promote learning.

2. Have the students identify some of the goals and results of effective assessment. Have them link their findings to topics they've studied in earlier chapters.

Among the goals and results the students identify, the following might be included:

- **Provides feedback about learning progress, which is essential according to attribution theory (discussed in Chapter 10).**
- **Provides information that helps learners modify their existing schemas.**
- **Helps students understand the teacher's expectations.**
- **Aids in task comprehension (one of the climate variables in the model for promoting learner motivation)**

3. Have them identify a number of informal assessments that teachers make on a daily basis. Some include:

- **Which students to call on and when.**
- **Whether to conduct a learning activity in a whole-group or a small-group arrangement.**
- **When to move from one learning activity to another.**
- **How much time to give students in a small-group activity.**
- **When to schedule a test, quiz, or performance assessment.**

As you discuss the results, emphasize that informal assessments are essential for conducting the daily activities in the classroom, but they should be used with caution as a basis for assigning grades.

4. **Define validity and reliability and then have the students think about a number of the tests they've taken. (Remind them to avoid any discussion of specific instructors.) Have them offer some examples of course content, learning activities, and tests or other assessments. Discuss the extent to which the tests and other assessments were valid and/or reliable.**

   (Since students sometimes feel tests are unfair, they are likely to be quite lively in this discussion.)

5. **To help the students understand the concepts of validity and reliability display PP 15.1 "*The Relationship Between Validity and reliability*," which provides a way of visualizing the relationships between the two.**

II. Traditional assessment strategies
  - A. Teachers' assessment patterns
  - B. Constructing valid test items: Instructional principles
    1. Multiple choice
       - a. The stem
       - b. Distracters
       - c. Assessing higher level learning
    2. Matching items
    3. True-false items
    4. Completion items
    5. Essay items: Measuring complex outcomes
    6. Using rubrics
  - C. Commercially prepared test items

Teaching Suggestions:

■ *To help the students understand teachers' assessment patterns:*

1. **Display PP 15.2 "*Teachers' Assessment Patterns*" which outlines some of the common assessment practices in schools. Ask the students why they believe these patterns exist.**

2. **Display PP 15.3 "*Characteristics of Teacher-Made Tests*," which outlines the characteristics of teacher-made test items. Again, you might have the students discuss why they believe these characteristics exist.**

■ *To help your students understand the characteristics of effective traditional assessments using different formats:*

1. **Display PP 15.4 "*Principles of Instruction for Constructing Valid Test Items*," and remind the students that these principles guide the construction of assessment items regardless of the format used.**

2. **Display PP 15.5 "*Guidelines for Preparing Multiple-Choice Items*" which summarizes suggestions for preparing effective multiple-choice items. Remind the students that "Checking Your Understanding" exercise 2.1 gives them the opportunity to assess a series of multiple-choice items using the guidelines.**

3. **Remind the students that, while popular, true-false and completion formats are generally considered to be weaker than multiple-choice and essay items, and they should be used with care.**

4. **PP 15.6 "*Guidelines for Preparing and Scoring Essay Items*" offers suggestions for preparing effective essay items and scoring them as reliably as possible. PP 15.7 "*Sample Rubric for Paragraph Structure*" illustrates a process for increasing the reliability of essay items.**

As with your multiple-choice and true-false items, having the students assess some of your essay items would be an effective way to help them understand and apply the information in this section.

5. **If you have access to some commercially prepared test items, have students assess the items according to the criteria suggested for the particular format.**

6. **Remind students that teachers' goals and emphasis may not match those of the publisher, so they should use commercially prepared items with caution.**

III. Alternative assessment
   A. Performance assessments
   B. Designing performance assessments: Instructional principles
      1. Specifying the performance
      2. Selecting the focus of assessment
      3. Structuring the evaluation setting
      4. Designing evaluation procedures
         a. Systematic observation
         b. Checklists
         c. Rating scales
   C. Portfolio assessment: Involving students in alternative assessment
   D. Putting traditional and alternative assessment into perspective

Teaching Suggestions:

■ *The suggestions in this section are designed to help your students understand the process of alternative assessment*

1. **If you have chosen to assign one or more of the projects suggested at the introduction to this Instructor's Manual, use these projects as a basis for discussing the content in this section. For instance, having them prepare knowledge representations or complete a peer-taught lesson represent alternative assessments with a high degree of realism.**

2. **PP 15.8 "*Designing Performance Assessments*" provides guidelines for designing performance assessments, and PP 15.9 "*Rating Scale for Content Representations*" illustrates a rating scale for the project that requires them to prepare content representations for a topic of their choice. If you have assigned this project, you might display the rating scale and definitions of values that you've used in assessing their work. PP 15.11 "*Definitions of Values for Rating Scale*" illustrates definitions for one of the dimensions in PP 15.9.**

3. **If you want to increase the emphasis on designing performance assessments, have students prepare performance assessments for a topic or set of topics.**

4. **Have the students identify an area of study, such as elementary math, middle school science, or secondary English and have them consider how they would design portfolio assessments for this area. Discuss the decisions involved in the design and implementation as a whole class.**

IV. Effective assessment practices: Instructional principles
   A. Planning for assessment
      1. Tables of specifications: Increasing validity through planning
   B. Preparing students for assessments
      1. Teaching test-taking strategies
      2. Reducing test anxiety
      3. Specific test-preparation procedures
   C. Administering assessments
   D. Analyzing results

Teaching Suggestions:

■ *To help your students understand effective assessment practices:*

1. **Display PP 15.10 "*Effective Assessment Practices*" which outlines a framework for effective assessment. Then, again use your class as a model. If you have followed the suggestions made at the beginning of the Instructor's Manual, your class can serve as a model in several ways:**
   - **You have given frequent announced quizzes.**
   - **You have specified the content of each quiz.**
   - **You have given them the chance to practice on items similar to those on the quizzes and tests by encouraging them to respond to the "Checking Your Understanding" questions, Self-Help Quizzes, the Application Exercises, and Practice Quizzes on the book's CW.**
   - **You have established positive expectations by encouraging them to study and suggesting that if they do, they will do well in your class.**
   - **You have provided adequate time for them to complete each assessment.**
   - **You have reminded them to focus on the quiz or test content as they try to respond.**
   - **You have promptly returned the quizzes and tests and have discussed frequently missed items.**

2. **To increase students' understanding of these practices, have them link the practices to the content of other chapters. Some of the connections might include the following ideas:**
   - **Giving frequent announced quizzes, specifying the content, and giving them adequate time to complete the quiz or test helps reduce test anxiety, and also aids in task comprehension.**
   - **Providing practice puts them in an active role and helps them develop well-organized schemas for the content.**
   - **Reminding them to focus on the content of the quiz helps reduce test anxiety by preventing the worry component from occupying working memory space.**
   - **Discussing frequently missed items provides feedback which allows them to reorganize and elaborate their schemas.**

V. Grading and reporting: The total assessment system
   A. Designing a grading system
      1. Formative and summative assessments
      2. Norm-referenced and criterion-referenced grading systems
      3. Traditional and alternative assessments
      4. Homework
   B. Assigning grades: Increasing learning and motivation
      1. Points or percentages
   C. Learning contexts: Assessment in urban classrooms

Teaching Suggestions:

■ *To help your students understand grading and reporting:*

1. **Display PP 15.12 "*The Total Assessment System*" which outlines the features of a total system.**

2. **You might point out that most school districts specify criteria for grading, and most teachers use criterion-referenced systems.**

3. **You might ask students how norm referencing compares to criterion referencing and how these relate to their study of motivation in Chapters 10 and 11. They should point out that a norm-referenced system tends to promote a performance-focused, rather than a learning-focused environment and an ego versus a task orientation. For these reasons, it is generally preferable to use a criterion-referenced system.**

4. **Remind the students of your rationale for the grading system you use in your class.**

5. **Point out that teachers tend to prefer a percentage system, because students and their parents understand and prefer it. Remind them that a percentage system can artificially increase the weight of assignments. (You might ask them to explain how this can happen.)**

6. **Emphasize that it is important for learners to understand the assessment system.**

7. **Ask them what variable in the Model for Promoting Student Motivation most closely relates to learners understanding the assessment system. (Task Comprehension).**

■ ***To help your students understand the possibilities of bias in measurement that can have an important impact on assessment in urban environments:***

1. **Remind the students about your efforts to be careful with wording that might be a problem for non-native English speaking students.**

2. **If you have students in your class who are not proficient in English, you probably arrange to give them extra time to complete your assessments. You can use this as another example of your efforts to reduce bias in assessment.**

ENRICHMENT MATERIALS

TEACHER PREP WEBSITE

The *Teacher Prep* website an online resource for students and instructors. Both you and students can access the *Teacher Prep* website by going to http://www.prenhall.com/teacherprep. Enter your user name and password and click on "Log In." The *Teacher Prep* website includes video episodes, student and teacher artifacts, teacher and research resources, and information about licensing and beginning a teaching career. The *Teacher Prep* website is described in detail in the Media Guide.

The following articles are recommended by the *Exploring Further* section titled "Assessment and Learning" on page 476 of the chapter.

Once into the *Teacher Prep* website access the articles by completing the following steps:

1. Click on "Research Resources" on the left panel of the screen, scroll down the middle of the page and again click on "Research Resources."
2. Go to "Classroom Processes" and click on "Assessment"
3. Click on the following articles:
   How Classroom Assessment Improves Learning, by T. Guskey (2003), Ref. No. 1723.
   Classroom Assessment for Learning, by S. Chappius and R. Stiggins (2002), Ref. No. 1736.

These articles describe how teachers can use assessment to improve learning in the classroom.

The following article is recommended by the *Exploring Further* section titled "Rubrics in the Classroom" on page 486 of the chapter.

Once into the *Teacher Prep* website access the articles by completing the following steps:

1. Click on "Research Resources" on the left panel of the screen, scroll down the middle of the page and again click on "Research Resources."
2. Go to "Classroom Processes" and click on "Assessment"
3. Click on the following article:
   Understanding Rubrics, H. Goodrich (1996), Ref. No. 2328.

This article describes the philosophy behind rubrics and how they can be integrated into a classroom's total assessment program.

The following article is recommended by the *Exploring Further* section titled "Grading and Standards" on page 502 of the chapter.

Once into the *Teacher Prep* website access the articles by completing the following steps:

1. Click on "Research Resources" on the left panel of the screen, scroll down the middle of the page and again click on "Research Resources."
2. Go to "Classroom Processes" and click on "Assessment"
3. Click on the following article:
   Helping Standards Make the Grade, by T. Guskey (2001), Ref. No. 1698.

This article describes the challenges teachers face when assigning grades in a standards-based environment. It also suggests ways to meet those challenges.

DISCUSSION STARTERS

You may choose to have your students discuss one or more of the following questions to further enrich their understanding of your learning activities.

1. Does assessment increase, decrease, or have no affect on learning? On what evidence is your opinion based?

2. How does assessment affect the intrinsic motivation of learners? The extrinsic motivation of learners? On what evidence is your opinion based?

3. Is assessment overemphasized, underemphasized, or appropriately emphasized in today's schools? On what evidence is your opinion based?

4. Teachers, particularly at the elementary level, tend to rely heavily on commercially prepared test items? Why do you think this is the case? How appropriate is the practice of using commercially prepared items?

5. Would an ideal assessment system for your level or content area use the following types of items? If so, how would they be used?
   Traditional assessments
   - essay
   - multiple choice
   - short answer
   - true/false
   - alternative assessments
   - performance assessments
   - portfolios

6. Is the emphasis on alternative assessment likely to increase or decrease in the future? Why do you think so?

7. Most teachers give grades based on district-mandated or suggested criteria, such as 94%-100% = A, 86-93 = B, etc... How appropriate is this practice? Why do you think so?

8. You are asked to meet with parents to hand out report cards and explain the grades on them. What kinds of information would be most helpful in this process? How would you present it to parents?

9. How could portfolios be used in your content area or grade level to supplement other data sources? What would go in them? How would the contents be evaluated?

BACKGROUND READINGS

Armour-Thomas, E. (2004). What is the nature of evaluation and assessment in an urban context? In S. R. Steinberg & J. L. Kincheloe (Eds.), *19 Urban questions: Teaching in the city*. New York: Peter Lang.
This chapter examines the role of assessment in promoting learning for urban students.

Gronlund, N. (2003). *Assessment of student achievement* (7th ed.). Boston: Allyn & Bacon.
A comprehensive look at assessment issues in the classroom.

Hambleton, R. (1996). Advances in assessment models, methods, and practices. In D. Berliner & R. Calfee (Eds.), *Handbook of educational psychology* (pp. 899–925). New York: Macmillan.
This chapter provides an overview of assessment practices including both traditional and alternative assessment.

Linn, R., & Miller, M. D. (2005). *Measurement and assessment in teaching* (9th ed.). Upper Saddle River, NJ: Merrill/Prentice Hall.
This classic text provides a comprehensive description of the assessment process.

Stiggens, R. (2005). *Student-centered classroom assessment* (4th ed.). Upper Saddle River, NJ: Merrill/Prentice Hall.
This text provides detailed descriptions of how to develop effective assessments with a learner-centered focus.

Venn, J. J. (2004). *Assessing students with special needs* (3rd ed.). Upper Saddle River, NJ: Merrill/Prentice Hall.
This text discusses the unique assessment challenges of assessing students with exceptionalities.

FEEDBACK

Developing as a Professional: Praxis Practice: Feedback for Short-Answer Questions

The feedback that appears here is for the short-answer questions that follow the case study on pages 505 and 506 of the text. The feedback is also available to students on the companion website.

1. How well were Ron's curriculum and assessment aligned? Explain specifically. What could he have done to increase curricular alignment?

Ron's curriculum was out of alignment. His stated learning objective was, ". . . you'll all be able to use pronouns correctly in your writing." This goal was congruent with the second part of his assessment, which asked the students to write a passage in which pronoun cases were used correctly. However, his learning activity was behaviorist; it focused on the sentences in isolation rather than on writing, so it was not congruent with his goal and the second part of his assessment. To make his instruction congruent with his goal, Ron needs to provide students with practice using pronouns correctly in their writing.

2. In the section on effective assessment practices, we discussed preparing students for assessments, administering them, and analyzing results. How effectively did Ron perform each task? Describe specifically what he might have done to be more effective in these areas.

Effective preparation for testing involves giving students the opportunity to practice on test-like items that are similar to those they will encounter on the test itself. Ron's students only responded to the specific and isolated sentences and they didn't practice using pronouns in their writing.

The only problem that existed with his administration of the test was the fact that the students were pressed for time, and he may have increased the anxiety of test-anxious students by his repeated reminders of the amount of time remaining. Giving students more time to finish the exam would remedy this problem.

In discussing the test results, Ron again de-emphasized their writing in favor of the specific items, and his feedback was somewhat vague. Unquestionably, providing feedback for every student is very demanding, but he could have written a model response to which the students could have compared their own paragraphs.

3. Ron teaches in an urban environment, so his students likely had diverse backgrounds. How effective was his teaching and assessment for urban students?

Ron's instruction for urban learners would have been more effective if he had made his instruction more concrete. For example, he could have prepared a personalized written passage that included examples of pronoun cases, and in this way his content would have been more meaningful for his students.

Research indicates that learners with diverse backgrounds benefit from explicit test preparation procedures. Had Ron provided more test preparation practice, particularly with writing, his assessment would have been more effective and valid.

4. What were the primary strengths of Ron's teaching and assessment? What were the primary weaknesses? If you think Ron's teaching and assessment could have been improved on the basis of information in this chapter, what suggestions would you make? Be specific.

Ron used his time well, his instruction was interactive, he had a clear learning objective for his students, and he provided practice for his students with respect to properly placing the pronoun in specific sentences. These were the strengths of his instruction and assessment.

His primary weaknesses were the fact that his learning objective, learning activity, and assessment were out of alignment, he didn't provide as much practice for his students as he might have, especially with using pronouns in their writing, and he didn't discuss the test results as thoroughly as he might have.

Feedback for Online Case Book Questions

The feedback below is for the *Online Case Book* for Chapter 7 (referenced on page 497 of the chapter). Both you and the students can access the case study by going to www.prenhall.com/eggen, selecting Chapter 15, and clicking on *Online Case Book.*

You may choose to assign the online case as homework or you may want to discuss the case in class. Answers to these questions *do not* appear on the companion website, so students *do not* have access to the feedback.

Multiple-Choice Items

1. Of the following, Sarah's matrix would be best described as a(n):
   a. rubric.
   b. formal assessment.
   c. interpretive exercise.
   d. table of specifications.
   d. A table of specifications helps teachers plan assessments by linking them to learning objectives. Sarah's matrix served this function.

2. Of the following, which is the best example of an informal assessment?
   a. Sarah reviewing the state standards
   b. Sarah seeing the confused looks on students' faces and deciding to give the students additional practice with fractions and percentages
   c. Sarah checking homework assignments, returning the assignments the next day, and providing the students with feedback
   d. Sarah giving the unit test.
   b. Seeing confused looks and deciding to give students extra practice is an example of gathering incidental information about learning progress and making decisions based on that information.

3. Of the instructional principles for effective assessment practices (on page 493 of the chapter), which is best illustrated by Sarah giving her opportunities to practice problems similar to those that would be on the test?
   a. Plan systematically to ensure a match between learning objectives and assessments.
   b. Prepare students so assessments measure their understanding and skills rather than test-taking strategies.
   c. Administer tests and quizzes under the best conditions possible to maximize student performance.
   d. Analyze results to ensure that current and future assessments are valid and reliable.
   b. By giving her students opportunities to practice problems similar to those that would be on the test, she was preparing her students for the assessment.

Short-Answer Questions:

4. Assess Sarah's attempts to create valid formal assessments.
   Sarah attempted to increase validity in at least three ways. First, she checked state and district guidelines to ensure that her unit would be aligned with these. Then she checked last year's standardized test results to make sure that unit content corresponded to the test. Finally, she produced a matrix that served as a table of specifications for the unit and test.

5. Provide an assessment of Sarah's efforts to prepare her students for her unit test?
   Sarah prepared her students for the test in several ways. First, she used her table of specifications to align the unit content with the test. Second, she provided practice quizzes to acquaint her students with the format and types of questions they would have on the test. Then she went over the test content thoroughly and shared sample items with them, and finally, she reassured them that they would do fine of the test and also helped reduce anxiety by providing plenty of time for the test.

CLASSROOM EXERCISES

The classroom exercises that follow appear *only here* in the instructor's manual. Students do not have access to *either the questions or the answers.*

The purpose of keeping the exercises only in the instructor's manual is to allow you to use them as class discussion items, or for homework, if you should choose to do so.

Feedback for the exercises follows immediately.

1. Karen Anderson gives a multiple-choice test to her biology students. She is careful to be sure her test is consistent with her goals. As it turns out, Karen inadvertently puts a clue in one of the items, so the students select the correct answer even though they don't understand the content. Is her test reliable? Is her test valid? Explain.

2. Greg Foster gives a multiple choice test to his biology students, and he is also careful to be certain that his test is consistent with his goals. As it turns out, Greg unintentionally writes the stem of one of the items in a misleading way, so that the students select a distracter rather than the correct answer, even though they understand the content measured on the item. Is Greg's test reliable? Is Greg's test valid? Explain.

3. Loretta Polanski is philosophically opposed to tests with her third graders on the grounds that it puts undue stress on them. She assigns grades based on their responses in class, arguing, "I call on all the students regularly, and I can tell from their answers whether or not they understand the content." Is Loretta's approach to measurement and evaluation reliable? Is it valid? Explain.

Eleanor Parker is emphasizing grammatically correct writing and expression of thought in writing with her students. She has begun using portfolios, where systematic collections of her students' work are placed for review and evaluation. She puts work samples in the portfolio at least three days a week, and she is careful to date the samples to help in assessing her students' progress. In examining her students' work, she checks for grammar, punctuation, spelling, and clear expression of thought, and she assigns grades on that basis.

4. Is Eleanor's behavior consistent with patterns identified by research; is she most likely an elementary teacher, a middle school teacher, or a high school teacher? Explain.

5. Are Eleanor's measurements reliable? Are they valid? Explain.

Four elementary teachers were discussing their handling of homework in their classes.

"They know they have to do it to do well on the tests," Jo Buck comments, "but I don't collect it or grade it."

"I don't grade it either, but I check to see if they did it, and they know they get a check mark in my grade book if they did it," Art Ames adds.

"It's a part of my grading system," Karen Warner continues. "I collect every assignment, score it, and record the scores."

"I spot check them," Lynn Peet adds. "They know it may or may not be collected, and I try to avoid falling into a pattern. I grade it and record the grades when I do collect it."

6. Based on research, which teacher's homework practice is most effective? Explain, using social cognitive theory as the basis for your explanation.

7. Based on research, which teacher's homework practice is least effective? Explain, again using social cognitive theory as the basis for your explanation.

8. Cal is in English Honors II as a 10th grader and is doing well, getting B's the first two grading periods--missing A's by 2 percentage points each time. Joanne Wilkes, his English teacher, consistently commented on the good work Cal did on his writing assignments. Cal took the PSAT and but scored only in the 40th percentile on the verbal section. The results were shared with Joanne, since she is an English teacher.

Cal's mother continued to proofread his essays as she had done the first two grading periods, but Cal got a C the third grading period. "I'll do better. I can do it," Cal said to himself, but he also got a C the fourth grading period, and received a C for the year.

Based on the information in the case study, what is the most likely explanation for the decline in Jim's grades?

9. Look at the following test item.

Formative tests:

a. are given at the beginning of instruction.
b. are given at any time during instruction.
c. are given at the end of instruction.
d. are given when the teacher wants diagnostic information.

Based on guidelines for preparing multiple-choice items, write an assessment of the item.

FEEDBACK FOR CLASSROOM EXERCISES

1. Her test is reliable, but it isn't valid. In spite of the scores, Karen will get consistent results. However, since the students are able to get a correct answer without understanding the topic, the test doesn't actually measure the objectives, so it isn't valid. (Technically, the misleading item doesn't make the entire test invalid. It invalidates that particular items. When the test, per se, becomes invalid is a matter of judgment.)

2. The same explanation applies in Greg's case as applied in Karen's. Greg will get consistent results, so his test is reliable, but it isn't valid (or, at least that particular item is invalid).

3. Loretta's approach is neither reliable nor valid. Since she isn't getting responses to the same questions from all the students, she isn't getting consistent measurements, which makes her measurements unreliable. Unreliable measurements cannot be valid.

4. Eleanor is most likely an elementary teacher. Elementary teachers tend to use performance measures and samples of student work to a greater extent than do middle, junior high, and high school teachers.

5. Eleanor is making an effort to gather consistent information from all the students. Research indicates that these efforts can produce acceptable levels of reliability (although difficulties with reliability are quite common with performance measures). Based on the evidence we have, we would conclude that Eleanor has achieved an acceptable level of reliability. Her measurements are consistent with her goals, so they are also valid.

6. Karen's practice is most effective. If students do homework, they expect to be reinforced for doing it. The reinforcer could be as simple as credit for doing it, and better yet, having it scored and recorded.

7. Jo's practice is least effective. Again, If students do homework, they expect to be reinforced for doing it. The nonoccurrence of the expected reinforcer acts as a punisher, making it less likely that the students will make an effort to conscientiously do the homework if it isn't collected or scored.

8. It is likely that Joanne's perception of Cal's ability was adversely affected by his PSAT results. As a result, her expectations were lowered, and she responded to her perceptions and expectations in evaluating Cal's performance.

9. More information should be included in the stem, so a clear problem or question is presented. Also, the item measures mere recall.

CHAPTER 16: ASSESSMENT THROUGH STANDARDIZED TESTING

CHAPTER OVERVIEW

This chapter begins by describing the functions and types of standardized tests, together with an examination of content, predictive, and construct validity. From there the chapter turns to a discussion of the teacher's role in standardized testing, descriptive statistics, the normal distribution, and an interpretation of standardized test results, including percentile ranks, stanines, grade equivalents, standard scores, and standard error of measurement. The chapter then examines accountability and diversity issues in standardized testing and closes with suggestions for eliminating test bias to the extent possible.

CHAPTER OBJECTIVES

- Identify functions and types of standardized tests in descriptions of decisions made by school officials and the types of validity addressed by the decisions.
- Explain standardized test results using statistics and standard scores.
- Describe the relationships between standards-based education, accountability, and high-stakes testing
- Describe potential types of testing bias and strategies teachers can use to minimize bias in the use of standardized tests with their students.

POWERPOINT SLIDES

PP 16.1 David Palmer's Achievement Test Report
PP 16.2 Functions of Standardized Tests
PP 16.3 Types of Standardized Tests
PP 16.4 Types of Validity for Standardized Tests
PP 16.5 Principles of Instruction for Using Standardized Tests Effectively
PP 16.6 Two Distributions of Scores
PP 16.7 Descriptive Statistics for the Two Distributions of Scores
PP 16.8 Normal Distribution
PP 16.9 Interpreting Standardized Test Scores: An Application
PP 16.10 Instructional Principles for Eliminating Bias in Standardized Testing
PP 16.11 Praxis Practice: Feedback for Short-Answer Questions
PP 16.12 Feedback for Online Case Questions
PP 16.13 Classroom Exercises

CHAPTER OUTLINE

I. Standardized tests
   A. Functions of standardized tests
      1. Assessment and diagnosis of learning
      2. Selection and placement
      3. Program evaluation and accountability
   B. Types of standardized tests
      1. Achievement tests
      2. Diagnostic tests
      3. Intelligence tests
         a. The Stanford-Binet
         b. The Wechsler Scales
      4. Aptitude tests
   C. Evaluating standardized tests: Validity revisited
      1. Content validity
      2. Predictive validity
      3. Construct validity
   D. The teacher's role in standardized testing: Instructional principles
      1. Matching tests and learning objectives
      2. Preparing students
      3. Administering tests
      4. Interpreting results
II. Understanding and interpreting standardized test scores
   A. Descriptive statistics
      1. Frequency distributions
      2. Measures of central tendency
      3. Measures of variability
      4. The normal distribution
   B. Interpreting standardized test results
      1. Raw scores
      2. Percentiles
      3. Stanines
      4. Grade equivalents
      5. Standard scores
      6. Standard error of measurement
III. Accountability issues in standardized testing
   A. Standards-based education and accountability
      1. No Child Left Behind
      2. High-stakes tests
   B. Testing teachers
      1. The Praxis series
IV. Diversity issues in standardized testing
   A. Student diversity and test bias
      1. Bias in content
      2. Bias in testing procedures
      3. Bias in test use
   B. Eliminating bias in standardized testing: Instructional principles
      1. Analyze test content
      2. Adapt testing procedures
      3. Use alternate assessment data sources
   C. Issues in standardized testing: Implications for teachers

PRESENTATION OUTLINE

The suggested activities can be completed in small groups and discussed as a whole group, or they can be conducted as whole-class activities. We encourage as much discussion–both in small groups and with the whole class–as possible.

I. Standardized tests
   A. Functions of standardized tests
      1. Assessment and diagnosis of learning
      2. Selection and placement
      3. Program evaluation and accountability
   B. Types of standardized tests
      1. Achievement tests
      2. Diagnostic tests
      3. Intelligence tests
         a. The Stanford-Binet
         b. The Wechsler Scales
      4. Aptitude tests
   C. Evaluating standardized tests: Validity revisited
      1. Content validity
      2. Predictive validity
      3. Construct validity
   D. The teacher's role in standardized testing: Instructional principles
      1. Matching tests and learning objectives
      2. Preparing students
      3. Administering tests
      4. Interpreting results

Teaching Suggestions:

■ *The purpose of this activity is to help students understand the characteristics of standardized tests.*

1. **Display PP 16.1 "*David Palmer's Achievement Test Report*" and have students make at least three conclusions about the information in the report. (If PP 16.1 is difficult to see because of the small print, you may have the students refer to Figure 16.1 on page 510 of their texts.) Remind them that PR stands for percentile rank, S stands for stanine, and GRADE EQUIV stands for grade equivalent. Discuss their findings.**

2. **Display PP 16.2 "*Functions of Standardized Tests*," which outlines the functions of standardized tests. After discussing David Palmer's standardized test results, have them relate the information on PP 16.1 to the functions of standardized tests.**

3. **Have the students recall some of the standardized tests that they've taken. Most of them will have taken the SAT or the ACT as part of the college admissions process. You can then have them identify the function of these tests.**

■ *To help the students understand the characteristics of different types of standardized tests:*

1. **Display PP 16.3 "*Types of Standardized Tests*." Have the students identify the type of test David Palmer took and the type of tests the SAT and ACT are.**

2. **Have students recall their experience with the sample intelligence test items to which they responded when you examined intelligence in Chapter 4. Then have them compare that experience to the functions and types of standardized tests. They will see that there is considerable overlap in the tests. For example, from their experience with the math problems**

on the sample intelligence test, they will see that items appearing on an intelligence test could also appear on an achievement test, and could even appear on a diagnostic test.

■ *To help students apply the concepts of content, predictive, and construct validity:*

1. **Display PP 16.4 "*Types of Validity for Standardized Tests.*" Discuss the descriptions and try to identify examples of each.**

■ *To help the students understand teachers' roles in the process of using standardized tests:*

1. **Display PP 16.5 "*Principles of Instruction for Using Standardized Tests Effectively.*" Point out that interpreting test results will be one of their most important roles, which will then lead to the next section of the chapter.**

II. Understanding and interpreting standardized test scores
   A. Descriptive statistics
      1. Frequency distributions
      2. Measures of central tendency
      3. Measures of variability
      4. The normal distribution
   B. Interpreting standardized test results
      1. Raw scores
      2. Percentiles
      3. Stanines
      4. Grade equivalents
      5. Standard scores
      6. Standard error of measurement

Teaching Suggestions:

■ *The purpose of this activity is to help the students understand descriptive statistics.*

1. **Display PP 16.6 "*Two Distributions of Scores*" and have students compare the distributions of scores. Ask them to decide if the students in the second sample performed better or less well than the students in the first sample and provide a rationale for their answer. They will see that the comparisons are difficult, since the numbers of students are different.**

2. **Have the plot a frequency distribution for the two classes and then predict whether or not the mean of the second sample will be higher than the mean of the first sample. Do the same with the standard deviation.**

3. **Have them calculate the mean, median, and mode for the two samples. Have the students estimate the standard deviation. (You may choose to have the students also calculate the standard deviation of the two samples.) Point out that these statistics help us "describe" the two samples.**

4. **Display PP 16.7 "*Descriptive Statistics for the Two Distributions of Scores.*" Discuss the statistics, and again remind them that in actual standardized testing situations the samples will be much larger than those used for the purposes of illustration here.**

5. **Display PP 16.8 "*Normal Distribution,*" and then ask students if the second class in PP 16.6 represents a normal distribution. Have them explain why or why not.**

6. **Have them examine both the measures of central tendency and the measures of variability. The mean, median, and mode of the second sample in PP 16.6 are the same, so in this regard the sample appears to have the characteristics of a normal distribution. However, a normal distribution has approximately 68% of the scores in the sample that fall within one standard**

deviation from the mean, whereas for the second class in PP 16.6 77% of the sample falls within this range. The class is not as "spread out" as is a normal distribution.

■ ***To help the students understand how to interpret standardized test results:***

1. **Point out that interpreting standardized test results will be one of the most important roles that teachers have in using standardized tests.**

2. **Display PP 16.9 "*Interpreting Standardized Test Scores: An Application*" and have students work to interpret the results of the problem. Have them explain their answers and discuss the results with the whole class.**

III. Accountability issues in standardized testing
   A. Standards-based education and accountability
      1. No Child Left Behind
      2. High-stakes tests
   B. Testing teachers
      1. The Praxis series

IV. Diversity issues in standardized testing
   A. Student diversity and test bias
      1. Bias in content
      2. Bias in testing procedures
      3. Bias in test use
   B. Eliminating bias in standardized testing: Instructional principles
      1. Analyze test content
      2. Adapt testing procedures
      3. Use alternate assessment data sources
   C. Issues in standardized testing: Implications for teachers

Teaching Suggestions:

■ ***The purpose of this activity is to help students understand some of the issues involved in standardized testing.***

1. **Standards-based education and accountability are controversial topics. Have students work in groups, take a position with respect to the effectiveness of these movements, and have the groups present and defend their position. Have them predict whether or not the emphasis on accountability is likely to increase, and have them give reasons for their predictions.**

2. **Have the students again reflect on their experiences with the sample items that they responded to in the activity on intelligence testing in Chapter 4. Ask them how bias in measurement—particularly bias in content and bias in test result use—could exist in measurements similar to the ones they experienced. Discuss their reactions in a whole-group activity.**

3. **To summarize this section display PP 16.10 "*Instructional Principles for Eliminating Bias in Standardized Testing.*" Remind the students that these are the most effective ways possible of helping reduce test bias.**

ENRICHMENT MATERIALS

TEACHER PREP WEBSITE

The *Teacher Prep* website an online resource for students and instructors. Both you and students can access the *Teacher Prep* website by going to http://www.prenhall.com/teacherprep. Enter your user name and password and click on "Log In." The *Teacher Prep* website includes video episodes, student and teacher artifacts, teacher and research resources, and information about licensing and beginning a teaching career. The *Teacher Prep* website is described in detail in the Media Guide.

The following article is recommended by the *Exploring Further* section titled "Standards-Based Education" on page 526 of the chapter.

Once into the *Teacher Prep* website access the articles by completing the following steps:

1. Click on "Research Resources" on the left panel of the screen, scroll down the middle of the page and again click on "Research Resources."
2. Go to "Classroom Processes" and click on "Assessment."
3. Click on the following article:
   Realizing the Promise of Standards-based Education, by M. Schmoker and R. Marzano (1999), Ref. No. 2313

This article describes the potential positive benefits of standards-based education.

The following article is recommended by the *Exploring Further* section titled "High-Stakes Testing" on page 526 of the chapter.

Once into the *Teacher Prep* website access the articles by completing the following steps:

1. Click on "Research Resources" on the left panel of the screen, scroll down the middle of the page and again click on "Research Resources."
2. Go to "Classroom Processes" and click on "Assessment."
3. Click on the following article:
   The Dangers of Testing, M. Neill (2003), Ref. No. 1745.

This article examines the practice of high-stakes testing from a critical perspective, focusing on potentially negative effects on motivation and learning for all students, and especially minorities.

The following article is recommended by the *Exploring Further* section titled "Minorities and Testing" on page 528 of the chapter.

Once into the *Teacher Prep* website access the articles by completing the following steps:

1. Click on "Research Resources" on the left panel of the screen, scroll down the middle of the page and again click on "Research Resources."
2. Go to "Classroom Processes" and click on "Assessment."
3. Click on the following article:
   First Do No Harm, by J. Heubert (2002), Ref. No. 1720.

This article describes some potential problems when high-stakes testing is used with minorities.

ADDITIONAL EXPLORING FURTHER SUGGESTIONS

Page 513 of the chapter suggests that students to go the *Exploring Further* module of Chapter 16 for a brief discussion of the history of intelligence tests.

DISCUSSION STARTERS

You may choose to have your students discuss one or more of the following questions to further enrich their understanding of your learning activities.

1. A great deal of criticism is being directed at education, the critics arguing that the nation's K-12 schools are doing an inadequate job of educating students for either the workplace or higher education. How much of this criticism is based on the results of standardized test scores? What are some other sources on which the criticisms are based?

2. You are responsible for explaining the results of a standardized achievement test to parents. What types of scores will be most useful to you? Least? Why?

3. You are explaining the same test results as in Question 2, but are working with the parents of students for whom English is a second language. What modifications would you have to make in your explanation?

4. What trends do you see in the future of standardized testing? Is the emphasis on standardized testing likely to increase or decrease in the next decade? Why do you think so?

5. What is the future of authentic assessment in standardized testing? Is the emphasis on authentic standardized testing likely to increase or decrease compared to the emphasis on "traditional" standardized testing? Why do you think so?

6. A great deal of emphasis has been placed on giving local districts and schools more autonomy. If the trend toward local control increases, how will standardized testing be influenced? Why do you think so?

7. Is emphasis on accountability likely to increase or decrease over the next decade? Why do you think so?

BACKGROUND READINGS

Aiken, L. R. (2003). *Psychological testing and assessment* (11th ed.). Boston: Allyn & Bacon
This text examines standardized testing in detail.

Amrein, A., & Berliner, D. (2003). The effects of high-stakes testing on student motivation and learning. *Educational Leadership, 60*(5), 32–38.
This article presents a strong criticism of high-stakes testing.

Corno, L., Cronbach, L. J., Kupermintz, H., Lohman, D. F., Mandinach, E. B., Porteus, A. W., & Talbert, J. E. (2002). *Remaking the concept of aptitude; Extending the legacy of Richard E. Snow.* Mahwah, NJ: Erlbaum.
An excellent overview of the history of aptitude testing.

Linn, R. L., & Miller, M. D. (2005). *Measurement and assessment in teaching* (9th ed.). Upper Saddle River, NJ: Merrill/Prentice Hall.
This classic text provides a detailed examination of standardized testing and some of the issues involved.

McIntosh, S., & Norwood, P. (2004). The power of testing: Investigating minority teachers' responses to certification examination questions. *Urban Education, 39*(1), 33–51.

This article examines the responses of teachers who are members of cultural minorities to questions on teacher certification examinations.

Popham, W. (2003). The seductive lure of data. *Educational Leadership, 60*(5), 48–51.
This article offers an analysis of the way data are used in making policy decisions.

Venn, J. J. (2004). *Assessing students with special needs* (3rd ed.). Upper Saddle River, NJ: Merrill/Prentice Hall.
This text examines the unique assessment challenges of assessing students with exceptionalities.

FEEDBACK

Developing as a Professional: Praxis Practice: Feedback for Short-Answer Questions

The feedback that appears here is for the short-answer questions that follow the case study on page 533 of the text. The feedback is also available to students on the companion website.

1. What type of standardized test would help Peggy determine "whether this class is really doing better than last year, or even my other classes this year"?

   Standardized achievement tests are specifically designed to provide information about how much students learn in various content areas. To be useful in answering her question the standardized achievement test would have to be carefully aligned with her curriculum.

2. What type of validity would be the primary concern with this test? Explain.

   Content validity, or the extent to which a standardized achievement test actually covers important content. This is essentially an issue of alignment.

3. One of Peggy's concerns was the prior knowledge of her students. What type of standardized test might Peggy use to gather data related to this concern?

   Because of their focus on specific content, standardized diagnostic tests would be most useful here. Diagnostic tests assess more narrowly, but do so more thoroughly, thus providing the teacher with more in-depth information about specific topics.

4. In investigating the problems that her students were having in math, Peggy checked out their overall test scores from past standardized tests. What else might she have done?

   The more information that teachers gather in their decision-making, the better their decisions. Other possible sources of information include specific subtests within the standardized tests, previous grades in math classes, and observations and evaluations from previous teachers.

Feedback for Online Case Book Questions

The feedback below is for the *Online Case Book* for Chapter 7 (referenced on page 224 of the chapter). Both you and the students can access the case study by going to www.prenhall.com/eggen, selecting Chapter 7, and clicking on *Online Case Book.*

You may choose to assign the online case as homework or you may want to discuss the case in class. Answers to these questions *do not* appear on the companion website, so students *do not* have access to the feedback.

Multiple-Choice Items

1. Jacinta commented, "We want to be able to document the fact that our student are learning something. That always is a major concern with charter schools." Of the following, which type of standardized test would best help them reach that goal?
   a. An achievement test
   b. A diagnostic test
   c. An intelligence test
   d. An aptitude test
   a. Documenting learning is the function of achievement tests.

2. Kyle said, "We also want to know where to place students in our math and language arts programs—especially if they are having difficulties with our initial placement." This comment suggests the need for a(n):

a. achievement test.
b. diagnostic test.
c. intelligence test.
d. aptitude test.
b. Concerns about specific placements suggests the need for a diagnostic test.

3. Gwen commented, "And we also need some type of test that we can use with students with special needs. We're going to get students who underperform, and we'll need to have some way of finding out if this is due to problems with general cognitive functioning." Which of the following tests would best help the teachers find out if students have problems with general cognitive functioning?

a. An achievement test
b. A diagnostic test
c. An intelligence test
d. An aptitude test
c. Intelligence tests are standardized tests designed to measure a student's ability to acquire knowledge, capacity to think and reason in the abstract, and ability to solve novel problems. Intelligence tests are often used to help diagnose learning problems with students with exceptionalities.

Short-Answer Questions:

4. Explain how concerns about the three types of validity discussed in the chapter were addressed in the meeting. Again, use specific information from the case.

Content validity refers to a test's ability to representatively sample the content taught and measure the extent to which students understand it. The statement best illustrating content validity was Jacinta's comment, "It also ought to match the State standards we examined. If it doesn't overlap with them, we're going to have problems."

Predictive validity refers to a test's ability to gauge future performance. The example best illustrating predictive validity was Gwen statement, "It also should match what students are going to encounter in the different high schools around here. If a student does well on the test, he or she should do well in a comparable subject in high school."

Construct validity describes the extent to which a test accurately measures a learning-related characteristic that is not directly observable. Kyle commented: "Well, first, it ought to match the goals we talked about last week. It should match our general philosophy that learning is thinking and not just accumulating facts." "Thinking" is not directly observable, so a test able to accurately measured students' ability to think would have construct validity.

5. Describe three ways in which the school could address Anita's concerns that the test scores they obtain from cultural minorities are valid?

First, they should examine the content of any test they are considering for possible bias in content. In this area they might enlist the help of parents or other adults who are members of a specific cultural minority.

Second, they should make a special effort to ensure that specific testing procedures do not unfairly affect any members of a cultural minority group. Bias could occur through procedures that aren't familiar to any specific group or through language problems.

A third check against bias in testing is to make sure that the results are used judiciously. This means that any test results should be compared with academic achievement in the classroom as well as observations of behavior in learning settings. In short, no standardized test score should be used in isolation from other data or information.

CLASSROOM EXERCISES

The classroom exercises that follow appear *only here* in the instructor's manual. Students do not have access to *either the questions or the answers.*

The purpose of keeping the exercises only in the instructor's manual is to allow you to use them as class discussion items, or for homework, if you should choose to do so.

Feedback for the exercises follows immediately.

1. A class had the following scores on a quiz:

					x				
					x	x			
				x	x	x			
			x	x	x	x			
	x	x	x	x	x	x			
	x	x	x	x	x	x	x	x	x
1	2	3	4	5	6	7	8	9	10

a. What is the mean for this quiz?

b. What is the mode for this quiz?

c. What is the median for this quiz?

2. A standardized test has a mean of 100 and a standard deviation of 10. Compute the t scores, z scores, and percentile for the following student scores on that test.

a. 110

b. 90

c. 130

d. 80

FEEDBACK FOR CLASSROOM EXERCISES

1. a. The mean is 5.84 (146/25).
   b. The mode, or most frequently occurring score is 6.
   c. The median, middle-point score, is also 6.

2. a. A score of 110 would result in a z score of 1, a t score of 60, and a percentile at approximately the 84th percentile.
   b. A score of 90 would result in a z score of -1, a t score of 40, and a percentile at approximately the 16th percentile.
   c. A score of 130 would result in a z score of 3, a t score of 70, and a percentile at approximately the 99th percentile.
   d. A score of 80 would result in a z score of -2, a t score of 30, and a percentile at approximately the 2nd percentile.

MEDIA GUIDE

to
accompany

Educational Psychology: Windows on Classrooms
Seventh Edition

CONTENTS

INTRODUCTION

The media resources for *Educational Psychology: Windows on Classrooms*, 7th Edition, appear in three forms:

- DVD Episodes That Accompany the Text
- Teacher Prep Website Resources
- Videos

ABOUT DVD EPISODES THAT ACCOMPANY THE TEXT (New to This Edition)

Two DVDs are found at the back of each textbook. These DVDs contain 25 classroom vignettes that range in length from 4 to 15 minutes. These classroom episodes illustrate specific chapter concepts, and references to them appear in the text.

An overview of the DVD Episodes that accompany the Seventh Edition of *Educational Psychology: Windows on Classrooms* is found in Table 1. Specific references to each episode are inserted into different chapters, provide a brief overview, and direct students to a specific DVD episode. These can be shown in class as a classroom instructional activity or given as homework.

Table 1: Overview of DVDs That Accompany the Text (New to This Edition)

DVD Episodes

Episode	Chapter	Title	Description	Approximate Length (minutes)
1 DVD 1	1	Demonstrating knowledge in classrooms	This episode illustrates a kindergarten teacher, middle school teacher, and two high school teachers demonstrating different forms of teacher knowledge.	14
2 DVD 1	2	Examining learner thinking: Piaget's conservation tasks	In this episode, students of different ages respond to Piaget's famous conservation tasks.	5
3 DVD 1	2	Developmental differences: Studying properties of air in first grade	This episode illustrates the thinking of first graders as they try to explain why water doesn't enter a glass inverted in a bowl of water and why a card doesn't fall off an inverted cup full of water.	4
4 DVD 1	3	Moral reasoning: Examining a moral dilemma	This episode illustrates the moral reasoning of students at different ages when they are presented with a moral dilemmas.	4
5 DVD 1	4	Culturally responsive teaching	In this episode a teacher discusses with an interviewer the accommodations she has made in her classroom for a student of Islamic faith, and the support her other students provide.	5
6 DVD 1	5	Reviewing an IEP	In this episode a teacher team discusses an IEP with a concerned parent	5
7 DVD 1	5	Using peer tutoring with students having exceptionalities	This episode illustrates children conducting a flashcard drill as a form of peer tutoring.	5

8 DVD 1	6	Using reinforcement in classrooms	In this episode a second-grade teacher uses a considerable amount of positive reinforcement combined with some presentation punishment as a part of her classroom management system.	7
9 DVD 1	6	Demonstrating problem solving in high school chemistry	This episode illustrates a high-school teacher using direct modeling to demonstrate the steps involved in solving chemistry problems.	8
10 DVD 1	7	Applying information processing: Attracting students attention	This episode illustrates two teachers attempting to begin their lesson with a demonstration that will attract students' attention.	8
11 DVD 1	7	Applying information processing: Organizing information	This episode includes four teachers using different ways of organizing information for students.	6
12 DVD 1	7	Applying information processing: The *Scarlet Letter* in high school English	This episode illustrates a teacher's attempts to help her students understand the characters in the novel *The Scarlet Letter*. (It is also chapter's closing case study.)	9
13 DVD 1	8	Constructing knowledge of beam balances	This episode illustrates the thinking of fourth graders as they attempt to construct understanding of the principle that makes beams balance. (It is also the chapter's opening case study, and it is integrated throughout the chapter.)	9
14 DVD 1	8	Constructing concepts: Using concrete examples	In this episode one middle school teacher uses a concrete example to illustrate the concept *bilateral symmetry* and a second middle school teacher uses the same strategy to teach the concept *concrete poem.*	10
15 DVD 1	9	Using a problem solving model: Finding area in elementary math	This episode involves fifth-graders' attempts to find the area of the carpeted portion of their classroom, which is an irregular shape. (It is also the chapter's opening case study.)	11
16 DVD 2	9	Guiding students' problem solving: Graphing in second grade	In this episode a second-grade teacher uses a problem solving approach to help her students understand bar graphs. (It is also the chapter's closing case study.)	14
17 DVD 2	10	Applying cognitive motivation theory: Writing paragraphs in 5th grade	In this episode a fifth-grade teacher has her students involved in writing, displaying and evaluating each others' paragraphs.	13
18 DVD 2	11	Applying the motivation model: Studying arthropods in 5th grade	The same teacher as in Episode 17 is attempting to use an intrinsically interesting activity to help her students understand the concept *arthropod.* (It is also the chapter's opening case study.)	13

19 DVD 2	12	Establishing and practicing classroom rules	In this episode, a second-grade teacher is attempting to help her students understand a set of classroom rules, and later in the episode she conducts a review of the rules.	6
20 DVD 2	13	Analyzing instructional alignment	In this episode a fifth-grade teacher covers a variety of topics related to the Civil War.	10
21 DVD 2	13	Essential teaching skills in an urban classroom	The teacher in this episode is attempting to demonstrate the Essential Teaching Skills with his middle school students.	13
22 DVD 2	13	Guided discovery in an elementary classroom	In this episode, a fifth-grade teacher uses *Guided Discovery* to help her students understand Haiku poetry.	10
23 DVD 2	14	Laptops for data in fifth grade	Students in this episode gather and enter information on laptop computers in their classroom	5
24 DVD 2	14	Using PowerPoint in the classroom	In this episode a world history teacher uses a PowerPoint presentation to provide her students with information on ancient Greece	5
25 DVD 2	15	Using assessment in decision making	The teacher in this episode uses a variety of assessment data to make instructional decisions about teacher her students to add fractions.	15

BOUT THE TEACHER PREP WEBSITE RESOURCES

tudents need an access code to enter the Teacher Prep Website. The website consists of five modules.

- **VIDEO CLASSROOM** captures real classrooms and real interviews with students and educators. Each clip is accompanied by a set of PRAXIS-style questions that spark analysis and prepare students for licensure.
- **STUDENT AND TEACHER ARTIFACTS** provide concrete opportunities to assess and respond to classroom artifacts. This collection contains authentic work from both students and teachers.
- **TEACHER RESOURCES** offer over 500 classroom-tested teaching strategies and lesson plans to use when becoming a practicing professional.
- **RESEARCH RESOURCES** provide access to articles from ASCD's renowned journal, *Educational Leadership,* and includes Research Navigator, a searchable database of additional educational journals.
- **GETTING YOUR LICENSE AND BEGINNING YOUR CAREER** shows how to navigate the first year of teaching, understand key educational standards, policies, and laws, pass the licensure exam, and assemble an effective portfolio.

,ocating Resources on the Teacher Prep Website

. Access the Merrill Teacher Prep Website at: http://www.prenhall.com/teacherprep
. Once on the website, enter your user name and password, and click on "Log In."
. After logging in, 5 options will appear on the left panel of the screen:
    a) Video Classroom
    b) Student and Teacher Artifacts
    c) Teacher Resources
    d) Research Resources
    e) Getting Your License and Beginning Your Career

Specific chapter-by chapter resources and directions are listed in the sections that follow.

Teacher Prep Website for Use with Chapter 1: Educational Psychology: Developing a Professional Knowledge Base

Research Resources **for Ch. 1**

Increasing Your Professionalism

1. From the Teacher Prep homepage, click on "Research Resources" on the left panel of the screen, scroll down the middle of the page, and again click on "Research Resources."
2. Then, go to "Classroom Processes" and click on "Refining Your Practice."
3. Finally, click on the following articles:
    - *Practicing Professional Responsibilities: Professional Development*, Ref. No. 729
    - *Practicing Professional Responsibilities: School Responsibilities*, Ref. No. 730
    - *Professionalism at Its Best: Effective Social Skills,* Ref. No. 734
    - *Professionalism at Its Best: Personal Attire*, Ref. No. 735.

Each of these articles offers practical suggestions for helping you develop as a professional.

Teacher Prep Website for Use with Chapter 2: The Development of Cognition and Language

Video Classroom **materials for Ch. 2**

From the Teacher Prep homepage, click on 'Video Classroom' in the left-hand menu, then 'Educational Psychology' on the drop-down menu. The videos that relate to this chapter's content are listed below.

Module #	Video #	Title
Module 1	Video 1	Cognitive Development
Module 5	Video 1	Memory & Cognition: Early & Middle Childhood
Module 5	Video 2	Memory & Cognition: Early & Late Adolescence
Module 6	Video 2	Discussion of the Properties of Air
Module10	Video 1	Motivation

Student and Teacher Artifacts **for Ch. 2**

From the Teacher Prep homepage, click on 'Student and Teacher Artifacts' in the left-hand menu, then 'Educational Psychology' on the drop-down menu. The artifacts that are appropriate for use with this chapter are listed below.

Module #	Artifact #	Name
Module 1	Artifact 1	Pet Story (Language Reading K–2)
Module 6	Artifact 1	Five Brain Corals (Science 6–8)
Module 6	Artifact 4	The Number 34
Module 7	Artifact 3	Me Too Iguana Book (Art, Music)

Research Resources **for Ch. 2**

Brain-Based Education

From the Teacher Prep homepage, click on "Research Resources" on the left panel of the screen, scroll down the middle of the page, and again click on "Research Resources."
Then, go to "Classroom Processes" and click on "Instructional Methods."
Finally, click on the following articles:

- *Brain Science, Brain Fiction,* Ref. No. 2227
- *Brain-Based Learning; A Reality Check*, Ref. No. 2238

he first article provides an overview of "brain science" and offers a critical analysis of its implications for assroom practice. The author then offers a skeptical view of *brain-based education* and what it suggests for creasing student learning.

he second article describes a number of common criticisms of *brain-based education* but offers a more optimistic iew of its potential for increasing student learning.

eacher Prep Website for Use with Chapter 3: Personal, Social, and Emotional evelopment

***ideo Classroom* materials for Ch. 3**

rom the Teacher Prep homepage, click on 'Video Classroom' in the left-hand menu, then 'Educational Psychology' n the drop-down menu. The videos that relate to this chapter's content are listed below.

odule #	Video #	Title
odule 2	Video 1	Moral Reasoning
odule 2	Video 2	Friendships
odule 2	Video 3	Emotions

***tudent and Teacher Artifacts* for Ch. 3**

rom the Teacher Prep homepage, click on 'Student and Teacher Artifacts' in the left-hand menu, then 'Educational sychology' on the drop-down menu. The artifacts that are appropriate for use with this chapter are listed below.

Module #	Artifact #	Name
odule 2	Artifact 1	Litter Letter (Social Studies 3–5)
odule 2	Artifact 2	Friendship Question (Social Development 6–8)
odule 2	Artifact 3	Qualities of 11-year-olds
odule 2	Artifact 4	Oklahoma Bombing

***esearch Resources* for Ch. 3**

Teaching Social Problem Solving Skills

1. From the Teacher Prep homepage, click on "Research Resources" on the left panel of the screen, scroll down the middle of the page, and again click on "Research Resources."
2. Then, go to "Classroom Processes" and click on "Classroom Management."
3. Finally, click on the following articles:
   - *Changing the Way Kids Settle Conflicts,* Ref. No. 219

- *Teaching Students To Be Peer Mediators,* Ref. No. 2236

These articles describe different strategies to develop students' perspective taking and problem solving skills.

Developing Emotional Awareness

1. From the Teacher Prep, click on "Research Resources" on the left panel of the screen, scroll down the middle of the page, and again click on "Research Resources."
2. Then, go to "Classroom Processes" and click on "Classroom Management."
3. Finally, click on the following articles:
   - *Portraits in Emotional Awareness,* Ref. No. 348
   - *Reaching Out to Grieving Students,* Ref. No. 357
   - *Down with Put-Downs,* Ref. No. 2297

These articles describe strategies to develop students' emotional awareness.

Different Instructional Approaches to Moral Education

1. From the Teacher Prep homepage, click on "Research Resources" on the left panel of the screen, scroll down the middle of the page, and again click on "Research Resources."
2. Then, go to "Grade Levels," click on "Primary" and then "Instructional Methods."
3. Finally, click on the following articles:
   - *The Socratic Approach to Character Education,* Ref. No. 786
   - *Teaching for Character and Community,* Ref. No. 1775.

These articles describe strategies to develop students' perspective taking and caring for others.

Teacher Prep Website for Use with Chapter 4: Group and Individual Differences

***Video Classroom* materials for Ch. 4**

From the Teacher Prep homepage, click on 'Video Classroom' in the left-hand menu, then 'Educational Psychology' on the drop-down menu. The videos that relate to this chapter's content are listed below.

Module #	Video #	Title
Module 3	Video 1	Bilingual Classroom

***Student and Teacher Artifacts* for Ch. 4**

From the Teacher Prep homepage, click on 'Student and Teacher Artifacts' in the left-hand menu, then 'Educational Psychology' on the drop-down menu. The artifacts that are appropriate for use with this chapter are listed below.

Module #	Artifact #	Name
Module 3	Artifact 1	Mural
Module 3	Artifact 2	Easier to Be a Girl
Module 3	Artifact 3	Valentine Card
Module 3	Artifact 4	Student with Class
Module 4	Artifact 1	South Africa (Social Development 6–8)
Module 4	Artifact 2	Name with Letters (Social Development 6–8)
Module 4	Artifact 3	What Hits Me (Social Development 3–5)

odule 4 Artifact 4 Dear Diary (Social Development 3–5)

search Resources **for Ch. 4**

Culturally Responsive Teaching

From the Teacher Prep homepage, click on "Research Resources" on the left panel of the screen, scroll down the middle of the page, and again click on "Research Resources."
Then, go to "Classroom Processes" and click on "Diverse Populations."
Finally, click on the following articles:
- *Bridging Cultures with Classroom Strategies*, Ref. No. 2242,
- *Exploring World Cultures in Math Class,* Ref. No. 1684
- *Closing the Achievement Gap,* Ref. No. 1789.

hese articles describe different ways that teachers can adapt instruction to meet the needs of diverse learners.

Eliminating Gender Bias

From the Teacher Prep homepage, click on "Research Resources" on the left panel of the screen, scroll down the middle of the page, and again click on "Research Resources."
Then, go to "Classroom Processes" and click on "Diverse Populations."
Finally, click on the following articles:
- *Gender Difference on Assessments,* Ref. No. 260
- *Gender Equity in Cyberspace,* Ref. No. 549
- *Raising Better Boys,* Ref. No. 2255

hese articles describe the different ways that teachers can deal with gender issues for both girls and boys in their assrooms.

Effective Instruction for Students Placed at Risk

From the Teacher Prep homepage, click on "Research Resources" on the left panel of the screen, scroll down the middle of the page, and again click on "Research Resources."
Then, go to "Classroom Processes" and click on "Diverse Populations."
Finally, click on the following articles:
- *Building on Urban Learners' Experiences,* Ref. No. 210
- *Strategies that Close the Gap,* Ref. No. 1688.

hese articles describe different strategies teachers can use in working with students placed at risk.

Teacher Prep Website for Use with Chapter 5: Learners with Exceptionalities

Video Classroom materials for Ch. 5

From the Teacher Prep homepage, click on 'Video Classroom' in the left-hand menu, then 'Educational Psychology' on the drop-down menu. The videos that relate to this chapter's content are listed below.

Module #	Video #	Title
Module 3	Video 1	Bilingual Classroom
Module 4	Video 1	Observing Children & Adolescents in Classroom Settings

Student and Teacher Artifacts for Ch. 5

From the Teacher Prep homepage, click on 'Student and Teacher Artifacts' in the left-hand menu, then 'Educational Psychology' on the drop-down menu. The artifacts that are appropriate for use with this chapter are listed below.

Module #	Artifact #	Name
Module 5	Artifact 1	Reflections of ADD (Social Development 9–12)
Module 5	Artifact 2	Behavioral Chart (Teacher Artifact K–2)
Module 5	Artifact 3	Group and Work Habits (Teacher Artifact K–2)
Module 5	Artifact 4	Story Note Taking Form (Social Studies 6–8)

Research Resources for Ch. 5

Inclusion

1. From the Teacher Prep homepage, click on "Research Resources" on the left panel of the screen, scroll down the middle of the page, and again click on "Research Resources."
2. Then, go to "Classroom Processes" and click on "Diverse Populations."
3. Finally, click on the following articles:
   - *Small Victories in Inclusive Classrooms,* Ref. No. 384,
   - *"Our School Doesn't Offer Inclusion" and Other Legal Blunders,* Ref. No. 1679
   - *Contemporary Issues: The Legal Basis of Inclusion,* Ref. No. 2265

These articles describe different ways that inclusion is changing classrooms in the United States.

Instructional Strategies

1. From the Teacher Prep homepage, click on "Research Resources" on the left panel of the screen, scroll down the middle of the page, and again click on "Research Resources."
2. Then, go to "Classroom Processes" and click on "Diverse Populations."
3. Finally, click on the following articles:
   - *What's in a Name? The Labels and Language of Special Education,* Ref. No. 2190
   - *Neverstreaming: Preventing Learning Disabilities,* Ref. No. 2275
   - *Understanding Disabilities,* Ref. No. 1721.

These articles describe the process of categorization within special education as well as different ways to help students with learning problems.

Teaching Students Who Are Gifted and Talented

From the Teacher Prep homepage, click on "Research Resources" on the left panel of the screen, scroll down the middle of the page, and again click on "Research Resources."
Then, go to "Classroom Processes" and click on "Diverse Populations."
Finally, click on the following articles:

- *For Gifted Students, Full Inclusion Is a Partial Solution,* Ref. No. 2272
- *Using Multiple Intelligence Theory to Identify Gifted Children*, Ref. No. 810.

hese articles describe different ways to identify and teach students who are gifted and talented.

The Teacher's Role in Inclusive Classrooms

. From the Teacher Prep homepage, click on "Research Resources" on the left panel of the screen, scroll down the middle of the page, and again click on "Research Resources."
Then, go to "Classroom Processes" and click on "Diverse Populations."
. Finally, click on the following articles:

- *Teaching in the Inclusive Classroom,* Ref. No. 2077
- *What to Do When Learners Make Mistakes,* Ref. No. 2207

hese articles describe effective instructional strategies for working with students with exceptionalities.

Teacher Prep Website for Use with Chapter 6: Behaviorism and Social Cognitive Theory

***ideo Classroom* materials for Ch. 6**

rom the Teacher Prep homepage, click on 'Video Classroom' in the left-hand menu, then 'Educational Psychology' n the drop-down menu. The videos that relate to this chapter's content are listed below.

Module #	Video #	Title
Module 8	Video 1	Cooperative Learning
Module 12	Video 1	Classroom Rules

***tudent and Teacher Artifacts* for Ch. 6**

rom the Teacher Prep homepage, click on 'Student and Teacher Artifacts' in the left-hand menu, then 'Educational sychology' on the drop-down menu. The artifacts that are appropriate for use with this chapter are listed below.

Module #	Artifact #	Name
Module 5	Artifact 2	Behavioral Chart (Teacher Artifact K–2)
Module 9	Artifact 1	Trip to Gettysburg (Social Studies 6–8)
Module 9	Artifact 2	Diary Entries (Language, Reading 3–5)
Module 9	Artifact 3	A Friend Is (Art, Music K–2)
Module 9	Artifact 4	Sportsmanship Trophy (Teacher Artifact K–2)

Research Resources **for Ch. 6**

Practicing What We Preach

1. From the Teacher Prep homepage, click on "Research Resources" on the left panel of the screen, scroll down the middle of the page, and again click on "Research Resources."
2. Then, go to "Classroom Processes" and click on "Classroom Management."
3. Finally, click on the following article:
   - *Attaining Credibility with Students: Teacher Attitude and Modeling Behaviors*, Ref. No. 454.

This brief excerpt offers examples of important behaviors that teachers should model in order to create a productive learning environment.

Teacher Prep Website for Use with Chapter 7: Cognitive Views of Learning

Video Classroom **materials for Ch. 7**

From the Teacher Prep homepage, click on 'Video Classroom' in the left-hand menu, then 'Educational Psychology' on the drop-down menu. The videos that relate to this chapter's content are listed below.

Module #	Video #	Title
Module 5	Video 1	Memory and Cognition: Early and Middle Childhood
Module 5	Video 2	Memory and Cognition: Early and Late Adolescence
Module 7	Video 1	Learning Charles' Law

Student and Teacher Artifacts **for Ch. 7**

From the Teacher Prep homepage, click on 'Student and Teacher Artifacts' in the left-hand menu, then 'Educational Psychology' on the drop-down menu. The artifacts that are appropriate for use with this chapter are listed below.

Module #	Artifact #	Name
Module 6	Artifact 1	Five Brain Corals (Science 6–8)
Module 6	Artifact 2	Thank You Note (Science 3–5)
Module 6	Artifact 3	Note Taking Hints (Social Development)
Module 6	Artifact 4	The Number 34

Research Resources **for Ch. 7**

Metacognition and Emotional Awareness

1. From the Teacher Prep homepage, click on "Research Resources" on the left panel of the screen, scroll down the middle of the page, and again click on "Research Resources."
2. Then, go to "Classroom Processes" and click on "Classroom Management."
3. Finally, click on the following article:
   - *Socratic Seminars: Engaging Students in Intellectual Discourse,* Ref. No. 385.

This article suggests that teachers use Socratic dialogue to help students become more metacognitive about their emotions and motivations. The approach is unique in that it relates metacognitive abilities to the affective domain.

eacher Prep Website for Use with Chapter 8: Constructing Knowledge

ideo Classroom materials for Ch. 8

om the Teacher Prep homepage, click on 'Video Classroom' in the left-hand menu, then 'Educational Psychology' the drop-down menu. The videos that relate to this chapter's content are listed below.

odule #	Video #	Title
lodule 6	Video 1	Discussion of *The Scarlet Letter*
lodule 6	Video 2	Discussion of the Properties of Air

tudent and Teacher Artifacts for Ch. 8

rom the Teacher Prep homepage, click on 'Student and Teacher Artifacts' in the left-hand menu, then 'Educational sychology' on the drop-down menu. The artifacts that are appropriate for use with this chapter are listed below.

lodule #	Artifact #	Name
lodule 7	Artifact 1	Quadrilaterals (Teacher Artifact 6–8)
lodule 7	Artifact 2	Map of Colonial Village (Art, Music 6–8)
lodule 7	Artifact 3	Me Too Iguana Book (Art, Music)
lodule 7	Artifact 4	Parallel Interval Graph (Social Studies 6–8)

esearch Resources for Ch. 8

Assessing Constructivist in Classrooms

1. From the Teacher Prep homepage, click on "Research Resources" on the left panel of the screen, scroll down the middle of the page, and again click on "Research Resources."
2. Then, go to "Classroom Processes" and click on "Instructional Methods."
3. Finally, click on the following article:
    - *Caution: Constructivism Ahead,* Ref. No. 2280.

This article provided an evenhanded analysis of "constructivist" approaches to instruction, neither wholeheartedly ndorsing, nor severely criticizing, these approaches.

Analyzing Authentic Instruction

1. From the Teacher Prep homepage, click on "Research Resources" on the left panel of the screen, scroll down the middle of the page, and again click on "Research Resources."
2. Then, go to "Classroom Processes" and click on "Instructional Methods."
3. Finally, click on the following article:
    - *Five Standards of Authentic Instruction*, Ref. No. 2282.

This article specifies and details standards the authors believe must be met in order for instruction to be validly described as "authentic."

Teacher Prep Website for Use with Chapter 9: Complex Cognitive Processes

***Video Classroom* materials for Ch. 9**

From the Teacher Prep homepage, click on 'Video Classroom' in the left-hand menu, then 'Educational Psychology' on the drop-down menu. The videos that relate to this chapter's content are listed below.

Module #	Video #	Title
Module 6	Video 1	Discussion of *The Scarlet Letter*
Module 6	Video 2	Discussion of the Properties of Air
Module 7	Video 1	Learning Charles' Law
Module 11	Video 1	Civil War Discussion

***Student and Teacher Artifacts* for Ch. 9**

From the Teacher Prep homepage, click on 'Student and Teacher Artifacts' in the left-hand menu, then 'Educational Psychology' on the drop-down menu. The artifacts that are appropriate for use with this chapter are listed below.

Module #	Artifact #	Name
Module 8	Artifact 1	Subtraction Explained (Math 3–5)
Module 8	Artifact 2	How We Became a Country (Language, Reading 6–8)
Module 8	Artifact 3	Common Standards (Teacher Artifact 9–12)
Module 8	Artifact 4	Island Map (Social Studies 6–8)

***Research Resources* for Ch. 9**

Problem-Based Learning

1. From the Teacher Prep homepage, click on "Research Resources" on the left panel of the screen, scroll down the middle of the page, and again click on "Research Resources."
2. Then, go to "Classroom Processes" and click on "Instructional Methods."
3. Finally, click on the following articles:
    - *Problem-Based Learning: As Authentic As It Gets,* Ref. No. 2288
    - *Problem Solved: How to Coach Cognition,* Ref. No. 2289.

These articles provide an overview and some examples of problem-based learning. The authors are strong advocates of the method, so they provide no critical review of the challenges involved in trying to implement it in classrooms. The articles do provide you with some additional information with respect to problem-based learning, which can give you some additional insights if you try to implement it in your classroom.

Teaching in Context

1. From the Teacher Prep homepage, click on "Research Resources" on the left panel of the screen, scroll down the middle of the page, and again click on "Research Resources."
2. Then, go to "Classroom Processes" and click on "Instructional Methods."
3. Finally, click on the following article:
    - *Strategies for Mathematics: Teaching in Context,* Ref. No. 2229

his article addresses the importance of context, experience, and application in promoting transfer of problem lving ability in math.

eacher Prep Website for Use with Chapter 10: Theories of Motivation

ideo Classroom materials for Ch. 10

rom the Teacher Prep homepage, click on 'Video Classroom' in the left-hand menu, then 'Educational Psychology' n the drop-down menu. The videos that relate to this chapter's content are listed below.

Iodule #	Video #	Title
Iodule 10	Video 1	Motivation

tudent and Teacher Artifacts for Ch. 10

rom the Teacher Prep homepage, click on 'Student and Teacher Artifacts' in the left-hand menu, then 'Educational sychology' on the drop-down menu. The artifacts that are appropriate for use with this chapter are listed below.

Iodule #	Artifact #	Name
Iodule 11	Artifact 1	Letter to Jefferson (Social Studies 3–5)
Iodule 11	Artifact 2	Book Project Choices (Teacher Artifact 6–8)
Iodule 11	Artifact 3	Pig Dissection (Science 3–5)
Iodule 11	Artifact 4	Count Dracula Story (Language, Reading 6–8)

esearch Resources for Ch. 10

Applying Goal Theory with At-Risk Students

. From the Teacher Prep homepage, click on "Research Resources" on the left panel of the screen, scroll down the middle of the page, and again click on "Research Resources."
. Then, go to "Classroom Processes" and click on "Diverse Populations."
. Finally, click on the following article:
    - *Using Motivational Theory with At-Risk Children*, Ref. No. 2294

This article describes one elementary school's efforts to create a learning-focused versus a performance focused nvironment and help students adopt learning goals instead of performance goals.

Teacher Prep Website for Use with Chapter 11: Motivation in the Classroom

Video Classroom materials for Ch. 11

From the Teacher Prep homepage, click on 'Video Classroom' in the left-hand menu, then 'Educational Psychology' on the drop-down menu. The videos that relate to this chapter's content are listed below.

Module #	Video #	Title
Module 10	Video 1	Motivation

***Student and Teacher Artifacts* for Ch. 11**

From the Teacher Prep homepage, click on 'Student and Teacher Artifacts' in the left-hand menu, then 'Educational Psychology' on the drop-down menu. The artifacts that are appropriate for use with this chapter are listed below.

Module #	Artifact #	Name
Module 11	Artifact 1	Letter to Jefferson (Social Studies 3–5)
Module 11	Artifact 2	Book Project Choices (Teacher Artifact 6–8)
Module 11	Artifact 3	Pig Dissection (Science 3–5)
Module 11	Artifact 4	Count Dracula Story (Language, Reading 6–8)

***Research Resources* for Ch. 11**

High-Stakes Testing and Student Motivation to Learn

1. From the Teacher Prep homepage, click on "Research Resources" on the left panel of the screen, scroll down the middle of the page, and again click on "Research Resources."
2. Then, go to "Classroom Processes" and click on "Assessment."
3. Finally, click on the following article:
   - *The Effects of High-Stakes Testing on Student Motivation and Learning,* Ref. No. 1725.

This research report begins with the questions: Do high-stakes testing policies lead to increased student motivation to learn? And do these policies lead to increased student learn? This article then provides a critical examination of the impact of high-stakes testing on students' motivation to learn, student dropout rates, and student learning.

What Urban Students Say About Good Teaching

1. From the Teacher Prep homepage, click on "Research Resources" on the left panel of the screen, scroll down the middle of the page, and again click on "Research Resources."
2. Then, go to "Classroom Processes" and click on "Instructional Methods."
3. Finally, click on the following article:
   - *What Urban Students Say About Good Teaching.* Ref. No. 1667.

This article provides a detailed look at urban students' perceptions of good teachers in a variety of areas. It contains a number of quotes from students.

Teacher Prep Website for Use with Chapter 12: Creating Productive Learning Environments: Classroom Management

***Video Classroom* materials for Ch. 12**

From the Teacher Prep homepage, click on 'Video Classroom' in the left-hand menu, then 'Educational Psychology' on the drop-down menu. The videos that relate to this chapter's content are listed below.

Module #	Video #	Title
Module 10	Video 1	Motivation

udent and Teacher Artifacts for Ch. 12

om the Teacher Prep homepage, click on 'Student and Teacher Artifacts' in the left-hand menu, then 'Educational ychology' on the drop-down menu. The artifacts that are appropriate for use with this chapter are listed below.

odule #	Artifact #	Name
odule 13	Artifact 1	Classroom Rules (Teacher Artifact 3–5)
odule 13	Artifact 2	Practice Writing Prompt (Language, Reading 3–5)
odule 13	Artifact 3	Homework Letter (Teacher Artifact K–6)
odule 13	Artifact 4	Letter Home (Teacher Artifact K–2)

esearch Resources for Ch. 12

Time Management

From the Teacher Prep homepage, click on "Research Resources" on the left panel of the screen, scroll down the middle of the page, and again click on "Research Resources."
Then, go to "Classroom Processes" and click on "Classroom Management."
Finally, click on the following article:
- *Time Management*, Ref. No. 1558.

his excerpt offers planning suggestions designed to help teachers use their time efficiently and maximize the mount of time available for instruction.

Improving Home-School Communication

From the Teacher Prep homepage, click on "Research Resources" on the left panel of the screen, scroll down the middle of the page, and again click on "Research Resources."
Then, go to "Classroom Processes" and click on "Classroom Management."
Finally, click on the following article:
- *Building Cultures with a Parent-Teacher Conference*, Ref. No. 537.

his article offers a Latina mother's perspective on a parent-teacher conference. It also outlines potential cross-ultural conflicts about values, and describes strategies teachers can use to help prevent or eliminate these conflicts.

eacher Prep Website for Use with Chapter 13: Creating Productive Learning nvironments: Principles and Models of Instruction

ideo Classroom materials for Ch. 13

rom the Teacher Prep homepage, click on 'Video Classroom' in the left-hand menu, then 'Educational Psychology' n the drop-down menu. The videos that relate to this chapter's content are listed below.

Module #	Video #	Title
Module 12	Video 1	Classroom Rules

***Student and Teacher Artifacts* for Ch. 13**

From the Teacher Prep homepage, click on 'Student and Teacher Artifacts' in the left-hand menu, then 'Educational Psychology' on the drop-down menu. The artifacts that are appropriate for use with this chapter are listed below.

Module #	Artifact #	Name
Module 12	Artifact 1	Journaling with Teacher (Teacher Artifact K–2)
Module 12	Artifact 2	Groupwork Instruction (Teacher Artifact 6–8)
Module 12	Artifact 3	Illustration of Plant Growth (Science 3–5)
Module 12	Artifact 4	Explanation of Plant and Animal Cells (Science 6–8)

***Research Resources* for Ch. 13**

Making Cooperative Learning Equitable

1. From the Teacher Prep homepage, click on "Research Resources" on the left panel of the screen, scroll down the middle of the page, and again click on "Research Resources."
2. Then, go to "Classroom Processes" and click on "Instructional Methods."
3. Finally, click on the following articles:
    - *Making Cooperative Learning Equitable*, Ref. No. 2240
    - *Varying Instructional Strategies,* Ref. No. 1936

The first article examines some of the issues that arise when socially dominant and socially isolated students work together in cooperative learning groups together with the causes of the inequality. It then goes on to offer suggestions for overcoming these obstacles.

The second article identifies some of the benefits of cooperative learning but also points out that it isn't appropriate for all learning situations and that instructional strategies need to be varied.

Teacher Prep Website for Use with Chapter 14: Learning, Instruction, and Technology

***Research Resources* for Ch. 14**

Plagiarism

1. From the Teacher Prep homepage, click on "Research Resources" on the left panel of the screen, scroll down the middle of the page, and again click on "Research Resources."
2. Then, go to "Classroom Processes" and click on "Technology."
3. Finally, click on the following article:
    - *Cut and Paste 101: Plagiarism and the Net,* Ref. No. 235

This article describes the recently discovered problem of plagiarism from the Internet and what teachers can do to combat this problem.

Teacher Support Applications of Technology

From the Teacher Prep homepage, click on "Research Resources" on the left panel of the screen, scroll down the middle of the page, and again click on "Research Resources."
Then, go to "Classroom Processes" and click on "Technology."
Finally, click on the following articles:
- *How Can I Use E-Mail for Professional Purposes?*, Ref. No. 113
- *How Can I Use the Web as a Lesson Planning Bank?,* Ref. No. 424, And
- *How Can I Use the Web as a Research Tool?* Ref. No. 425

hese articles describe different ways to use technology to increase your instructional effectiveness.

'eacher Prep Website for Use with Chapter 15: Assessing Classroom Learning

'*ideo Classroom* materials for Ch. 15

rom the Teacher Prep homepage, click on 'Video Classroom' in the left-hand menu, then 'Educational Psychology' n the drop-down menu. The videos that relate to this chapter's content are listed below.

lodule #	Video #	Title
lodule 13	Video 1	Portfolios

***tudent and Teacher Artifacts* for Ch. 15**

rom the Teacher Prep homepage, click on 'Student and Teacher Artifacts' in the left-hand menu, then 'Educational 'sychology' on the drop-down menu. The artifacts that are appropriate for use with this chapter are listed below.

lodule #	Artifact #	Name
lodule 14	Artifact 1	A Stressful Situation (Social Development 9–12)
lodule 14	Artifact 2	Speed Tests (Language, Reading)
lodule 14	Artifact 3	Colonial Economics Rubric (Social Studies 6–8)
lodule 14	Artifact 4	Music Standards (Teacher Artifacts 3–5)

***esearch Resources* for Ch. 15**

Assessment and Learning

. From the Teacher Prep homepage, click on "Research Resources" on the left panel of the screen, scroll down the middle of the page, and again click on "Research Resources."
. Then, go to "Classroom Processes" and click on "Assessment."
. Finally, click on the following articles:
- *How Classroom Assessment Improves Learning*, Ref. No. 1723.
- *Classroom Assessment for Learning,* Ref. No. 1736.

These articles describe how teachers can use assessment to improve learning in the classroom.

Rubrics in the Classroom

1. From the Teacher Prep homepage, click on "Research Resources" on the left panel of the screen, scroll down the middle of the page, and again click on "Research Resources."
2. Then, go to "Classroom Processes" and click on "Assessment."
3. Finally, click on the following article:
   - *Understanding Rubrics*, Ref. No. 2328.

This article describes the philosophy behind rubrics and how they can be integrated into a classroom's total assessment program.

Grading and Standards

1. From the Teacher Prep homepage, click on "Research Resources" on the left panel of the screen, scroll down the middle of the page, and again click on "Research Resources."
2. Then, go to "Classroom Processes" and click on "Assessment."
3. Finally, click on the following article:
   - *Helping Standards Make the Grade*, Ref. No. 1698.

This article describes the challenges teachers face when assigning grades in a standards-based environment. It also suggests ways to meet those challenges.

Teacher Prep Website for Use with Chapter 16: Assessment Through Standardized Testing

Video Classroom **materials for Ch. 16**

From the Teacher Prep homepage, click on 'Video Classroom' in the left-hand menu, then 'Educational Psychology' on the drop-down menu. The videos that relate to this chapter's content are listed below.

Module #	Video #	Title
Module 13	Video 1	Portfolios

Research Resources **for Ch. 16**

Standards-Based Education

1. From the Teacher Prep homepage, click on "Research Resources" on the left panel of the screen, scroll down the middle of the page, and again click on "Research Resources."
2. Then, go to "Classroom Processes" and click on "Assessment."
3. Finally, click on the following article:
   - *Realizing the Promise of Standards-Based Education*, Ref. No. 2313

This article describes the potential positive benefits of standards-based education.

High-Stakes Testing

1. From the Teacher Prep homepage, Click on "Research Resources" on the left panel of the screen, scroll down the middle of the page, and again click on "Research Resources."
2. Then, go to "Classroom Processes" and click on "Assessment."
3. Finally, click on the following articles:
   - *The Dangers of Testing*, Ref. No. 1745